Maura O'Connell Foley

My Wild Atlantic Kitchen

Recipes & Recollections

Maura O'Connell Foley

Extract from The Irish Times 1971 including recipes from Maura
Photo of Maura and her sister Grainne by George Morrison (Theodora FitzGibbon's husband)
Maura's old menu planning notes from the early 1970s

Foreword

By Derry Clarke

I first met the wonderful Maura Foley when she was cooking at The Lime Tree Restaurant in her native Kenmare in the late 1980s. Her husband Tom was front of house in those days in the beautiful and charming 19th century building. My memories of that evening are of spectacular fresh fish cooked to perfection with flair and imagination. We had a great chat that night when she had finished in the kitchen. Being a chef myself, I was very eager to meet the lady who was working her magic in the kitchen.

There were not that many female chefs in the kitchen in those days. Maura was and is a trailblazer. She had started The Purple Heather Tea & Cake Shop with her mother Agnes in 1961. They then moved to a larger property serving high teas and more substantial meals, with a bar to the rear and a piano, which became a Piano Bar. Maura was soon serving mixed grills and fresh fish and it quickly evolved into a restaurant with Maura in the kitchen and Agnes front of house. Maura became famous for her fresh fish, which she got straight from the trawler of a friend directly to her kitchen. Remember there were very few restaurants in Ireland in those days, especially ones where you could get fish fresh from the sea hours after it was caught and cooked with tender loving care.

When Maura opened Packie's, it was our go-to restaurant in Kenmare. Indeed, we would travel miles to eat there, even if we were staying in Dingle or anywhere in the vicinity. Her menu not only had the fresh fish she had become famous for but her meat, poultry and vegetarian dishes were delicious and well worth the distance we travelled to be there. Again, imaginative vegetarian dishes were not the norm on menus in those days and we have a daughter who is a strict vegetarian just like Maura's daughters. Maura understands the wants and needs of her guests and was constantly evolving her menu to be ahead of the trend. Kenmare is now synonymous with great food and this is down to Maura Foley and her progressive ideas, dedication and ambitions for her home town. Personally, I feel it was Maura who put Kenmare firmly on the map as a food destination.

This book is the culmination of 60 years of passion, hard work and imagination and is a summary of her life working in busy kitchens. These recipes are timeless, classic and detailed. This is a book I feel every cook should have in their kitchen as there are so many brilliant and varied recipes. This is a book recording Maura's legacy through the many years she has been at the forefront of Irish cooking. As a fellow chef, I am very proud to know her and respect her for all her achievements.

Is Mise Le Meas

Derry Clarke
Chef

Contents

Introduction 10

Maura's Cooking Notes 32

Breakfast 41

Starters 75

Fish 139

Meat 201

Vegetables 251

Desserts & Baking 283

Sauces, Stocks & Staples 337

Dinner Parties 387

Glossary 394

Index 397

Acknowledgements 406

Contributions 408

Introduction

Introduction

I have loved food and cooking all my life. It was a lucky day for me when my mother, Agnes O'Connell, rented a property from Gerald O' Shea on Henry Street in Kenmare where together we started a tearoom. This enabled me to pursue a career in cooking which gives me so much joy.

Keeping food simple, cooking with care and using the best produce is the key, in my opinion. Throughout the years, seeking out quality fresh ingredients for cooking was my number one focus. However, another important aspect when people eat out is that they relax and enjoy the surroundings, therefore ambience and lighting are up there with the food and service in creating a whole experience for a restaurant.

Over the years in the restaurants, I was approached on many occasions to write a book, but just didn't make the time. I have finally put pen to paper and I can tell you it has been a tremendous effort! The recipes are a diverse collection of the food I have loved to cook at various times in my life.

One should use a recipe as a guide only as there are so many factors that will determine the outcome; for that reason, tasting as you cook is vital. Cook to one's own taste and do not be afraid to veer from the recipe and add or omit as you please. Baking is the exception, where quantities and methods matter.

When writing this book, I found getting exact weights and measurements quite difficult and it nearly drove me mad at times! We have tried to be as specific as possible.

The book includes recipes from my various business ventures. The first was our little tea shop which my mother Agnes and I opened in 1961, The Purple Heather Tea & Cake Shop. Two years later we moved to a larger property where The Purple Heather is today, and this is where I started my real life as a cook. Today my dear sister Grainne continues to run The Purple Heather Bar & Bistro as a day business. Later in 1985 with my husband Tom, we opened The Lime Tree Restaurant on Shelbourne Street, in what was originally the school house that I had attended as a young girl. In 1992 we converted my uncle Packie's grocery into Packie's restaurant. At the same time we bought a Georgian farmhouse, Shelburne House, as a renovation project. It opened as Shelburne Lodge Guesthouse in 1996 and we continue to run it today.

Each business served a variety of interesting and tasty dishes. I hope you enjoy reading the book and more importantly recreating the food for your own table. I very much hope it will be a source of happy cooking.

Maura

My Life in Food

Early Life and Influences

I was surrounded by food from an early age as my mother Agnes spent her time baking and cooking. She was my first influence. She cooked exquisitely and had an excellent palate which I luckily also developed. She was fortunate in having a brilliant mother, Hanora 'Nonie' Crowley Hanley (née Harrington of Drombouhilly, Tuosist on the Beara Peninsula) who, in the late 1800s at the age of 15, travelled as a young teenage girl alone to Boston where she worked in a kitchen as a maid. She was married twice and both husbands died young and when her children were very little. She had five children in total. She met her first husband Timothy Crowley when she travelled back from Boston to Ireland and they had three children, Michael 'Dugsie', Maureen Mary Jane and Kathleen.

On the early death of her husband, the children went to Tuosist to live with their grandparents in Drombouhilly and Hanora crossed the Atlantic by boat for the second time and trained as a cook in the same kitchen. This was an amazing achievement. She returned to Ireland for the second time and married Michael Hanley and they had two children, Agnes (my mother) and Patrick 'Packie' (my uncle).

Nonie built No. 35 Henry Street in 1926 and started a grocery store. She was well known as a great cook, particularly for her hare soup and rabbit casserole. She bought butter, eggs, chickens and rabbits all year round and, at Christmas time, turkeys from local farmers. She sold real homemade ice-cream made by herself and her family. The custard was made on the stove in the kitchen, cooled and hand churned in a vat using blocks of ice delivered from the old Kenmare railway station, which is sadly no longer there. Nonie was a big card player, playing every night with friends in the kitchen and later Packie carried on that tradition.

My parents moved to London in 1941 during the second world war and I was born a year later. We lived on Parkhill Road in Hampstead. My mother Agnes worked as a professional cake maker at Fraser's Tea and Cake Shop on Haverstock Hill, a beautiful tea shop with an abundance of delightful homemade cakes. I loved visiting and can still remember eating the lemon flavoured iced cakes, decorated with little mimosa balls on a sprig with pretty leaves. My interest in food was born.

We returned to Kenmare in 1950 and my mother opened a tea shop on Bridge Street called Riverside. She made the cakes by hand and baked them in a Stanley cooker. At the same time my father John, who had trained in the 1930s as a mechanical engineer at Bolton Street in Dublin, ran a successful garage with uncle Packie. It had a sub agency for VW Beetles which sold like hot cakes. At that time there were very few petrol stations with the garage being a regular petrol stop en route to the Parknasilla Great Southern Hotel. One of our clients who never passed the door without stopping was Dan Langan

Packie, Anna Mai and friends outside his grocery shop with the reflection of Gerald O'Shea's, where the Purple Heather Tea & Cake Shop first opened in 1961

of Caltex, a subsidiary of Texaco. Interestingly, his son Peter was one of the owners along with Michael Caine of the famous Langan's Brasserie in London, which never left the social columns in the late 1970s and early 1980s. I loved going there when I visited London. I was amazed at the cars such as Bentleys, Rolls-Royces and Daimlers that stopped on their way to Parknasilla, which is beautifully situated by the sea and is now thriving under the expert direction of Tony Daly.

My mother closed the tea shop after a few years as the garage business became very busy. Another food venture was started around the same time by my aunt Kathleen who opened and ran The Wander Inn, formerly Falvey's pub. She subsequently bought Vickery's pharmacy next door and combined both places to form a splendid family hotel where my cousins Therese, Nuala, Agnes, Nancy and Jerry grew up.

In 1957, I returned to London and lived with my remarkable aunt Maureen (Jane Burton) who worked for the Foreign Office in Whitehall and had received an MBE in 1952 for her service. I attended school for a few years at the Convent of La Sagesse in Golders Green, which was run by French nuns. During this time, I learned so much about food, exploring markets and tasting food from all varieties of cuisines, and I loved to travel into town and explore Soho.

My favourite market, where we went each Saturday, was the Berwick Street market because of the bustling atmosphere, the fabulous displays of fresh fruit and vegetables and the characters selling their produce. Maureen didn't have a family and I was very fortunate as she took me to her favourite restaurants throughout London, one regular being the Hostario Romano in Dean Street – she became good friends with the family who ran the restaurant. Here, they had the most amazing veal dishes, homemade pastas and creamy gorgonzola. On special occasions, we dined at Quo Vadis which is still there today. Another of my aunt's favourites was Maison Suisse in North Soho, run by two Swiss sisters who were superb cooks; they had a beautiful chicken dish with a white wine cream sauce which I can remember vividly. My aunt went there especially for that same dish. They served globe artichokes with hollandaise sauce which I was amazed by, this being my first time having hollandaise.

All these experiences helped to develop my palate and further my love of food. I came home to Ireland in 1960 when I was 18 and helped with the accounts for the garage. Circumstances changed for the garage and it was at this point that my mother decided to re-open a tea shop.

The Purple Heather Tea & Cake Shop (1961)

The first Purple Heather opened in Gerald O'Shea's, where The White Room is today. Gerald agreed to rent the premises at £6 per week for two years and 11 months, not to exceed three years which was the legal requirement at the time. Through a loan of £200 from the Munster and Leinster Bank secured by my good uncle Packie, we purchased an oven, tables and chairs. In the first year I made all the cakes by hand, starting very early each morning, and while it was hard work I absolutely loved it. We sold Génoise sponges, Madeira cakes, layer cakes of all flavours, éclairs, tarts, meringues, choux pastries, puff pastry made with butter and an abundance of biscuits. The second year we bought a Hobart mixer for £115, which is still in use in The Purple Heather kitchen today.

The original 1962 Hobart mixer which is still in use today in The Purple Heather

The Purple Heather

Cakes were sold at 2p, sandwiches 3p, cream cakes 3p, tea and coffee 2p. Currency was 12p to 1 shilling, 20 shillings to £1. Just to give you an idea, on 15th August, 1961, the big fair day in Kenmare, we took £70 in total which is a lot of cakes and sandwiches.

From the very early days in Kenmare, we were blessed with a small tourism sector because of the Great Southern Hotels, including Parknasilla which first opened in 1895 and the Great Southern Hotel Kenmare, now the Park Hotel Kenmare, which opened in 1897. Tourism largely expanded from the 1960s onwards. Both hotels had a constant flow of English and Irish merchants and professionals. When we first started The Purple Heather, very few if any went for a cup of coffee; it wasn't the norm. A few people would have celebrated special occasions in the Great Southern Hotels, but times were changing.

The Purple Heather (Christmas 1963 to The Present Day)

In 1963, my mother purchased part of Lizzie Flynn's former pub for £1,100 from PDM O'Sullivan. This formed part of a cluster of buildings including Florry Batt's and Tangney's built from the remaining sandstone and limestone from the beautiful Holy Cross Church. At the time the building was semi-derelict and following some renovations, in Christmas 1963 we opened a tea shop at the front. The property held a six-day licence and we bought a seven-day licence from the Harrington Bakery in Castletownbere (cousins of my father). We opened a lovely bar at the rear that had a patio entrance with clematis on the walls, which was an oasis.

In the mid 1960s during the winter, I travelled back to London and completed a six-week advanced Cordon Bleu course on Marylebone Lane, the original premises of Rosemary Hume. These were the days of the Swinging Sixties and we had to go to the King's Road every Saturday to soak up the atmosphere. I also did various *stages* and courses to further develop my skills and learn as much as possible from great chefs in busy kitchens.

The Ryan family of the Arbutus Lodge in Cork were friends and in the 1960s I was lucky enough to work with Declan, later a Michelin starred chef, who taught me a huge amount during my first time in a professional kitchen. He trained with one of Europe's top chefs, Pierre Rolland, in one of Europe's top hotels, Dublin's famous Russell Hotel, which was owned by Ken Besson. Pierre originally came to Ireland to Jammet's, one of Ireland's first top-class restaurants, which operated for over 60 years and closed in 1967.

The Purple Heather gradually evolved from a tea shop to a restaurant. Agnes looked after the front of house and I did the cooking. The main reason The Purple Heather became a restaurant was as a result of a daily supply of fresh fish from a friend, Kevin Cooper, who had recently bought a trawler. This was amazing produce and was the ultimate in freshness, direct from a small boat. It was such a treasure to be able to get fish of that quality.

My cousins, the Hurleys, were butchers and they supplied us with prime meat.

During those days, Agnes loved to go out to visit her great friend Mai who ran The Lakehouse by the stunning Cloonee Lakes, now run by her daughter Mary and husband Sean. It offered a nice break from The Purple Heather – they would go out on the boat and fish for trout.

At that time, I was influenced by Theodora FitzGibbon, Elizabeth David, Declan Ryan, Jane Grigson (Sophie's mother) and especially Julia Child's *Mastering the Art of French Cooking*. I laughed so much when I saw the film, *Julie & Julia*, which was released in recent years and brought me right back to my early cooking days.

The Purple Heather at this stage was a thriving business; the place had a club atmosphere with tasty simple food and a piano bar at the rear. Our regulars were locals and visitors with holiday homes in Kenmare and hotel staff from the Great Southerns, including Terry McCoy, later of The Red Bank in Skerries; Conal O'Sullivan, one of the hotel managers at the time and son of Toddy O'Sullivan; Aidan White, who later worked for many years in Bunratty Castle; Tom Mythen, who went on to become a president of the Restaurant Association of Ireland (RAI); and Rory Murphy, who became one of the leading hoteliers in Ireland including the management of Ashford Castle. The Purple Heather was one of the first bars in town to welcome females as regular clientele. Up until the early 1960s, women did not go into or were not really permitted in bars or pubs in Ireland, but times were rapidly changing for the better and last orders at the bar stretched into the early hours of the morning. Harp lager was popular at the time and we had to have Angostura bitters available for our customers who drank pink gin.

The restaurant business was only just beginning in the country. Up until then, hotels had restaurants, but they generally catered for residents and it wasn't the norm for locals to eat out. To give you an idea, I attended the very first meeting of the RAI, which was not until 1970, co-founded by Mike Butt of the Golden Orient in Dublin. He was an astounding man who opened one of Ireland's first Indian restaurants in 1956 with his wife Terry. In the early 1960s Ernie Evans, who trained in Lausanne, and his wife Miriam of The Towers Hotel in Glenbeigh changed the whole scene. Theirs was the first restaurant that became well known in the south; one would have dinner in the restaurant for a social evening out followed by a fantastic dance with terrific music. Even in Dublin, Jammet's was one of the few established restaurants in Ireland. People like Ernie Evans of Glenbeigh, the Ryan family of Arbutus Lodge, Myrtle Allen of the wonderful Ballymaloe House who opened her Yeats Room in 1964, and our Purple Heather in Kenmare were becoming well known as food destinations.

Photographs in The Purple Heather of the Sheen River including a salmon leaping upstream

menu

Starters – Cream of Mussel Soup   1.
Fresh Prawn Cocktail   6
Fresh Lobster Cocktail   7.
Smoked Kerry Salmon   7–

Entrées – Lobster American   20.
Black Sole on the bone from   13.
Black Sole with prawns, cream and brandy sauce   18.
Grilled or poached Roughty River Salmon with hollandaise sauce   15
Scallops in white wine sauce   12
Scampi   13
Fresh fillets of Plaice   9
Fresh Salmon mayonnaise   13
Lobster mayonnaise   18

The Purple Heather menu created by Maura for Les Fruits De Mer festival in the early 1970s

menu

Vegetables –	Peas	1-6
tossed in butter	French Beans	1-6
	Mushrooms	1-6
	Broccoli	2-6
	Tossed Salad	1-6
	Potatoes creamed or chipped	1-6

Sweets –	Apple Tart	1-9
all served	Gateau	2-0
with fresh	Fresh Fruit Salad	2-6
cream.	Icecream + chocolate Sauce	1-6
	Asst. Cheeses.	2-0

Tea or coffee inclusive

Irish Coffee   4-6
Wine by the glass 2-6

In the early 1970s, we had a seafood festival in Kenmare called Les Fruits De Mer. It was a tremendous success. There were two main events: a seafood buffet competition, with chefs from the top hotels around the country each preparing a seafood display of all kinds of fish and shellfish with spectacular butter carvings as the centrepiece (p143), and the seafood banquette which was the finale. The banquette was held in the Silver Slipper Ballroom with the catering provided by the Great Southern Kenmare, always followed by dancing with a big showband. The festival raised the profile of Kenmare at a national and international level, with supporters including Charles Heidsieck who sponsored the champagne reception each year. The town was alive with activity and people returned especially for the festival – there was even a horse racing event held in Dunkerron on the O'Sullivan's farm. All the bars and restaurants participated; the bars provided free mussels and periwinkles on their counters. With the growth of the festival, one of the years the seafood banquette was held in different venues across Kenmare including The Purple Heather. I catered for about 50 guests including Theodora FitzGibbon, who became a good friend – she particularly enjoyed my avocado mousse which I served as a starter with crab.

During the festival in 1973 my friend Jim Foley from Limerick, who was the secretary of the festival, introduced me to his brother Tom who was home from Kenya. Following a whirlwind romance, we got engaged two months later and married in January 1975. I went with Tom to Kenya and, on the insistence of my mother Agnes I returned to work in The Purple Heather by Easter. Soon after this we closed the restaurant upstairs and focused on serving seafood and fish in the bar downstairs for a simpler life.

My father died in February 1980 and my mother died 10 months later. From my father I inherited a love of bridge; he was involved in starting the Bridge Congress in Kenmare which remains one of my annual highlights to this day. My mother Agnes was a tremendously charismatic and generous lady who thrived in a sociable environment. Her customers loved to chat with her, many of them returning over the years to reminisce about her vivacious and engaging character. Both were an immense loss to Grainne and me. We continued to run the business. Grainne took on the sole running of the business in the early 1980s and continues to run The Purple Heather Bar & Bistro with a longstanding team – notably Mag McCarthy (née Harrington), who has been there since 1985.

The Lime Tree Restaurant (1985-1991)

In 1984, Tom and I bought a former schoolhouse from Ernst Weeland. I had attended the school as a young girl when it was run by Ms Moore and Mr O'Connor. The school was located right beside the former Great Southern Hotel, which was bought by Ernst in 1977 and re-opened in 1980 as the Park Hotel Kenmare, a luxury five-star hotel under the excellent management of Francis Brennan. Francis and his brother John, now owners, continue to successfully operate the superb hotel to this day.

The schoolhouse had become run-down and after renovations and redesign by architect Hugh Elliott, a close friend of Tom's, we opened The Lime Tree restaurant in 1985 – named after the beautiful tree at the front of the property. This was an exciting business from the very start. I cooked and Tom was a wonderful front of house host with an excellent knowledge of the wine we served. Jim Whelan of Ballymaloe had the George Duboeuf agency for wines and many other labels, and as an expert in wine was a tremendous help to Tom. He advised Tom on the different grape varieties, regions and which wines to stock.

I had a large American clientele and the style of restaurant was compared to Chez Panisse in California. At this time, I was interested in the cooking style of Alice Waters, thanks to my cousin James O' Shea who kept me in touch with the kitchens in America. He especially kept me abreast of the hot American cooks, before the internet! He is an experienced restaurateur with several restaurants since the 1980s and now runs a restaurant, The West Street Grill, in Litchfield, USA. At the time he sent me many books, including those by Alice Waters and Wolfgang Puck. His sister Bernadette O'Shea had Truffles in Sligo and Luna in Leitrim – both brilliant restaurants. I spent quite a few summer holidays in Templenoe with my cousin Margaret and her family. I loved it there. Another example of the influence of food in our family.

We didn't have our own garden in The Lime Tree but Billy Clifford, a local organic grower, supplied us with wonderful organic produce and still does to this day. Annie Goulding cooked with me at The Lime Tree and introduced me to the wonders of collecting your own food such as wild mushrooms, elderflower, wild garlic, spring nettles, wild sorrel and more. At the time, another great influence was Sonia Stevenson, a master chef of Great Britain, who first opened the Horn of Plenty restaurant in 1967 in Devon, England. Sonia is a brilliant chef and was the first woman to cook at Maxim's in Paris and the first British woman to be awarded a Michelin star. I did a stage in her restaurant in Devon in the early 1980s and learned a huge amount from her. I was also highly influenced by Michel Guérard, Nico Ladenis (known as 'Nico') and Pierre Koffmann.

I also had the opportunity to briefly work with the great Colin O'Daly at his famous restaurant The Park in Blackrock, Co. Dublin. Colin was formerly head chef at the Park Hotel in Kenmare and earned a Michelin star there in 1983. At that time James Mulchrone, who had been a chef at the Park Hotel, was part of Colin's team and he was very helpful to me in a highly pressurised kitchen. James now runs a very successful

Above left: The Lime Tree today
Above right: Our renovation of the old mid-nineteenth century schoolhouse into The Lime Tree restaurant in the early 1980s

chain which started in Kenmare called Jam Café, Deli & Bakery, with cafés in Killarney, Ballincollig and Cork as well as Kenmare. In the 1980s, I continued to attend various workshops including one given by Ruth Rogers and Rose Gray of The River Café in London at Darina Allen's marvellous Ballymaloe Cookery School. I was also fortunate that John Desmond – of the amazing Island Cottage restaurant in Heir Island, Co. Cork and a former teacher at École de Cuisine La Varenne in Paris and Burgundy – is a close friend, and I was able to attend one of his nouvelle cuisine courses which he gave at Ballymaloe.

The Lime Tree was a very happy and satisfying place. The kitchen was airy and Therese, Annie Goulding and I had massive fun while we worked! Cyril O'Donoghue, who started to work with me in the kitchen during the school holidays, went on to become one of my main chefs at The Lime Tree and for a while in Packie's before turning to another passion of his, fishing. The O'Donoghue family formed an integral part of my team over the years.

In The Lime Tree, I was able to express my keen interest in interior design, another love of mine. The dinner service, lamps, vases and many other items were all from Louis Mulcahy in Dingle. All the chairs were covered with Irish tweed. The place was truly rustic, and a mezzanine over half the dining room created an interesting eating space.

The cutlery was from David Mellor. We were fortunate that many great local artists lived in the area, many of whom are my good friends and The Lime Tree was a showcase of Irish art and craft.

Favourite dishes at The Lime Tree included: prawn & spinach pastries with a mousseline sauce (p119), wild Atlantic seafood soup (p80), seafood mousse (p122) with oyster and leek beurre blanc, rack of lamb with paloise sauce (p229), tornados of monkfish with lobster, scallops with ginger beurre blanc, coeur de fromage with fresh raspberry sauce, and zabaglione ice-cream (p322). Delicious!

It was during The Lime Tree days that I was invited to join Euro-Toques by Myrtle Allen, one of the co-founders along with other European chefs including Paul Bocuse from France. Myrtle was an astounding woman and was always extremely enterprising. One of my most memorable dinners was an evening hosted by Euro-Toques at my friend Derry Clarke's restaurant, L'Ecrivain, in the 1990s. We were served the most amazing tasting menu cooked by Derry and the talented Ross Lewis of Chapter One. It was a privilege to be there that evening and Evan Doyle brought us to a wonderful night club where Tom and I danced the night away – the perfect night!

The Lime Tree reached Red M status with Michelin and became a hugely successful restaurant. At the time, we were looking for something simpler. We sold The Lime Tree in 1991 and opened a smaller restaurant in 1992 – Packie's on Henry Street.

Packie's, Henry Street: From Grocery to Restaurant (1992–2003)

My uncle Packie's grocery shop used to be called Packie's. He had continued to run his mother's business, with his wife Anne Mai (née O' Sullivan Rodger from Kilgarvan), from the 1940s until he passed away in 1991. Eileen O'Leary worked with Packie in the shop for many years and later was a great help to me in Shelburne Lodge.

It was a big local business with a unique personal service. Packie travelled in his van during the 1940s, 1950s and 1960s around the Beara and Iveragh peninsula, going as far as Ardgroom on a Tuesday and Castlecove on a Friday. He sold his groceries to those living in the countryside, including sugar and loose tea that came from India in large wooden chests (believe it or not, these empty tea chests were later used as play pens for children). In turn Packie bought their local farm produce such as poultry, rabbits, eggs and homemade butter which he sold in his shop or directly to Murphy's butter merchants in Little Hanover Street in Cork for export. Prior to the introduction of the big supermarkets, the locally run family shops were great social centres and people went in for a chat just as much for their shopping. At Christmas time, he had salted ling fish hanging at the door which was a staple for Christmas Eve suppers, being a day of abstinence with no meat. Also during Christmas, hundreds of turkeys were plucked and prepared, some of which were sent abroad, including to my parents when we lived in London.

For Packie's restaurant, I had hoped originally to open a casual eatery with good food and no bookings, but Packie's became a smaller version of The Lime Tree. One of the new dishes I introduced was crispy crumbed mustard crubeens (pig's trotters), which were a favourite of my chef customers. I got the tasty recipe for these from Richard Corrigan who was working in Mulligan's at the time, before starting his culinary empire.

Martin Hallissey standing outside Packie's

Packie's has been leased to Martin Hallissey since 2003. Martin first started working with me during his school summer holidays in The Lime Tree. He is very passionate about his cooking and has maintained a wonderful standard over the years.

Maura and Cyril O'Donoghue in Packie's in the 1990s, The Irish Times

Shelburne Lodge – Restoration to Guesthouse – 1990 to Present

In 1990 we bought Shelburne House, an old mid-18th century Georgian farmhouse. The restoration was a big undertaking and took five years. In 1996 we opened the lovingly restored Shelburne Lodge as a registered guesthouse.

I had a super team at Packie's and we managed to operate both the restaurant and Shelburne Lodge at the same time. My daughter Senga, who has a natural creativity for flower arranging and a particular talent for baking, worked with me both at Packie's and later at Shelburne Lodge.

My Life in Food : 25

More recently, my close friend Liz Murphy has been a great help and advisor to me at Shelburne Lodge. She has a lifetime of experience having taught at a catering school in Switzerland and worked throughout her career in top five-star hotels in Ireland, including The Park Hotel Kenmare when it first opened in 1980, The Adare Manor Hotel and the beautiful Sheen Falls Lodge Hotel situated on the Sheen River.

Having a great team is absolutely crucial to any hospitality business. Throughout our business ventures, we have always fostered a friendly environment and been surrounded by excellent staff to whom I am very thankful. Lasting friendships have been formed and I love catching up with them, often reminiscing about our times together.

Over the years we have been fortunate with national and international review articles in the media such as *The New York Times*, *The Times* and *The Irish Times*. These have been incredibly supportive for our businesses. John and Sally McKenna, originally of the *Bridgestone Guide* and now the *McKenna's Guide*, in particular, wrote some wonderful tributes to me over the years for which I am hugely grateful.

Shelburne Lodge

It has been a pleasure for me to see Kenmare develop and grow into an established holiday destination. Tourism is an integral part of our town, with mostly family run businesses that span over several generations. Locals and visitors enjoy a high standard of food with a superb choice of hotels, restaurants, cafés and bars and the beautiful and unique surroundings that Kenmare has to offer. I love Kenmare for its vibrancy and its people – it is a very special place to live. Many have come here to work and have settled and contributed greatly to the town and its ethos, including young chefs.

With a long career in food, I wanted to bring this cookbook together for all my dear family, friends, staff and customers; to share the stories and food that has enriched my life and, hopefully, also the life of others. Included are a diverse collection of recipes, gathered from a life of cooking in Kenmare.

Below: Shelburne Lodge today
Overleaf: Detail from Maurice Henderson painting (1986)
hanging in Shelburne Lodge

My Life in Food 27

Maura's Cooking Notes

Cooking Notes

In writing this book, I found getting exact measurements difficult. It doesn't always provide perfect results and when I cook in my kitchen it is 'taste, taste, taste' to my liking. Tasting is vital as there are many factors that will determine the outcome. Cook to your own taste and make what you feel is enjoyable and delicious.

One of my favourite sayings is by Paul Bocuse, the great master chef, for its brilliant reference to the wonders of butter: "du beurre, encore du beurre, toujours du beurre". Cooking to what pleases your palate in terms of flavour is important as balance varies with the individual. Don't be afraid to veer from the recipe and add or omit as you please. Use recipes as a guide or as inspiration.

Equipment

Julia Child said to "always start out with a larger pot than what you think you need" and I have always followed her advice.

Here are a few important tools for the kitchen:

- A good selection of heavy stainless steel saucepans with riveted handles
- Heavy Tefal frying pans with riveted handles in varying sizes are best for frying
- Heavy casserole pots, preferably two of different sizes
- A few heavy roasting pans
- One or two heavy iron griddle pans, especially for steak and meat
- One or two omelette pans; old heavy iron pans are best or use a non-stick heavy Tefal pan
- A few good knives – I love the small Kitchen Devils but a variety of knives is important in your kitchen; different coloured handles with allocations are great for hygiene
- A few different kitchen scissors for specific purposes, for example one for trimming fish, one for snipping herbs
- A selection of stainless steel flexible whisks including a few small whisks for sauces
- A few spatulas to always scrape the bowls and reduce waste
- Flat straight fish slices, slotted spoons, sieves and a versatile grater
- A heavy pestle and mortar
- A variety of chopping boards
- Accurate weighing scales for measuring
- A good quality hand blender

Quality of Ingredients

It is vital you aim to source the best ingredients, especially if you want the best outcome. Only a little help is required once you have wonderful raw ingredients. Aim to source local, fresh and seasonal. In my experience it is impossible to improve a bad ingredient.

Butter

All butter in this book is salted butter unless specified as unsalted in a few recipes. In Ireland we are lucky as there are excellent quality dairy butters available. Kerrygold is available worldwide and is a good option outside of Ireland, or use locally made dairy butters which are now becoming more available.

Clarified Butter

Clarified butter is actually very simple to make and can be stored. It is used for frying foods and reaches a very high temperature before it burns. The method is included in the Sauces, Stocks & Staples chapter (p376). If you opt for regular butter, including a little oil into the pan at the same time will enable a higher temperature before it burns. Unsalted butter can also reach a high temperature. Salted butter alone is trickier and it can burn fast; if this happens it really is unusable.

Eggs

We have local organic farm eggs and all recipes in the book refer to organic eggs. Fresh eggs are important. In a fresh egg, the white is well coagulated and stays together; on cracking an egg if the white runs out, it is not a fresh egg. It is best to store eggs at room temperature.

Herbs

Fresh herbs are delicious and nutritious. It is very simple to grow a kitchen garden or window box and having a variety to choose from can finish a dish beautifully in terms of flavour. Alternatively, seek fresh herbs from your market or supermarket. They are very different to the dried version and the recipes included in the book refer to fresh herbs unless specified as dried.

- **Bay leaf, sage and rosemary:** these are strong herbs and should be used carefully. Sage is good in duck or pork stuffing and used a lot in Italian cooking. Bay leaves are added to pâtés, strong stews and casseroles (except lamb); usually one bay leaf will do. Rosemary is lovely with lamb, tomatoes, marinades and barbecuing and in oil infusions.
- **Basil:** a great summer herb, can be difficult to digest for some people. Used in Italian food, great in salads, pastas, tomatoes, soups, pestos and sauces.
- **Oregano:** great in salads with similar uses as basil.
- **Thyme:** an all-round herb which can be used with a variety of meats, soups, stocks, stuffings, potatoes and poultry; adds great flavour.
- **Chives:** delicate oniony flavour not for cooking, should be snipped over salads or sauces just before service.
- **Coriander:** a summer herb, used widely in Indian and Middle Eastern cooking. Distinctive flavour which can transform a dish, excellent with spicy food and all savoury food, especially if you love it, it can go with everything.
- **Tarragon:** used in classic French cooking, great with fish, chicken, pasta, vinegars and a key flavour in béarnaise sauce.
- **Fennel:** aniseed flavoured herb associated with fish; used a lot in my kitchens as a garnish for its beautiful colour and texture; bronze variety is equally beautiful, and the flower can be used for garnish also. The bulbs work well with fish and are great roasted. Fennel flowers are great for arrangements and fennel seeds are super in soups or with fish.
- **Mint:** lots of varieties; great for teas, dressings, salads, mint sauce for lamb or garnishing desserts; used a lot with coriander in Vietnamese cooking, a great combination.
- **Borage:** its edible purple flowers are used for garnishes and brews.
- **Sweet cicely:** lacy fern-like leaves with an aniseed flavour, used for garnish in our kitchens for fish and fruits.
- **Salad burnet:** leaves are serrated and are cucumber-like in flavour, delicate, good in salads or chopped into mayonnaise. Also used in summer cocktails.
- **Lemon verbena or lemon balm:** great for decorative use and garnish of desserts. Verbena is also used as a tea infusion.

Tarragon Vinegar

This can be difficult to find readymade. To make, add multiple fresh tarragon sprigs to a bottle of good quality white wine vinegar. Push the herb right down to the bottom. Leave on a warm sunny windowsill for a week to infuse.

Noilly Prat

This is a dry vermouth and is best added to a sauce just a few minutes before it is complete. It does not require a long period of cooking out, like brandy or wine for example. It will give your sauce that extra oomph.

Nuts

Need to be fresh; always get the current season. Last year's nuts lose their flavour and can go rancid. Best roasted in the oven to enhance their flavour for about 20 minutes at around fan 130°C / fan 265°F / gas mark 2.

Seasoning

Good quality sea salt is important; if it is very coarse then it is better to grind it, especially when seasoning flour. When black pepper is used, it is always freshly cracked from the mill or ground in a pestle and mortar. Seasoned flour is used a lot for the fish and chicken recipes. Use plain white flour, then season with a few grinds of sea salt and freshly ground black pepper per tablespoon of flour.

Shallots

The sweetness of slow cooked shallots is superb. My mother Agnes only used shallots and I mostly do the same, especially for certain recipes. She had a supplier, a farmer from The Two Mile Bridge near Kenmare, and he grew them especially for her. She used to get a large netted bag of sweet shallots regularly. They can be used instead of onions and have a sweeter flavour. When using regular onions, try and get local and fresh.

Spices

Spices are always better as fresh as possible, dry roasted and pounded in the pestle and mortar for maximum flavour.

Vanilla Pods

Vanilla pods have become expensive. They are required for a few recipes in the book, particularly custard and the ice-cream. Do not buy dry pods; they need to be moist and plump. When sold in a glass vial they are at their best. To use the pod, split the vanilla pod horizontally and open out the pod with the seeds exposed. Use a flat knife to scrape out the seeds; the seeds will come off in lumps and are very precious. Once they are added to liquid they will disperse right through the liquid. The pod can also be added to the liquid for infusion, then removed and used to make vanilla sugar. Clean the pod and dry briefly by placing in a warm oven for a few minutes. Place in a jar of caster sugar to infuse.

Conversion Tables

Ovens

All recipes referred to in the book provide fan-assisted, fan oven or 'convection' oven temperatures. If you are using a conventional oven (not fan-assisted) the rule of thumb is to add 10-20°C or 25-30°F to the recommended fan temperature. Of course, every oven behaves differently, so factor in your knowledge of your own oven and the manufacturer's guidance.

The temperatures provided here are a guide only. Cooking times can also vary and take longer in a conventional oven. If using a fan or 'convection' oven, depending on the recipe, it is a good idea to check 5 to 10 minutes before recommended cooking times.

Know your own oven and use some common sense!

Fan °C Degrees Celsius	Fan °F Degrees Fahrenheit	Gas Mark	Conventional Oven
100	210	½	A rough rule of thumb is to add 10-20°C or 25-30°F for a conventional oven e.g. fan 180°C to conventional 190-200°C or fan 350°F to conventional 375-380°F.
120	250	1	
130	265	2	
140	275	3	
160	325	4	
170	340	5	
180	350	6	
200	400	7	
220	425	9	

Weight Conversions

Dry Ingredients – Conversions used are approximate

Metric	Imperial	Metric	Imperial
15g	½oz	225g	8oz / ½lb
30g	1oz	255g	9oz
45g	1½oz	285g	10oz
55g	2oz	310g	11oz
85g	3oz	340g	12oz / ¾lb
100g	3½oz	370g	13oz
115g	4oz	400g	14oz
130g	4½oz	450g	16oz / 1lb
140g	5oz	500g	1lb 2oz
170g	6oz	900g	2lb
200g	7oz	1.8kg	4lb

Liquid Ingredients – Conversions used are approximate

Metric	Imperial	Metric	Imperial
30ml	1fl oz	285ml	½ pint
55ml	2fl oz	310ml	11fl oz
85ml	3fl oz	340ml	12fl oz
115ml	4fl oz	370ml	13fl oz
140ml	¼ pint	400ml	14fl oz
170ml	6fl oz	450ml	16 fl oz
200ml	7fl oz	510ml	18 fl oz
225ml	8fl oz	570ml	1 pint
255ml	9fl oz	1140ml	2 pints

Breakfast

Irish Brown Soda Bread	46
Spiced Apple & Cinnamon Compote	48
Gooseberry & Elderflower Compote	49
Dried Prune & Apricot Fruit Compote	50
Summer Berry Compote	51
Blackberry or Blackcurrant & Apple Compote	53
Rhubarb & Orange Compote with Irish Strawberries	54
Spicy Plum Compote with Star Anise	55
Poached Pears in Ginger	57
Drop Scone Pancakes with Dry Cured Bacon and Apple Syrup	58
Organic Porridge with Whiskey Cream	60
Organic Whole Natural Yoghurt with Honey, Nuts & Seeds	61
Shelburne Lodge Omelette with Gubbeen Chorizo	62
Purple Heather Omelette	64
Smoked Salmon Omelette	65
Shelburne Lodge Eggs Benedict, Florentine and Royale	66
Scrambled Eggs with Smoked Salmon and a Chive Crème Fraîche	68
Fish of the Day	69
Irish Farmhouse Cheese Selection	71

For more breakfast ideas try…

Potato Pancakes with Garlic or Herb Butter (p94)

Wild Chanterelle Mushrooms with Bruschetta (p99)

Date, Orange & Sunflower Seed Loaf (p301)

Breakfast

When you make time for breakfast, it can be one of the most special meals of the day. Broken down, the word is as literal as it sounds: 'break' the overnight 'fast'. In the old days in Ireland, people especially needed a good breakfast. Bicycles were the main mode of transport and people mainly worked physically so one needed good nourishment. Eggs, porridge and homemade breads were mostly eaten.

Being on my feet most of the day, I still try to have a good breakfast and sit down to eat porridge and brown bread daily with Tom. My morning porridge is usually accompanied by local honey and some form of fruit compote, the spiced apple being my particular favourite (p48).

In Ireland, breakfast had a special tradition of its own on Sundays. People fasted from midnight to mass on Sundays and afterwards would have a cooked breakfast, which included black pudding. The tradition of a cooked Irish breakfast is continued today. Made in varying forms and combinations, black pudding is one of the earliest puddings made. The key ingredient is fresh pig's blood, which is rich in iron and goes willingly with varying flavours. We serve some wonderful local black puddings from near Kenmare, including the delicious Putóg De Róiste from Ballyvourney with an oatmeal texture and the more smooth-textured Sneem Black Pudding baked in a loaf style. Good quality dry cured bacon rashers and handmade pork sausages are also essential for a full Irish breakfast. I like to use a mix of both green (unsmoked) and smoked dry cured bacon rashers. There are some great suppliers in the south west region such as Ashe's from Annascaul who make delicious breakfast sausages.

Irish soda bread (or 'brown bread') is a daily breakfast staple, and like all old recipes each household has their own take on the classic. We make our bread daily and serve it with soft butter and local jams and marmalades, alongside a country loaf and barmbrack from Harrington's, our local bakery. According to master baker Johnny Moriarty, my good friend and bridge partner, breads should be baked in an oven with a dropping heat. Johnny and his brothers had the most wonderful bakery for many years in Kenmare with large, deep brick fired ovens dating back to the 1930s. The ovens were heated by a log fire until they were bright red, then raked out. The bread was then put in the oven and baked by the hot bricks. The base heat and the top heat allowed for the crust which baked it from the inside out. Making all their bread by hand, they offered a fabulous choice of breads including butter loaves, seed loaves, round browns, barmbracks, tea buns, twin pans and basket loaves. Renowned in Ireland for their barmbracks, at Christmas time they would have carefully packaged and posted seven to eight hundred loaves abroad to the UK and the US – a very special delivery. The bakery was also a great local meeting place for storytelling and interesting conversations, particularly in the afternoons when all the bread was baked.

On the daily menu for breakfast at Shelburne Lodge is fish of the day. Fish is one of my favourite ingredients and what I am best known for. Some of our regular guests stay especially for the fish. We are spoiled with the great fresh fish from the wild Atlantic and it makes for a wonderful start to the day. As a young girl in the early 1950s, my parents and I spent many weekends fishing together. Mostly, we fished at the Black Valley, a beautiful valley near Kenmare, or in Gleninchaquin on the Tuosist side on the Beara Peninsula. My father also fished many evenings in the summer and I often went with him up to Lough Barfinnihy near Moll's Gap. We loved it. I have fond memories of my mother cooking the trout that we had caught the previous evening and we always ate it with a smoked rasher for breakfast. Plain and simple.

Growing up, the rest of our breakfast staples came local as well. We lived near the creamery. I used to hop over the wall and into the dairy where there were big churns of cream and they would give me a little carton to take home, which we would eat with our porridge. Our milk came morning and evening from our next door neighbour, Den McCarthy, who had a big farm. I would also collect eggs from our neighbour Cas when we lived on Bridge Street, a time when 'organic eggs' were just 'eggs'. Thankfully, we continue to have beautiful fresh organic eggs in Kenmare. The quality of the egg is so important to the finished dish; always try to source good fresh eggs if you can and store outside of the fridge at room temperature.

Conveniently, many of the recipes in this chapter work equally well for brunch, a light lunch or even supper. The fruit compotes are best served with organic whole natural yoghurt and could also be used as a dessert or served with some good cheese. I vary my compotes depending on which fruits are in season. Considering fruit varies in sweetness or tartness, it is essential to taste your compote and adjust accordingly. If it is too sweet add a little lemon juice, or if too tart add some caster sugar or serve with local honey.

We continue to offer full service for our breakfast in Shelburne Lodge, for a special and thoughtful way to start the day.

Enjoy.

Irish Brown Soda Bread

Irish brown soda bread is a staple for an Irish breakfast, being both simple and nutritious. There are many variations across the households of Ireland, some including rolled oats, honey or treacle, whereas my mother's was a rich bread with butter, eggs and not too much sugar.

The type of flour is important for texture. I mainly use an extra coarse stoneground wholemeal flour as I prefer a nutty texture. Buttermilk is another key ingredient, as it interacts with the bicarbonate of soda to rise the loaf. The amount of buttermilk needed will vary depending on the texture of the flour you use; 'extra coarse' absorbs less moisture than 'coarse' and requires less buttermilk. If you have no buttermilk available, substitute with sour milk or fresh milk soured with 1 tsp of white wine vinegar. Oven temperatures vary, so know your oven and adapt; the bread should be golden brown all over.

My favourite way to eat the bread is fresh out of the oven with some butter and local honey spread on top. It is also delicious with a good olive oil or tapenade. In The Purple Heather, it is served in baskets and as the base for their open sandwiches.

The bread freezes well, and the batch can be easily doubled or sliced up and frozen to be toasted individually later.

Ingredients

Makes 900g / 2lb loaf tin

- **Sunflower oil, to grease**
- **115g / 4oz plain white flour, sieved**
- **1 round tsp bicarbonate of soda, sieved into the flour**
- **340g / 12oz extra coarse stoneground wholemeal flour**
- **¼ tsp sea salt**
- **1 tbsp demerara sugar or honey**
- **1 egg, beaten**
- **55g / 2oz butter, melted**
- **Approximately 400ml / 14fl oz buttermilk or sour milk (it will depend on the type of wholemeal flour used, for example 'extra coarse' absorbs less moisture than 'coarse' and requires less buttermilk)**

Method

Preheat the oven to fan 180°C / fan 350°F / gas mark 6. Grease a 900g / 2lb loaf tin with sunflower oil and cut a long rectangle of greaseproof paper to line the length of the tin. Over a bowl, sieve in the flour with the bicarbonate of soda to combine well. Add the remaining dry ingredients (if using honey, add to the milk) and combine well. It is critical that the dry ingredients are thoroughly mixed. In another bowl, mix together the egg, butter and buttermilk (and honey if using).

Add the wet ingredients into the dry ingredients and mix together gently. Be careful not to overmix, as this will toughen the bread. The dough should be a fairly wet consistency. Add the bread mixture to the tin and even the surface on top. Bake in the oven for 55-60 minutes or until golden brown and cooked.

Leave the bread in the tin for about 5 minutes, then carefully remove to cool on a wire rack. When completely cool, store in a sealed container for up to 5 days.

Spiced Apple & Cinnamon Compote

This compote has infinite breakfast and even dessert serving options; try it with porridge or whiskey cream.

With such a huge variety of apples to choose from, I use large Bramley cooking apples and Cox's as my preferred eating apple. Use whichever eating apple you like best. You will need to adapt this recipe to taste according to the apples you use as their tartness will vary. Adjust the water depending on the size and texture of your apples.

Ingredients

Serves 6-8

- 6 large cooking apples, e.g. Bramley
- 6 firm eating apples, e.g. Cox's
- 570ml / 1 pint cold water
- 200g / 7oz demerara sugar
- 1 stick of cinnamon, broken into around 5cm / 2in pieces
- 2 tsp ground cinnamon
- Zest and juice of 1 lemon, plus extra to taste if needed
- Caster sugar, to taste if needed
- Cream, Whiskey Cream (p60) or porridge, to serve
- A few little vertical pieces of cinnamon stick from the compote, optional garnish

Method

Peel, core and thickly slice all the apples (about the size of an average orange segment). In a medium saucepan, combine the water with the sugar, cinnamon, and lemon zest and juice. Bring to the boil over a medium-high heat, stirring for the sugar to dissolve, then add the apples to the pan. Bring back to the boil, then reduce to a low heat. With a large stainless steel spoon, periodically bring the apples at the base to the top to allow the apples to cook evenly, being sure to keep them firm and not cooking too long to avoid the apples disintegrating. (The cooking apples will tend to be softer and the eating apples will retain their shape.) Taste the compote, adding a little caster sugar if too tart, and more lemon juice if too sweet.

Allow to cool, then store in a sealed container in the fridge for up to 5 days.

Serve warm with cream, Whiskey Cream (p60) or with porridge. Garnish with a few little pieces of cinnamon stick from the compote.

Gooseberry & Elderflower Compote

To me, gooseberries are the Cinderella of the berry family. Incredibly versatile, I serve them with savoury dishes, such as salmon (**p178**). My good friend Annie Goulding, who cooked with me at The Lime Tree, prepared them in a delicious gooseberry fool. The gooseberries I remember the most are the ones of my childhood, the dessert gooseberries – sweet enough to eat straight off the bush, although rarely seen now. Gooseberries will vary in levels of bitterness, so additional sugar may be needed; adjust this to your taste.

Ingredients

Serves 6-8

- 4 tbsp water
- 225-340g / 8-12 oz demerara sugar, depending on bitterness of the gooseberries
- 450g / 1 lb gooseberries, topped, tailed and washed
- Zest and juice of 1 lime
- 4 large elderflower heads, stems washed and cut to separate stems and heads
- Sugar Syrup (p365) or caster sugar, to taste if needed
- Organic whole natural yoghurt, to serve
- Lemon balm and elderflower, optional garnish

Method

In a saucepan, add the water and sugar and stir to dissolve over a medium-high heat. Add the gooseberries, lime zest and juice, and elderflower stems and heads to the pan. Reduce heat and simmer gently, stirring occasionally for 20 minutes or until the gooseberries are soft and burst a little. Take the pan off the heat and remove the elderflower stems from the pan. Set aside to cool.

Once cooled, store in a sealed container in the fridge for up to 5 days.

Serve chilled with organic whole natural yoghurt and garnish with lemon balm and elderflower.

Dried Prune & Apricot Fruit Compote

Unlike the other compotes, this one can be made anytime of the year. Delicious for breakfast with muesli or organic whole natural yoghurt, it is nourishing and healthy. If not for breakfast, use for a Moroccan-style tagine or as a stuffing for slow-cooked boned pork shoulder. It can also be served as a sweet accompaniment with a good salty cheese.

Ingredients

Serves 6

- 425ml / 15fl oz cold water
- 1 tbsp honey
- Zest and juice of ½ orange
- Zest and juice of ½ lemon
- 2 Earl Grey tea bags
- 225g / 8oz dried prunes
- 225g / 8oz dried apricots
- Organic whole natural yoghurt or cream, to serve
- Lemon balm or mint, optional garnish

Method

In a medium saucepan, add the water. Over a low heat add the honey, zest and juice and stir. Add the tea bags, prunes and apricots. Bring to the boil, then cover with a tight lid and reduce heat to the lowest heat possible, cooking the fruit gently until plumped for about 30-40 minutes.

Allow to cool, then store in a sealed container in the fridge for up to 1 month.

Serve cold with organic whole natural yoghurt or cream. Garnish with lemon balm or mint.

Summer Berry Compote

A compote bursting with the freshness of the berries. The sugar syrup (p365) is an excellent base for many other fruit compotes, such as ripe sliced nectarines, peaches or apricots. Spread the compote or spoon onto drop scone pancakes, meringues, organic whole natural yoghurt or good quality ice-cream for a delicious dessert.

Ingredients

Serves 8-10

- 600ml / 21fl oz sugar syrup (p365)
- 100g / 3½oz blackcurrants
- 100g / 3½oz loganberries, if you can source them
- 310g / 11oz strawberries, quartered
- 125g / 4½oz raspberries
- 125g / 4½oz blueberries
- Additional caster sugar or lemon juice, to taste if needed
- Organic whole natural yoghurt, to serve
- Wild strawberry leaves and flowers, optional garnish

Method

Pour the syrup into a large saucepan and heat over a medium heat. Add the blackcurrants and simmer for 5 minutes or until they start to burst. Add the remaining berries and cook for 5 minutes or until the strawberries start to soften – you want them to keep their texture. Taste the compote, adding a little caster sugar if too tart, or more lemon juice if too sweet.

Allow to cool then store in a sealed container in the fridge for up to 5 days.

Serve chilled with organic whole natural yoghurt or with drop scone pancakes (p58). Garnish with some wild strawberry leaves and flowers.

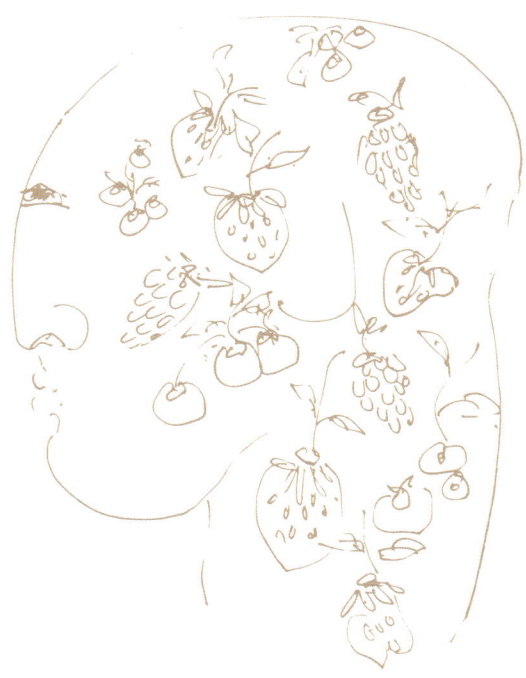

Blackberry or Blackcurrant & Apple Compote

Picking blackberries is a pure shared joy; children absolutely love it. Seamus Heaney, who has been a guest of ours, wrote a marvellous poem, 'Blackberry Picking', portraying the activity's joys and disappointments. One of my daughters based her school art project on the vivid imagery of his poem showing the blackberries "leaving stains upon the tongue and lust for picking" and our hands being "peppered with thorn pricks". We're fortunate because we can pick lots of blackberries given the many briars in our semi-wild garden.

Ingredients

Serves 8

- **5 large cooking apples e.g. Bramley**
- **100ml / 3½fl oz cold water**
- **200g / 7oz demerara sugar**
- **225g / ½lb blackberries or blackcurrants**
- **Additional caster sugar or lemon juice, to taste if needed**
- **Organic whole natural yoghurt, to serve**
- **When using blackcurrants: a sprig of blackcurrant leaves with some fresh blackcurrants, optional garnish**
- **When using blackberries: mint, lemon balm or borage flowers, optional garnish**

Method

Peel, core and thickly slice all the apples (about the size of an average orange segment). In a medium saucepan, add the water, sugar and apples and cook over a medium heat stirring occasionally for about 10 minutes or until the apples soften. Add the berries, bring to a simmer and stir and cook until the berries start to break up – about 6-8 minutes for the blackcurrants and about 4-6 minutes for the blackberries, both depending on the ripeness. It is important to stay with the pot while the berries are cooking and stir occasionally to ensure that it is not sticking to the pan. Taste the compote, adding a little caster sugar if too tart, or more lemon juice if too sweet. Cover with a lid to cool and allow the flavours to infuse.

Once cooled, store in a sealed container in the fridge for up to 5 days.

Serve chilled with organic whole natural yoghurt and garnish with blackcurrant leaves and blackcurrants or herb of choice.

Rhubarb & Orange Compote with Irish Strawberries

I make this popular compote in the early summer when rhubarb is in season. Using homegrown organic rhubarb from Billy Clifford and served with fresh Irish strawberries (when in season), the tart rhubarb pairs beautifully with the sweet strawberries.

The pink rhubarb at the start of the season will take less cooking time and need less sugar. As the season progresses, the rhubarb changes texture and becomes greener and will require more cooking time and more sugar.

Ingredients

Serves 8

- 2 bundles of red rhubarb (about 800g / 1lb 12oz), washed, trimmed and chopped into 2.5cm / 1in pieces
- Zest and juice of 1 orange
- 100-200g / 3½-7oz demerara sugar (as the season progresses, the rhubarb gets more green and bitter and will need a lot more sugar to taste)
- 2 tbsp water
- 450g / 1lb strawberries, to serve
- Organic whole natural yoghurt, to serve
- Wild strawberry leaves and flowers or a sprig of lemon balm or borage flowers, optional garnish

Method

Preheat the oven to fan 180°C / fan 350°F / gas mark 6. Add the rhubarb, zest, juice, sugar and water into a large ovenproof ceramic or Pyrex dish and toss everything together until the rhubarb is coated with sugar and juice. Cover tightly with foil and bake for 15 minutes. Remove from the oven; the sugar should have dissolved. Using a large spoon, scrape the bottom of the dish to ensure the sugar hasn't stuck and to disperse the sugar, and gently move the rhubarb around. Re-cover with the foil and bake for another 5-12 minutes until the rhubarb is tender but still retains its shape. Cooking time will depend on the time of season.

Allow to cool, then store in a sealed container in the fridge for up to 5 days.

Serve the compote chilled with sliced strawberries on top. Garnish with herbs of your choice or wild strawberry flowers and leaves if you have them. Even better with a spoon of organic whole natural yoghurt.

Spicy Plum Compote with Star Anise

The star anise adds a delicate, and almost mysterious, flavour to the compote. Taste a sliver of the plum before making the compote to determine how much sugar may be needed, judging based on the sweetness or tartness of the fruit. Use dark purple plums for the best results and cook very slowly so the plums hold their shape yet become sufficiently tender.

Ingredients

Serves 4-6

- 400g / 14oz demerara sugar, more or less depending on the ripeness of the plums
- 400ml / 14fl oz cold water
- Zest and juice of 1 orange
- 6 star anise
- 12 cloves
- 1kg / 2lb 4oz whole dark purple plums (around 12-14 plums, depending on size)
- Organic whole natural yoghurt, to serve
- Borage flowers, optional garnish

Method

Into a large heavy-based saucepan, add the sugar, water, zest, juice, star anise and cloves. Stir over a medium heat to dissolve the sugar then bring to the boil. Add the plums and reduce to a very low heat (as low as possible to avoid the plums from breaking up too much) and cook slowly for 10-15 minutes until the plums are soft. The plums will vary in cooking time based on their variety and degree of ripeness. They should hold their shape but be sufficiently tender. Gently shake the pot occasionally to move the plums around so that they can cook evenly but don't break up as they would with stirring. Once ready, remove from the heat and cover with a lid to allow the flavours to infuse and allow to cool.

Once cooled, store in a sealed container in the fridge for up to 5 days.

Serve chilled with organic whole natural yoghurt. Garnish with borage flowers.

Poached Pears in Ginger

Ginger has natural soothing properties making for a great start to the day. This recipe is for breakfast and it is critical that the pears are unripe. It is one of the most requested recipes by guests staying in Shelburne Lodge.

For dessert, the recipe can be adapted and the poached pears caramelised. In a non-stick frying pan over a high heat, add 3 tbsp of the ginger syrup from the poached pears and 2 tbsp of butter and allow to caramelise a little. Add the four half poached pears and cook for 3-4 minutes. These can be served with a scoop of vanilla ice-cream (p320) and a shortbread biscuit (p324) on the side.

Ingredients

Serves 4-6

- 850ml / 1½ pints sugar syrup (p365, making with demerara sugar instead)
- 5cm / 2in piece fresh ginger, peeled and julienned
- Zest and juice of 1 lemon
- 6 under ripe pears, peeled and halved with the seeds removed, retaining the stalk on one half of the pear (Conference pears are best)
- Organic whole natural yoghurt, muesli or porridge, to serve
- A sprig of chocolate mint leaf or bronze fennel, optional garnish

Method

In a small saucepan, heat the syrup with the ginger, zest and juice over a gentle heat. Add the pears and poach gently for 25-30 minutes or until tender.

Allow to cool, then store in a sealed container in the fridge for up to 5 days.

Serve chilled with your choice of organic whole natural yoghurt, muesli or porridge and garnish.

Drop Scone Pancakes with Dry Cured Bacon and Apple Syrup

These old-fashioned style pancakes were widely cooked in Irish country farmhouses, mostly because they were both economical and delicious. They are traditionally eaten with homemade butter and jams, much like how my mother would make them for me. I now serve them in more of a savoury way at Shelburne Lodge with bacon for a welcome saltiness. When cooking bacon, it should always be on a high heat, ideally using a hot griddle pan.

I serve the pancakes with maple syrup or a homemade apple syrup (p364). They are also great with warm spiced apple compote (p48) or summer berry compote (p51). The batter keeps for up to 2 days in the fridge. If stored in the fridge the pancakes will be thicker and need longer to cook.

Ingredients

Makes 12-14 pancakes

- 90g / 3¼oz plain white flour
- A pinch of sea salt
- 2 rounded tsp baking powder
- 1 tsp demerara sugar
- 2 eggs
- 100ml / 3½fl oz milk
- 40g / 2¾oz butter, melted and cooled
- Butter for cooking (preferably use clarified butter p376)
- 6 rashers dry cured bacon
- 6 rashers unsmoked bacon
- A little jug of homemade apple syrup (p364) or maple syrup, to serve
- Oregano flower, sweet cicely or any seasonal herb, optional garnish

Method

Into a bowl, add the flour, salt and baking powder then mix in the sugar and blend thoroughly with a whisk. Beat the eggs lightly, add the milk and beat until blended (about 30 seconds). Add the eggs and milk to the dry ingredients and gently mix to combine, being careful not to overmix. Lastly, add the melted cooled butter.

In a large heavy-based frying pan lightly grease with ½ tsp butter over a medium-high heat until it sizzles (be careful that the butter does not burn). Using a dessert spoon, dollop spoons of the mixture into the pan, allowing a little space for the mixture to spread. Cook until the pancakes start to rise and bubbles appear on the surface for about 3-4 minutes, then quickly flip over and cook for 3 minutes or until the pancakes are cooked through. They will need longer if the batter is thick and has been left overnight in the fridge. Add ½ tsp butter to the centre of the pan again, turn once more briefly, then turn out onto a hot plate.

While the pancakes are cooking, heat a griddle pan over a high heat and lightly grease with a little oil. When the pan is hot, add the bacon rashers and fry for 1 minute on either side until golden brown.

Serve the pancakes with bacon and a small jug of homemade apple syrup or maple syrup.

Organic Porridge with Whiskey Cream

I have been serving whiskey porridge for nearly 25 years since we opened Shelburne Lodge. With the smooth cream and warm whiskey, it really gets the blood flowing in the morning.

For the Celtic people, oats and cream were classic ingredients and whiskey was the drink of the gods drunk before battles (fitting considering that whiskey in Irish is 'uisce beatha' meaning 'water of life or energy'). I have always had a fondness for Bushmills Whiskey, which is what I use at Shelburne Lodge. For me, honey is the food of the gods and I always add a swirl of local organic honey to my porridge and for our guests. I also use Flahavan's organic porridge oats and allow them to soak overnight ready for the morning.

Ingredients

Makes 4 good portions

- 1 cup of organic porridge oats
- Pinch of sea salt
- 3 cups cold water
- ½ cup of milk
- Whiskey Cream:
  100ml / 3 ½ fl oz cream
  2 caps full of good Irish whiskey
- 1 dessert spoon of local organic honey, to serve

Method

To a large stainless steel pot, add the oats, salt and water, cover and soak overnight. Cook over a medium-low heat, stirring occasionally while bringing to the boil. Add the milk and bring back to the boil, stirring continuously. Turn off the heat and pop the lid on to keep warm and avoid a skin from forming. Rest for at least 15 minutes, which will allow the grains to absorb more liquid.

To make the whiskey pouring cream, combine the whiskey and cream in a little jug.

To serve, warm the porridge over a medium heat, stirring continuously. Pour the porridge into a warm bowl, swirl the honey around and serve with the little jug of whiskey cream on the side. The porridge also works very well with some of the fruit compotes, including the warm spiced apple and cinnamon (p48).

Organic Whole Natural Yoghurt with Honey, Nuts & Seeds

This is super simple and if, like me, you love the combination of honey and nuts, you must try it.

Ingredients

Serves 1

- 125g / 4½ oz whole organic natural yoghurt e.g. Glenilen Farm or Glenisk

- 1 tbsp local honey, depending on your preference

- A selection of nuts of your choice e.g. walnuts broken up a little, toasted hazelnuts roughly chopped, toasted flaked almonds

- A section of seeds of your choice e.g. chia seeds, sunflower seeds, sesame seeds

Method

Spoon the yoghurt into a bowl. Swirl the honey on top and sprinkle over the nuts and seeds.

Shelburne Lodge Omelette with Gubbeen Chorizo

I have been serving omelettes since the 1960s and know a good omelette pan is crucial; if you can get a heavy iron omelette pan, they are the best. Fresh organic farm eggs at room temperature seasoned with sea salt and freshly cracked black pepper is another essential. The eggs must not be overmixed, just lightly beaten, and although cream hasn't been used in my omelettes in the past, I definitely do so now.

For this omelette we use Gubbeen chorizo, which has a distinct and refined flavour. The chorizo is locally produced by Fingal Ferguson in Schull of the Ferguson family famed for their Gubbeen Cheese, which features in our Irish farmhouse cheese selection (p71).

Ingredients

Makes 1 omelette

- Generous knob of butter, for cooking
- 1 tbsp Gubbeen chorizo or good quality chorizo, cut thickly and diced (about 1.5x1.5cm / ½ x½in)
- Few leaves of wild garlic (when in season), plus an extra leaf and the flower to garnish or 1 small garlic clove, finely chopped
- 1 small cooked potato, diced (about 1.5x1.5cm / ½ x½in)
- 1 tsp snipped fresh thyme leaves, plus extra to garnish
- 3 eggs, seasoned and lightly beaten with a fork
- 2 tbsp cream

Method

In a heavy-based omelette pan or medium frying pan, melt the butter over a medium heat. Add the chorizo, potato, garlic leaves or garlic and half the thyme leaves and sauté gently for a few minutes until the chorizo starts to crisp. Gently mix the cream into the lightly beaten eggs. Pour the egg mixture into the pan and allow to set and start to coagulate. With a wooden spoon, gently move the cooked outer parts of the omelette into the centre; continue doing this until all the egg is cooked, being careful not to stir too much (the gentler you are, the lighter the finished omelette will be). Sprinkle the remaining thyme leaves over the centre and gently fold the omelette in half in the pan.

Serve immediately, garnishing with garlic leaves and flowers if available or a few fresh thyme leaves.

Purple Heather Omelette

On the menu since the mid-1960s at The Purple Heather, the pub and bistro that my dear sister Grainne continues to run, this omelette is a remaining bestseller. There isn't any cream in this recipe, but should you want a richer omelette, some can be added. In The Purple Heather it is served with an organic green salad and homemade brown soda bread.

Ingredients

Makes 1 omelette

- Generous knob of butter, for cooking
- 1 shallot or small onion, diced
- 1 small cooked potato, diced
- 3 eggs, seasoned and lightly beaten with a fork
- ½ tsp fresh thyme leaves
- 1 tbsp mature cheddar cheese, grated
- Green salad and brown soda bread, to serve
- Freshly chopped parsley, optional garnish

Method

In a heavy-based omelette pan or medium frying pan, melt the butter over a medium heat. Add the potato, thyme and the shallots and sauté gently for a few minutes or until the shallots are softened. Pour in the eggs and allow to set and start to coagulate. With a wooden spoon, gently move the cooked outer parts of the omelette into the centre; continue doing this until all the egg is cooked, being careful not to stir too much (the gentler you are, the lighter the finished omelette will be). Sprinkle the cheese over the centre and gently fold the omelette in half in the pan. Turn the omelette out onto the plate and serve immediately with a fresh green salad and brown bread.

Smoked Salmon Omelette

There was a time when I served wild smoked salmon as a standard, but nowadays it is at a premium just like caviar. While it is available, be prepared to pay. Ireland is blessed with a great choice of organic smoked salmon with many excellent smokehouses across the nation. In Shelburne Lodge, we use a lot of organic smoked salmon in our breakfasts including a simple smoked salmon platter with a chive crème fraîche.

For the smoked salmon omelette, it is particularly important not to overbeat or overcook the eggs; it should be very light.

Ingredients

Serves 1

- Generous knob of butter, for cooking
- 2 tbsp cream
- 3 eggs, seasoned and lightly beaten with a fork
- 55g / 2oz organic smoked salmon
- Wedge of lime, to serve
- A sprig of fennel, optional garnish

Method

In a heavy-based omelette pan or medium frying pan, melt the butter over a medium heat. Gently mix the cream into the lightly beaten eggs. Pour the egg mixture into the pan and allow to set and start to coagulate. With a wooden spoon, gently move the cooked outer parts of the omelette into the centre, being careful not to stir too much (the gentler you are, the lighter the finished omelette will be). Place the salmon slices on the upper half of the omelette, and once the egg is sufficiently cooked, gently fold over the lower half the omelette and turn out onto the plate. Arrange a rosette of smoked salmon on the plate and garnish with a sprig of fennel.

Serve immediately with a wedge of lime.

Shelburne Lodge Eggs Benedict, Florentine and Royale

I used to make hollandaise almost every single day in the restaurants, serving thousands of portions over the years. At Shelburne Lodge I serve hollandaise flavoured with lemon juice (p342) with our eggs Benedict, Florentine and Royale, and with asparagus when in season. The eggs in this recipe are of the utmost importance. We use wonderful fresh local organic farm eggs stored at room temperature, and instead of serving on muffins we prefer toasted batch country bread from Harrington's local bakery. Try and source the freshest eggs possible to achieve plump poached eggs.

Ingredients

Serves 2

- 4 eggs

- 4 tbsp hollandaise
  (p342, with lemon juice),
  warm

- ½ tbsp butter, softened

- 2 thick slices of
  country-style bread

- Sweet cicely or thyme,
  optional garnish

- Benedict:
  4 medium slices of smoked
  ham, off the bone (we use
  smoked Limerick ham)

- Florentine:
  2 large handfuls of fresh
  local organic spinach, gently
  wilted and seasoned

- Royale:
  4 slices organic
  smoked salmon

Method

Preheat the oven to fan 100°C / fan 210°F / gas mark ½. To be prepared to serve while the eggs are still warm, toast the bread and keep it crisp in the oven.

Fill a tall stainless steel pot with water and over a high heat bring to a gentle bubbling point; this prevents the eggs from sticking to the bottom. Crack the eggs into a small bowl. Give the water a few round stirs, then gently drop the eggs into the water and turn the heat down so it's just barely bubbling. Cook for 3 minutes for a soft egg and runny yolk, or longer depending on preference. Remove the eggs with a slotted spoon, being careful to drain off all the water. The eggs must be well drained.

Cut both slices of toast in half and butter lightly, dividing between two plates. Place the eggs on top of each slice of toast and lay either the ham, spinach or salmon on top, partially covering the eggs. Spoon over the warm hollandaise. Garnish with the herb of choice and serve immediately while still warm.

Benedict
Along with the toast in the oven, warm the ham too. Partially cover the eggs with the ham and finish as directed above.

Florentine
To wilt the spinach, wash and dry the spinach, keeping some moisture. In a saucepan, melt a knob of butter over a medium-high heat, add in the spinach and gently stir – it will wilt immediately. Season to taste. Partially cover the eggs with the wilted spinach, placing some of the spinach on the plate as well. Finish as directed above.

Royale
Along with the toast in the oven, warm the salmon too. Partially cover the eggs with the salmon and finish as directed above.

Scrambled Eggs with Smoked Salmon and a Chive Crème Fraîche

Scrambled eggs are a soothing and easy breakfast. I use the same mixture as I do for my omelettes. As mentioned before, use fresh organic eggs, where possible storing the eggs at room temperature and once your egg mixture is prepared use it straight away. Be sure to have all elements of your breakfast ready, as the scrambled eggs should be prepared last and served immediately.

I prefer large creamy curds rather than small finer curds in my scrambled egg, so I gently move the eggs in the pan, rather than vigorous stirring.

Ingredients

Serves 2

- Generous knob of butter, for cooking
- 4 eggs
- 40ml / 1½fl oz cream
- 2-3 slices organic smoked salmon

Chive Crème Fraîche:

- 1 tbsp crème fraîche
- Freshly snipped chives
- Wedge of lime, to serve
- A sprig of fennel, optional garnish

Method

For the chive crème fraîche, add the freshly snipped chives to the crème fraîche and mix to combine.

Snip the dark flesh off the base of the smoked salmon slices. To serve, pinch in the base of each slice to form a large fan of smoked salmon for presentation on the plate.

Season the eggs with sea salt and cracked black pepper. Lightly beat the eggs with a fork, being careful not to overbeat. Gently mix in the cream. Heat a large non-stick frying pan over a medium heat. Add the butter and once melted, pour in the egg mixture and turn down to a medium-low heat. Let the egg mixture settle in the pan and then gently move it around using a wooden spoon to cook the eggs to your liking.

Remove from the heat and place the scrambled egg at the base of the fanned slices of salmon. Serve immediately with a wedge of lime and the chive crème fraîche and garnish with fennel.

Fish of the Day

In Ireland, we are fortunate enough to have access to the cold water fish from the Atlantic. At Shelburne Lodge, we have many regular guests who come predominantly to eat the fresh fish of the day on our breakfast menu. I have a marvellous fish supplier, Paudie Spillane, who calls me three mornings a week. Paudie, and his parents Michael and Finola before him, have supplied me with fresh fish since the 1980s. The fish on the menu varies according to the time of year, what is freshly available and, of course, what Paudie has to offer. When buying fish for yourself, follow your fish supplier's recommendations for what's best and good value as this can vary from day to day.

The following fish recipes work well for breakfast or brunch and have all featured as our Fish of the Day at Shelburne Lodge:

Crab Cakes with Tartare Sauce — p116

Smoked Cod Cakes — p126

Dover Sole Meunière — p154
Dover slip soles are smaller and more suitable for breakfast

Pan-Fried Fillet of Mackerel in an Oatmeal Crust — p174

Fillet of Salmon with Lime and Coriander Butter — p177

Fillet of Salmon with Hollandaise or Wild Sorrel Sauce or Gooseberry, Lime and Elderflower Sauce — p178

Fillet of John Dory — p176
Choose small fillets for breakfast with a citrus butter (p377)

Irish Farmhouse Cheese Selection

We like to have a good selection of farmhouse cheese for our guests. We have a lot of American, Swiss, French, German, Italian and Dutch guests who love cheese for their breakfast. They are sometimes surprised at how good our Irish cheeses are!

Annie Goulding, one of my chefs at The Lime Tree and a great friend of Norman and Veronica Steele, always brought a full round of Milleens cheese from Eyeries for our restaurant. This was one of the earliest farmhouse cheeses to be recognised for its very high standard and got many international awards from the late 1970s on. At first we didn't refrigerate it to have it in perfect condition but now we most certainly do. Annie was also a friend of Jeffa Gill who set up Durrus cheese in the late 1970s.

The Steeles, Gordons of St Tola, Jeffa Gill and the Fergusons set the standard for great artisan cheese making in Ireland. Siobhán Ní Ghairbhith's St Tola, Grubbs' Cashel Blue & Crozier, Fergusons' Gubbeen, Mahers' Cooleeney, Jeffa Gill's Durrus, Willems' Coolea and, very local to us, Séan Coles-O'Sullivan's Knockatee Kerry Blue – these great names are all family businesses who produce wonderful cheese and we use them for our selection. There are many, many more cheese producers all around Ireland.

One of my food heavens is cheese. In the 1990s I sadly developed an intolerance to blue cheese and it was my favourite food to eat after service with a sip of wine. It's off my list and I now eat the mature hard cheeses and goat's cheese. I'm hoping my doctor doesn't take these cheeses off my list!

We vary the selection and serve our local cheese board very simply at Shelburne Lodge, the cheese speaks for itself. Cheese is delicious with fruit, but I serve it with walnuts and Grainne's delicious homemade oatmeal biscuits (p333). Scrumptious!

Starters

Soups

Wild Atlantic Seafood Soup	80
Curried Parsnip Soup	82
Cauliflower Soup	83
Nettle & Spinach Soup	84
Roast Red Pepper & Tomato Soup	86
Mushroom Soup	87
Asparagus Soup	88
Carrot & Coriander Soup	89
Celeriac & Apple Soup	92
Leek & Potato Soup	93

Vegetarian

Potato Pancakes with Garlic or Herb Butter	94
Red Onion Tart with Kerry Blue Cheese	96
Wild Chanterelle Mushrooms with Bruschetta or Tagliatelle	99
Globe Artichokes with Hollandaise	102
Moroccan Vegetable Parcels	104
Twice Baked Hazelnut Cheese Soufflé	106
Goat's Cheese Parcels with Toasted Hazelnuts and Apple	108
St Tola Irish Goat's Cheese & Warm Red Pepper Salad	111
Salad of Summer Fruits with St Tola Divine Irish Goat's Cheese	112
Rocket, Pear & Irish Blue Cheese Salad with Apple & Walnut Oil Dressing	114
Salad Suggestions	115

Fish

Crab Cakes with Tartare Sauce	116
Crab & Coriander Bundles	117
Prawn & Spinach Pastry with Mousseline Sauce	119
Seafood Mousse or Sausage with Beurre Blanc	122
Soused Mackerel	124
Smoked Cod Cakes	126
Smoked Cod Mousse	128

Meat

Smoked Bacon & Bread Stuffing Rolls	129
Confit Duck Leg with Pear & Ginger Salad	131
Chicken Mousseline with Carrots & Citrus Sauce	132
Chicken Liver Pâté with Cumberland Sauce	133
Irish Black Pudding, Caramelised Apple & Citrus Vinaigrette Salad	134

Starters

A memorable start to your meal is important. Included in this chapter is a selection of starter recipes which can also be used as a luncheon or light supper. It is advisable when planning a meal to choose a starter that is balanced with the main course and dessert, if you are having one.

Soups are very nourishing and great to have at hand. When making soups, aim to keep them seasonal. Your ingredients will be at their best when in season, adding to the flavour of your soup. Keep your ingredients simple, letting the main ingredient speak for itself along with a good stock base. To increase richness, cream and a dash of Noilly Prat vermouth can be added. Always use fresh herbs. The most important point when making a soup is to allow the flavours to infuse and then taste, taste, taste! I have included a great seasonal variety in this section. They can be batch frozen which is ideal for families, lunch or as a starter for dinners and parties.

Two of my daughters are vegetarian, and Tom just loves vegetarian food, so I am always planning meals that have adaptability and tend to omit meat stocks for this reason. I have included a lot of vegetarian starters but of course these can also be eaten for dinner. Denis Cotter, vegetarian chef and owner of the renowned Cafe Paradiso (now Paradiso) in Cork, is fantastic. His recipes are wonderful – I often refer to his books for inspiration.

There are four recipes in this section using filo pastry. It was the great Sonia Stevenson – a master chef of Great Britain and the first female chef in the UK to be awarded a Michelin star for her restaurant, The Horn of Plenty in Devon – who first introduced me to filo pastry in the 1980s. I find it a rather wonderful ingredient because it is so light. It doesn't take in any way from the main ingredient but rather gives a lovely light, crispy texture in contrast to the filling. Sonia told me to only use Theo's, which I continue to use to this day. I have tried others, but they are just simply not as light and crispy. Try and source Theo's if you can for the best outcome for my recipes; it is available in some of the larger supermarkets.

Mousse was very fashionable in the 1970s and 1980s. I still love it and have included a few mousse recipes here. It makes such a great starter. I had the most memorable sole mousse for my starter in Nico Ladenis' restaurant Chez Nico in London with Tom. It was smooth as silk and bursting with flavour. I can still remember the feeling of pure enjoyment! Simply known as 'Nico' in the food world because he was so remarkable, Nico is one of my favourite chefs and is also self-taught. The time we visited Nico's we were about to open The Lime Tree; I spilled red wine on their cream carpet and a young Irish chef who trained with a friend of mine, Gerry Galvin of Drimcong Restaurant in Galway, came out from the kitchen to help clean it. I was very embarrassed. We did learn from the experience: we were choosing a carpet for The Lime Tree at the time and had fallen in love with a cream Jacob's fleece sheep wool carpet. After this incident, we chose dark brown instead – far more practical!

Wild Atlantic Seafood Soup

This is one of the more luxurious fish soups, best served with fresh crusty bread or rouille (p353) for seafood lovers. Ours is a tomato base and the flavour stems from the great shellfish stock (p373). We are so fortunate to live by the Irish Atlantic with its cold water. I think cold water fish is superior; it has immense flavour and texture. This soup is not a cream-based chowder and is a very individual soup, more like bouillabaisse in flavour.

Enjoy.

Ingredients

Serves 8

- 2 tbsp olive oil
- 55g / 2oz butter
- 4 garlic cloves, finely chopped
- 6 shallots, finely chopped
- 1 leek, washed and finely chopped
- 1 fennel bulb, finely chopped
- 2 carrots, peeled and finely chopped
- 1 tbsp tomato purée
- 1140ml / 2 pints shellfish stock (p373)
- 4 ripe tomatoes, skinned, deseeded and chopped
- Zest of 1 orange
- 2 tsp chopped thyme leaves
- 2 tsp chopped tarragon leaves
- ¼ tsp fennel seeds
- 3 star anise, wrapped and tied in muslin
- ½ tsp saffron threads
- 225g / ½lb crab meat (white and brown)
- 900g / 2lb fresh fish, skinned and chopped (e.g. a mixture of sea bass, John Dory, haddock or cod. The sea bass and John Dory cook more slowly than haddock and cod, so need to be chopped into smaller pieces)
- 225g / ½lb Atlantic prawns, cooked and shelled
- 1 large lobster, cooked and sliced (optional)
- Sea salt and cracked black pepper, to taste

Serving suggestions:

Crusty bread and rouille (p353), to serve

Method

In a large saucepan, heat the olive oil and butter over a low heat. Add the garlic, shallots, leek, fennel and carrots and sweat, covered, for 15 minutes or until the vegetables have softened, stirring occasionally. Remove the lid and add the tomato purée then the stock, tomatoes, orange zest, thyme, tarragon, fennel seeds, the star anise and saffron. Turn up the heat and bring to the boil, then lower the heat and simmer for 5 minutes. If you would like the soup base without chunks of vegetable, it can be blitzed at this stage with a hand blender or food processor in batches, but be sure to remove the star anise before blending. If using a food processor, return to the saucepan. Add the crab meat and fish and cook for 5 minutes to cook through, stirring occasionally.

Serve with 3-4 cooked prawns per bowl with a few slices of lobster each. Divide the soup between warm soup bowls, evenly distributing the fish.

Curried Parsnip Soup

Parsnips – some people hate them, some people love them. I am in the category of parsnip lovers. This is a gently spiced soup that turns the earthy and sweet flavour of the parsnips into a heart-warming bowl of goodness. I particularly enjoy making this soup with the aromas from the spices filling up the kitchen. Perfect in the autumn and winter months with some brown or crusty bread.

Ingredients

Serves 6-8

- 1 tbsp coriander seeds
- 1 tbsp cumin seeds
- 115g / 4oz butter
- 450g / 1lb onions, finely chopped
- 6 garlic cloves, finely chopped
- 1 tbsp ginger, peeled and finely chopped
- 1.35kg / 3lb parsnips, peeled and finely sliced
- 1 litre / 1¾ pint vegetable stock (p374)
- 1 tbsp apple chutney (p378)
- Sea salt and cracked black pepper

Serving suggestions:

2 tbsp toasted desiccated coconut or roughly chopped coriander and cream, to serve

Method

In a dry frying pan, toast the coriander and cumin seeds over a low heat for 3-4 minutes or until aromatic and lightly coloured. Crush with a pestle and mortar.

In a large saucepan, melt the butter over a low heat. Add the onions and garlic and sweat with the lid on for 10 minutes or until soft, but not coloured. Add the ground spices, ginger and parsnips and sweat with the lid on for a further 5-8 minutes, stirring occasionally. Add the vegetable stock, turn up the heat and bring to the boil then reduce the heat and simmer for about 30 minutes. Stir in the apple chutney to sweeten.

Remove from the heat and blitz using a hand blender, or food processor in batches. If it is too thick, add a little more stock. If using a food processor, return to the saucepan and heat it very gently. Strain the soup if you would like it smoother. Season to taste.

Serve hot with a swirl of cream and a sprinkle of coconut or coriander.

Cauliflower Soup

Cauliflower is a vegetable that always remains a staple in my kitchen and more recently has become quite fashionable. Cauliflower is superb with roast beef in a creamy sauce. Delicious with some spices or simply with Mornay sauce (p345) as a gratin. The best cauliflower soup I ever had was from my dear friend Colin O'Daly when he was a chef at the Park Hotel, Kenmare; for such a strong vegetable, it was creamy, delicate and delicious – so memorable. My version is below and is not as good as Colin's!

Ingredients

Serves 6-8

- 900g / 2lb cauliflower, cut into small florets
- 115g / 4oz butter
- 450g / 1lb onions, finely chopped
- 4 garlic cloves, finely chopped
- 450g / 1lb floury potatoes (e.g. Golden Wonder or Kerr's Pink), peeled and diced
- 1 litre / 1¾ pint of vegetable stock (p374)
- 140ml / ¼ pint cream
- Sea salt and cracked black pepper

Serving suggestions:

Croûtons, to serve
2 tbsp snipped fresh chives or chive flowers, to serve

Method

Bring a medium saucepan water with a pinch of sea salt to the boil. Add the cauliflower florets and blanch for 5-10 minutes or until tender. Drain in a colander.

In a large saucepan, melt the butter over a low heat. Add the onions, garlic and cauliflower florets and sweat with the lid on for 10 minutes or until soft, stirring occasionally. Turn up the heat, add the potatoes and stock and bring to the boil, then reduce the heat and simmer for 20 minutes or until the vegetables are soft. Remove from the heat and blitz using a hand blender, or food processor in batches. If using a food processor, return to the saucepan. Stir in the cream over a medium heat.

Season to taste and serve with croûtons and some snipped fresh chives or chive flowers.

Nettle & Spinach Soup

This is a wonderful green springtime soup, using only young nettles. Young nettles are more delicate in flavour. There is an Irish song which includes a reference to nettles, 'Down by the Glenside', about the Fenian revolution in the 1860s after the Famine in Ireland. Fenians were young men who challenged the older politicians and there was an attempted revolution but it wasn't successful. Quite a lot of them then emigrated to America. The song's opening lines are: "Twas down by the glenside, I met an old woman, aplucking young nettles, she n'er saw me comin." In the old days Irish people believed that the blood needed to be cleansed and they used young nettles in springtime in their broths, after the long winter with no sun. They also drank it as a brew. This soup is delicious, nourishing and has such a beautiful vibrant green colour.

Ingredients

Serves 6-8

- 115g / 4oz butter
- 2 large onions, finely chopped
- 6 garlic cloves, finely chopped
- 2 floury potatoes (e.g. Golden Wonder or Kerr's Pink), peeled, cooked and diced
- 900g / 2lb fresh spinach, washed
- 2 handfuls of young nettle leaves, stems removed (using gloves) and thoroughly washed
- 1140ml / 2 pints vegetable stock (p374)
- Some freshly grated nutmeg (optional)

Serving suggestion:

Serve with cream

Method

In a large saucepan, melt the butter over a low heat. Add the onions and garlic and gently sweat with the lid on for 10 minutes or until soft, stirring occasionally. Stir in the washed spinach and nettles. Add the cooked potatoes followed by the vegetable stock, turn up the heat and bring to the boil then reduce the heat and simmer for 5 minutes. Blitz the soup using a hand blender, or food processor in batches. Season the soup to taste, adding some freshly grated nutmeg if you'd like.

Serve hot with a swirl of cream on top.

Roast Red Pepper & Tomato Soup

The flavour in this soup will be predominantly red pepper – the poor tomatoes get lost, however they are necessary to give a balance and reduce the intensity of the pepper flavour. I have included two chillies in this recipe which gives a mild heat to the soup; add or omit chillies depending on the level of heat you would like.

Ingredients

Serves 6-8

- 4 red peppers, split and seeded
- 3 tbsp olive oil
- 55g / 2oz butter
- 3 onions or 6 shallots, sliced
- 4 garlic cloves, crushed and finely chopped
- 900g / 2lb ripe vine or sweet tomatoes or very good quality tinned tomatoes, chopped
- 45g / 1½oz good quality tomato purée
- 2 red chillies, seeded and finely chopped (optional)
- 1140ml / 2 pints vegetable stock (p374) or chicken stock (p370)
- Sea salt and cracked black pepper
- 2 tbsp pesto (p356)

Method

Preheat the oven to fan 200°C / fan 400°F / gas mark 7. Lay out the peppers on a baking tray, drizzle over the olive oil and season. Roast in the oven for 20-30 minutes, or until softened but not charred. Set aside to cool and slice with the skins on.

In a large saucepan, melt the butter over a low heat, along with any oil/juices from the baking tray. Add the onions or shallots and garlic, cover and sweat with the lid on for 20 minutes or until soft, stirring occasionally. Add the tomatoes, tomato purée, red chillies and sliced red peppers. Stir together, cover and sweat for 10 minutes. Add the stock, turn up the heat and bring to the boil, then reduce the heat and simmer for 10-15 minutes. Remove from the heat and blitz using a hand blender, or food processor in batches. If using a food processor, return to the saucepan and heat it very gently. Season to taste.

Serve hot with a swirl of pesto.

Mushroom Soup

Use large flat field mushrooms for the best flavour in this deliciously comforting soup.

Ingredients

Serves 6-8

- 115g / 4oz butter
- 450g / 1lb onions, peeled and finely chopped
- 4 garlic cloves, peeled and finely chopped
- 900g / 2lb flat field mushrooms, finely chopped
- 100ml / 3½fl oz port
- 100ml / 3½fl oz Noilly Prat
- 1 litre / 1¾ pint vegetable stock (p374) or chicken stock (p370)
- Sea salt and cracked black pepper

Method

In a large saucepan, melt the butter over a low heat. Add the onions and garlic and sweat with the lid on for 10 minutes or until soft. Add the mushrooms, port and Noilly Prat and stir. Place a double layer of dampened greaseproof paper pressing down directly over the mushroom mix, checking frequently that the contents do not dry out, and cook slowly for 10 minutes. This helps intensify and sweeten the flavours. At this stage, the mushrooms should be nice and soft. Add the stock, turn up the heat and bring to the boil, then reduce the heat and simmer for 5 minutes. Remove from the heat and blend using a hand blender, or food processor in batches. If it is too thick, add a little more stock. If it is too thin, add a little beurre manié (p394). If using a food processor, return to the saucepan and heat it very gently. Taste and season accordingly.

Serve with a good swirl of cream.

Asparagus Soup

This is a very seasonal soup using green asparagus native to Ireland when available.

Ingredients

Serves 6-8

- 115g / 4oz butter
- 450g / 1lb onions, peeled and finely chopped
- 4 garlic cloves, peeled and finely chopped
- 900g / 2lb asparagus, stalks trimmed and finely chopped, keeping the tips for soup garnish
- 100ml / 3½fl oz port
- 100ml / 3½fl oz Noilly Prat
- 1 litre / 1¾ pint vegetable stock (p374) or chicken stock (p370)
- Sea salt and cracked black pepper

Method

In a large saucepan, melt the butter over a low heat. Add the onions and garlic and sweat with the lid on for 10 minutes or until soft. Add the asparagus, port and Noilly Prat and stir. Place a double layer of dampened greaseproof paper pressing down directly over the asparagus mix, checking frequently that the contents do not dry out, and cook slowly for 7-10 minutes, depending on the thickness of the stalks, until tender. This helps intensify and sweeten the flavours. At this stage, the asparagus should be nice and soft. Add the stock, turn up the heat and bring to the boil then reduce the heat and simmer for 5 minutes. Remove from the heat and blend using a hand blender, or food processor in batches. If it is too thick, add a little more stock. If it is too thin, add a little beurre manié (p394). If using a food processor, return to the saucepan and heat it very gently. Taste and season accordingly. Blanch and refresh the asparagus tips.

Serve the soup with a swirl of cream and garnish with the asparagus tips.

Carrot & Coriander Soup

A light summer soup, delicious with lots of fresh coriander snipped on top.

Ingredients

Serves 6-8

- 1 tbsp coriander seeds
- 115g / 4oz butter
- 450g / 1lb onions, peeled and finely chopped
- 4 garlic cloves, peeled and finely chopped
- 900g / 2lb carrots, peeled and finely chopped
- 1 tsp ground coriander
- 100ml / 3½fl oz port
- 100ml / 3½fl oz Noilly Prat
- 1 litre / 1¾ pint vegetable stock (p374) or chicken stock (p370)
- Zest of 1 orange
- Bunch of coriander, roughly chopped, plus extra for garnish
- Sea salt and cracked black pepper

Method

In a dry frying pan, toast the coriander seeds over a low heat for a few minutes or until fragrant and turning lightly golden. Crush finely using a pestle and mortar.

In a large saucepan, melt the butter over a low heat. Add the onions and garlic and sweat with the lid on for 10 minutes or until soft. Add the carrots, ground coriander, port and Noilly Prat and stir. Place a double layer of dampened greaseproof paper pressing down directly over the carrot mix, checking frequently that the contents do not dry out, and cook slowly for about 20 minutes. This helps intensify and sweeten the flavours. At this stage, the carrots should be nice and soft. Add the stock and orange zest, turn the heat up and bring to the boil, then reduce the heat and simmer for 5 minutes. Remove from the heat and blend using a hand blender, or food processor in batches. If it is too thick, add a little more stock. If using a food processor, return to the saucepan and heat it very gently. Taste and season accordingly. Just prior to serving, stir in the crushed coriander seeds and fresh coriander.

Serve the soup with a swirl of cream and garnish with fresh coriander.

Celeriac & Apple Soup

A lovely autumn or winter soup.

Ingredients

Serves 6-8

- 115g / 4oz butter
- 450g / 1lb onions, peeled and finely chopped
- 4 garlic cloves, peeled and finely chopped
- 800g / 1¾lb celeriac, peeled and finely diced
- 3 eating apples of your choice, peeled and chopped
- 100ml / 3½fl oz port
- 100ml / 3½fl oz Noilly Prat
- 1 litre / 1¾ pint vegetable stock (p374) or chicken stock (p370)
- Sea salt and cracked black pepper

Method

In a large saucepan, melt the butter over a low heat. Add the onions and garlic and sweat with the lid on for 10 minutes or until soft. Add the celeriac, apple, port and Noilly Prat and stir. Place a double layer of dampened greaseproof paper pressing down directly over the mixture, checking frequently that the contents do not dry out, and cook slowly for 20 minutes. This helps intensify and sweeten the flavours. At this stage, the celeriac should be nice and soft. Add the stock, turn up the heat and bring to the boil, then reduce the heat and simmer for 5 minutes. Remove from the heat and blend using a hand blender, or food processor in batches. If it is too thick, add a little more stock. If using a food processor, return to the saucepan and heat it very gently. Season to taste.

Serve the soup with a swirl of cream.

Leek & Potato Soup

A wonderful hearty soup for a cold winter's day.

Ingredients

Serves 8-10

- 4 large leeks
- 55g / 2oz butter
- 2 medium floury potatoes (e.g. Golden Wonder or Kerr's Pink), peeled and diced
- 3 onions or 6 shallots, sliced
- 4 garlic cloves, crushed and finely chopped
- 2 tsp fresh thyme leaves
- 1140ml / 2 pints vegetable stock (p374) or chicken stock (p370)
- 100ml / 3½fl oz Noilly Prat
- Sea salt and cracked black pepper
- 4 tbsp cream, to serve
- 2 tbsp snipped fresh chives or chive flowers, snipped to serve

Method

Trim off the green top and roots of the leeks, split them in half and slice finely. Wash thoroughly to get rid of any sand and grit and drain in a colander.

In a large saucepan, melt the butter over a low heat. Add the leeks, potatoes, onions or shallots, garlic and thyme; stir so they are coated in the butter and season. Cover and sweat for 20 minutes, stirring occasionally. Add the stock and Noilly Prat, turn up the heat and bring to the boil then reduce the heat and simmer for 20 minutes.

Remove from the heat and blend using a hand blender, or food processor in batches. If it is too thick, add a little more stock. If using a food processor, return to the saucepan and heat it very gently. Season to taste.

Serve hot with a swirl of cream and chives or chive flowers on top.

Potato Pancakes with Garlic or Herb Butter

These savoury pancakes are one of my signature dishes. They were one of the most popular dishes I served in The Lime Tree and remain on the menu in Packie's. Cooking them in the pan followed by the oven makes them surprisingly light and fluffy. A hot oven is a crucial step as otherwise they can be heavy and soggy. They need an accompaniment and my favourite way to serve them is with thyme or garlic butter. They also work well with smoked salmon and crème fraîche, like blinis. The most important ingredient here is well cooked floury potatoes. I love Golden Wonders; I think they are the best floury potato variety in Ireland – if you can get these, use them. Waxy potatoes will not work. Clarified butter (p376) is also an important step. When my daughter and her friends were hungry, I would often cook a small batch for them and they would eat them on the street. Healthy street food back in the 1990s! The batter will keep for about 2 days in the fridge.

Ingredients

Makes about 14-18 small pancakes (about 6cm / 2½in in diameter when cooked)

- 225g / ½lb floury potatoes (e.g. Golden Wonders or Kerr's Pink), peeled, cooked, cooled and weighed after cooking, chopped

- 100g / 3½oz plain white flour

- ½ level tsp sea salt

- 1 tsp fresh thyme leaves

- 50ml / 1¾fl oz whole milk

- 50ml / 1¾fl oz cream

- 2 eggs

- Clarified butter (p376) for frying (about 1 tbsp per batch, as pancakes need to be cooked in batches)

- Garlic or thyme butter (p376-377) or smoked salmon and crème fraîche, to serve

Method

Preheat the oven to fan 220°C / fan 425°F / gas mark 9.

In a food processor, pulse the potatoes, flour, salt and thyme to a breadcrumb-like texture. This will only take about 30 seconds, so watch carefully; if over-pulsed the mixture will form a solid mass and is not usable. Add the milk, cream and eggs and blend until a smooth paste. Check the consistency; you're after a thick batter, much thicker than a crêpe batter, but with a dropping consistency. The consistency will depend on the potatoes. If necessary, add a little more whole milk.

Cook the pancakes in batches. Melt 1 tbsp of the clarified butter (p376) per batch in a large ovenproof frying pan over a medium heat. Spoon 1 dessert spoon of the batter per pancake into the pan – they will spread naturally and form a round shape, so leave enough room between the pancakes to avoid them touching. Cook the pancakes until the underside is golden brown (around 2-3 minutes). Turn over and cook the other side for about a minute to a similar golden colour.

Ensuring that the oven is hot – this is a very important step to ensure the pancakes are crisp and light – move the pan into the oven and cook for 4-5 minutes. You'll see them theatrically puff up in the oven.

Serve the pancakes straightaway, otherwise they will go soggy. Serve up to 5 per person.

Best with garlic or thyme butter at room temperature; spoon a little on top of each pancake before serving. Also good with smoked salmon and crème fraîche.

Red Onion Tart with Kerry Blue Cheese

This recipe was featured in the UK Good Housekeeping in 1998. At that time, I used Cashel Blue Cheese. We now also have a great local blue cheese in Kenmare which my family love, called Kerry Blue, which comes from Knockatee Dairy, Tuosist. It is uncanny that my grandmother Hanora Crowley Hanley was born in Drombouhilly, under Knockatee Mountain, in this same valley. The business was started by the Iresons and has been taken over by Séan Coles-O'Sullivan, whose family originate from Tuosist post office. Séan is settled in Tuosist and also rears pigs on his farm. His blue cheese is creamy and tangy, with lovely sweetness too.

I was sent to Drombouhilly on my holidays regularly when I was a young girl. One time, my mother sent me out with my cousin Nancy, I think I was around 10. The big fair day was on in Kenmare, the 15th August, and my cousin did not want to miss it, so we took off in the early morning through the fields, so we weren't seen going down the road. We kept walking as far as Dinish Island (six miles), then got a lift and ended up in town for the day. We couldn't miss out on the town buzz! We were very naughty and caused a lot of upset in the family with our lovely cousins in Drombouhilly. At the time of course we didn't understand.

The pinhead oats add a lovely crunch to the simple savoury pastry. The pastry is very quick to make and easy to roll out, ideal to be made in advance and frozen. The onion filling is very versatile and can also be used as an onion pickle served with cold meats and cheese such as toasted goat's cheese.

Ingredients

Makes 6 small tarts

Pastry:

- 55g / 2oz wholemeal flour
- 70g / 2½oz plain white flour
- 30g / 1oz pinhead oats
- 70g / 2½oz butter, softened
- 45g / 1½oz freshly grated mature cheddar
- Pinch of sea salt
- 1 tsp fresh thyme leaves, plus extra to garnish
- 3 tbsp cold water

Onion filling:

- 450g / 1lb red onions, peeled and sliced
- 120ml / 4fl oz good quality balsamic vinegar, or half balsamic vinegar and half water to reduce the intensity
- 1 tbsp honey
- Sea salt and cracked black pepper
- Chopped fresh thyme, to garnish
- 115g / 4oz Kerry Blue cheese, for topping

Equipment:

- 6 x 10cm / 4in loose base tart tins
- Baking beans or dried pulses, for blind baking

Method

To make the pastry, use a food processor to blend together the flours, oats, butter, cheese, salt and thyme to a fine crumb texture. Add the cold water and pulse until the dough comes together to form a ball. Tip the dough out, wrap in clingfilm and rest for 30 minutes in the fridge.

Preheat the oven to fan 160°C / fan 325°F / gas mark 4. Roll out the dough on a lightly floured surface to a thickness of 1-2mm, then cut 6 pastry circles large enough to line the tins. Use these to line the tins. Prick the base of the pastry with a fork and chill for another 30 minutes in the fridge. Cover the pastry with baking paper, fill with ceramic baking beans or dried pulses and blind bake for 15 minutes or until cooked, then remove the beans and bake for another 2-5 minutes until golden brown. Turn the oven up to fan 220°C / fan 425°F / gas mark 9.

To make the onion filling, combine the onions and vinegar in a medium stainless steel saucepan, cover with a lid and sweat gently for 30 minutes. Take off the lid, drizzle in the honey, stir and continue to cook until almost all the liquid has evaporated. Season to taste.

To serve, remove the baked pastry from the tins, fill with the warm balsamic onions and crumble the blue cheese on top. Cook the tarts briefly in the hot oven for about 5 minutes or until the cheese is melted.

Garnish with thyme and serve warm.

Horst delivering chanterelles

Wild Chanterelle Mushrooms with Bruschetta or Tagliatelle

When first served at The Lime Tree, chanterelles weren't well known. So much so, a delivery en route to the restaurant had to spend the night at the local Garda station. James Riney, who cycled the countryside to secret locations to pick chanterelles and trompette des morts, was on his way to deliver when he was stopped by a young Garda who couldn't quite identify the mushroom. He suspected them to be magic mushrooms, and promptly confiscated them. The following day, James went to the barracks to retrieve his mushrooms where fortunately the Sergeant was a customer at The Lime Tree and he confirmed they were in fact on the menu! Fortunately, chanterelles are now well known within Kenmare and make seasonal appearances on menus.

Chanterelles require particular care when being picked, and Horst, who now provides me with the mushrooms, picks and cleans them beautifully. There are very few people as knowledgeable about wild mushrooms as Horst and his expertise is regularly sought after. The chanterelles must be picked without the earthy base and cleaned with a dry brush, rather than washed. Water will rot and destroy them quickly.

Ingredients

Serves 4

Chanterelles:

- 2 tbsp extra virgin olive oil
- 55g / 2oz butter
- 300g / 10½oz chanterelles
- 4 garlic cloves, finely chopped
- ½ tbsp fresh thyme leaves
- 1 tbsp chopped flat leaf parsley
- 2 tbsp cold water

Bruschetta:

- 8 slices of baguette
- 2 tbsp extra virgin olive oil
- 1 large garlic clove, peeled
- Sea salt and cracked black pepper
- Sprigs of fresh thyme, for garnish

Tagliatelle:

- 500-600g (1lb 2oz-1lb 5oz) fresh tagliatelle
- Shavings of Parmigiano Reggiano

Method

For the bruschetta, preheat the oven to fan 180°C / fan 350°F / gas mark 6.

For the chanterelles, heat the oil with the butter in a heavy-based frying pan. Add the chanterelles to the pan, toss to coat, and fry for 3 minutes over a high heat. Turn the heat to low and add the garlic, herbs and water, then cook for 3-4 minutes or until softened and fragrant. Season with sea salt and cracked black pepper.

For the bruschetta, place the baguette slices on a baking tray and drizzle over the olive oil on both sides. Bake in the oven until crisp and golden brown. Remove from the oven, then rub one side of each of the baguette slices with the peeled garlic. These can be stored in an airtight container in the fridge for up to 1 week.

Top each of the bruschetta with a generous spoonful of the chanterelles and garnish with a few fresh thyme leaves.

For the pasta, bring a large saucepan of water with a good pinch of salt to the boil. Add the fresh tagliatelle and cook until al dente. Drain and return to the saucepan and toss in a generous drizzle of extra virgin olive oil, sea salt and cracked black pepper. Divide the pasta between serving bowls, top with the chanterelles and a generous shaving of Parmigiano Reggiano.

Globe Artichokes with Hollandaise or Vinaigrette

Globe artichokes are beautiful and exotic. I first saw and tried them in the 1950s at the Maison Suisse restaurant in London; this was also my first encounter with hollandaise. They were both as memorable as the other. While the globe artichokes in Ireland aren't as large as those in France, they are equally wonderful with delicate hearts. Tom, my husband, has beautiful artichokes growing in Shelburne Lodge.

Our plants came from a good friend, Tom Bambury, who had a beautiful garden at the front of his house, full of globe artichokes amongst much more! People would photograph his garden. He split them for us, and he used to come out and chat with us and check on how they were growing. He also produced amazing honey from his bees.

This recipe can be served as a starter at a dinner party or as part of a very light luncheon. It is a fair amount of effort, but certainly worth it. This is really just to tease the appetite and not substantial.

Ingredients

Serves 4 as a starter

- ½ lemon, cut into wedges
- 4 globe artichokes, with stems cut to the base

Serve with any of the following accompaniments (2 tbsp per portion) in a dipping bowl for each person:

- Hollandaise (p342, with lemon juice)
- Citrus vinaigrette (p381), Purple Heather vinaigrette (p384) or vinaigrette of choice
- Melted butter

Method

Fill a large saucepan or pot with water, add the lemon wedges and warm over a low heat. Add the globe artichokes, bring to the boil then simmer for around 30 minutes or until the leaves come off easily. Remove and drain the artichokes. To prepare the artichokes, push out the outer leaves to access the top part of the artichoke. Remove the central leaves, they should easily lift out, to reveal the choke. Using a spoon, carefully remove the choke from the centre – this is the fibrous non-edible part so be sure to remove all the fibres, although be careful to not remove any of the heart, which is at the base. This part is a little laborious, but essential.

Serve the artichokes with a small dipping bowl of the chosen accompaniment with the leaves picked off on the platter, keeping the flesh to eat as well. For me, the heart of the artichoke is the highlight.

Moroccan Vegetable Parcels

I make these at home for special family lunches and gatherings. At Christmas, I roll them into a cracker shape. In the winter and autumn, instead of the peas or sugar snaps, spinach, celeriac and cauliflower florets can be used.

Ingredients

Makes 12 small parcels if using Theo's Filo Pastry (30x34cm / 11¾x13½in per sheet). Number of parcels will vary depending on filo used.

- 12 sheets of filo pastry (e.g. Theo's brand if possible)
- 120g / 4½oz clarified butter (p376), melted, (plus a brush for buttering pastry)

Filling:

- 75g / 2¾oz golden sultanas
- In spring/summer: 200g / 7oz frozen garden peas or sugar snaps, sliced at an angle
- In autumn/winter: 100g / 3½oz spinach, 150g / 5¼oz small cauliflower florets (2.5cm / 1in), 100g / 3½oz celeriac, peeled and finely chopped
- 1 tbsp olive oil

- 1 tsp fennel seeds
- 3 tsp coriander seeds
- 2 tsp whole black mustard seeds
- A few nuts of butter (about 50g / 1¾oz)
- 4 onions, finely chopped
- 8 garlic cloves
- 200g / 7oz carrots, peeled and finely chopped
- 100g / 3½oz celery, peeled and finely chopped
- ¼ tsp ground cinnamon
- ½ tsp turmeric

- ½ tsp dried chopped chilli
- 100ml / 3½fl oz cream
- Zest of 1 orange
- Sea salt and cracked black pepper
- 100g / 3½oz pine nuts, toasted, or hazelnuts, toasted and chopped
- 2 tbsp pomegranate seeds
- 1 large bunch coriander, roughly chopped leaves and stems

Serving suggestions:

Mango salsa (p215), organic whole natural yoghurt and coriander & mint green salad tossed in a dressing of your choice

Method

Preheat the oven to fan 200°C / fan 400°F / gas mark 7 and place a non-stick tray in the oven to preheat.

In a heatproof bowl, cover the sultanas in boiling water and set aside for 15 minutes to soak and become plump.

Bring a small pot of boiling water with a pinch of sea salt to the boil. Blanch the garden peas or sugar snaps for 2 minutes or until bright green and tender. If using cauliflower, blanch for 3-4 minutes. Drain and refresh in ice-cold water.

In a dry frying pan, toast the fennel and coriander seeds over a low heat for a few minutes or until fragrant and turning lightly golden. Crush with a pestle and mortar.

In a saucepan, heat the butter and oil over a low heat. Add the onions and garlic, cover and sweat for 10 minutes or until soft. Add the carrots, celery, celeriac, chopped fresh spinach and cauliflower if using and sweat with the lid on for 5 minutes over a medium heat. Stir in the ground seeds, mustard seeds, spices and chilli and cook for a few minutes. Add the cream, bring to the boil for about 2-3 minutes and turn off. Add the orange zest, stir and season to taste. Set aside to cool. Once cool, stir in the sultanas, peas or sugar snaps (if using), toasted nuts, pomegranate seeds and coriander.

To prepare the pastries, have the melted clarified butter and pastry at hand, keeping the filo pastry well covered in clingfilm to prevent it from drying out. Further cover it with a damp tea towel to prevent it from crumbling, but do not allow the damp tea towel to touch the pastry directly.

Lay out one sheet of filo and brush with butter, ensuring the sheet is entirely coated with butter right out to the edges. Lay a second sheet carefully on top for a double layer and immediately brush with butter.

Using a sharp knife, cut the pastry lengthways down the centre, which will give you two good size parcels (if you want smaller parcels for a snack size, cut into four).

Place a good amount of filling in the centre of the pastry. Fold the long part first from the bottom over the filling. Brush with butter again. Then fold down from the top part. Butter, then fold under the outer sides and butter. Repeat with the remaining filo and filling to make 12 parcels in total.

Place the folded filo parcels on the preheated oven tray and bake until golden all over (for about 20-25 minutes – it will depend on your oven).

Twice Baked Hazelnut Cheese Soufflé

Served at The Lime Tree and Packie's in autumn when fresh hazelnuts were available. Twice baked soufflés are ideal for dinner parties, baked with a first initial rise, then a second time just before serving. Lovely served with a small organic green salad with hazelnut vinaigrette (p381). Instead of goat's cheese, for the hard cheese a mature cheddar can be used and for the soft cheese a soft blue cheese would work well.

Ingredients

Makes 4

Ramekin Lining:

- 30g / 1oz hazelnuts (about 20 hazelnuts)
- 55g / 2oz soft white breadcrumbs
- 30g / 1oz soft butter

Soufflé:

- 15g / ½oz butter
- 15g / ½oz plain white flour
- 100ml / 3½fl oz milk
- 65g / 2¼oz hard goat's cheese, grated
- 2 egg yolks, beaten
- 6 egg whites
- 65g / 2¼oz soft goat's cheese for centre filling, chopped
- ½ tsp lemon juice
- Sea salt

Serving suggestion:

Organic green salad with hazelnut dressing

Method

To toast and skin the nuts, preheat the oven to fan 160°C / fan 325°F / gas mark 4. Arrange the nuts in a single layer on a baking tray and toast in the oven for about 10-15 minutes, turning occasionally until the skins crack and the nuts are light golden. Once roasted, rub the nuts in a dry cloth to remove the skins. Pulse in a processor for a few seconds to bring the nuts to a coarse crumb consistency. Combine the hazelnut crumbs and breadcrumbs.

To prepare the ramekins, generously brush the butter over the sides and bottoms of the ramekins. Coat with a generous layer of hazelnut breadcrumbs. Set aside.

Increase the oven temperature to fan 170°C / fan 340°F / gas mark 5.

Make the base of the soufflé by melting the butter in a saucepan over a low heat. Add the flour and cook, stirring, to a pale golden colour. Gradually add the milk, continuing to stir, to a smooth consistency. Bring to the boil, then take off the heat and allow to cool. Stir in the hard goat's cheese, egg yolks and season with sea salt.

In a large dry bowl (essential for whipping egg whites), beat the egg whites with the sea salt until slightly thickened.

Add the lemon juice and whisk to stiff peaks. Take a quarter of the egg white mixture and mix this into the cooled cheese sauce until well combined. Gently fold in the remaining egg white mixture until well combined.

Half fill the ramekins with the soufflé mix, place the soft goat's cheese in the centre then cover with the remaining soufflé mixture, filling the ramekin to the top. Run your thumb around the ramekins to clean the top edge – this helps the soufflé to rise. Place each of the ramekins in a roasting tin and pour in enough hot water to come up an inch around the ramekins. Bake for 15 minutes to partially bake. Remove from the oven and allow to cool for at least 15 minutes.

At this point, the soufflés can be set aside until the second bake. If making ahead, chill in the fridge for up to 6 hours only.

Increase the oven heat to fan 200°C / fan 400°F / gas mark 7. Loosen the soufflés in the ramekin with a palette knife or small knife. Return the soufflés to the oven, this time with no water in the roasting tray, and bake for 10 minutes or until lightly risen. Serve immediately.

Goat's Cheese Parcels with Toasted Hazelnuts and Apple

These filo parcels work well as a lunch with a salad or smaller as a snack or starter for dinner parties. They can be prepared well in advance and frozen for up to 1 month.

Ingredients

Makes 14 small parcels if using Theo's Filo Pastry (30x34cm / 11¾x13½in per sheet). Number of parcels will vary depending on filo used.

- 14 sheets of filo pastry (e.g. Theo's brand if possible)

- 200g / 7oz clarified butter, melted, plus a brush for buttering pastry

Filling

- 6 eating apples (e.g. Cox's), peeled, cored and cut into small chunks

- 55g / 2oz hazelnuts

- 540g / 1lb 3oz crumbly local goat's cheese (e.g. St Tola Original)

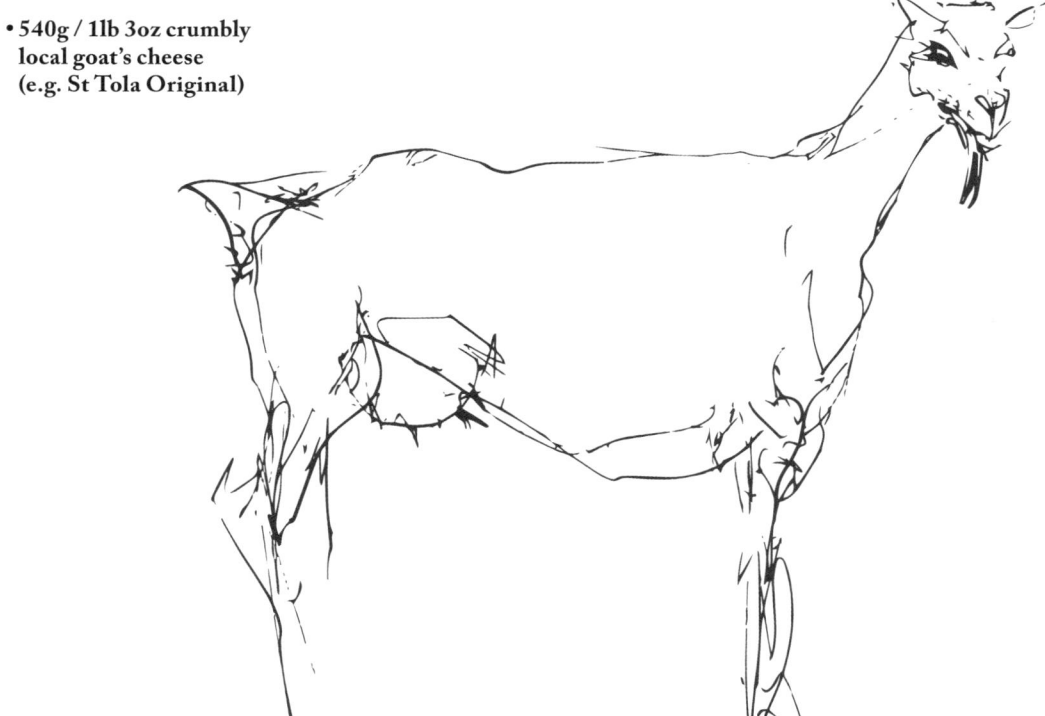

Method

Preheat the oven to fan 200°C / fan 400°F / gas mark 7 and place a non-stick tray in the oven to preheat.

To toast and skin the nuts, preheat the oven to fan 160°C / fan 325°F / gas mark 4. Arrange the nuts in a single layer on a baking tray and toast in the oven for about 10-15 minutes, turning occasionally until the skins crack and the nuts are light golden. Once roasted, rub the nuts in a dry cloth to remove the skins.

In a food processor, add the hazelnuts and pulse to roughly chop. Peel, core and chop the apples into small chunks. Crumble the goat's cheese to be the same size. In a large bowl, gently combine the hazelnuts, apples and goat's cheese making sure the ingredients stay separate rather than form a pâté-like mix.

To prepare the pastries, have the melted clarified butter and pastry at hand, keeping the filo pastry well covered in clingfilm to prevent it from drying out. Further cover with a damp tea towel to prevent it from crumbling, but do not allow the damp tea towel to touch the pastry directly.

Lay out one sheet of filo and brush with butter, ensuring the sheet is entirely coated with butter right out to the edges. Lay a second sheet carefully on top for a double layer and immediately brush with butter.

Using a sharp knife, cut the pastry lengthways down the centre and then again across to quarter the pastry, which will give you two good size parcels (if you want smaller parcels for a snack size, cut into four). Place a good amount of filling in the centre of the pastry. Fold the long part first from the bottom over the filling. Brush with butter again. Then fold down from the top part. Butter, then fold under the outer sides and butter. Repeat with the remaining filo and filling to make 14 parcels in total.

Place the folded filo parcels on the preheated oven tray and bake for about 10 minutes or until golden all over (baking time will depend on your oven).

Serve with a little green salad and a hazelnut vinaigrette dressing (p381).

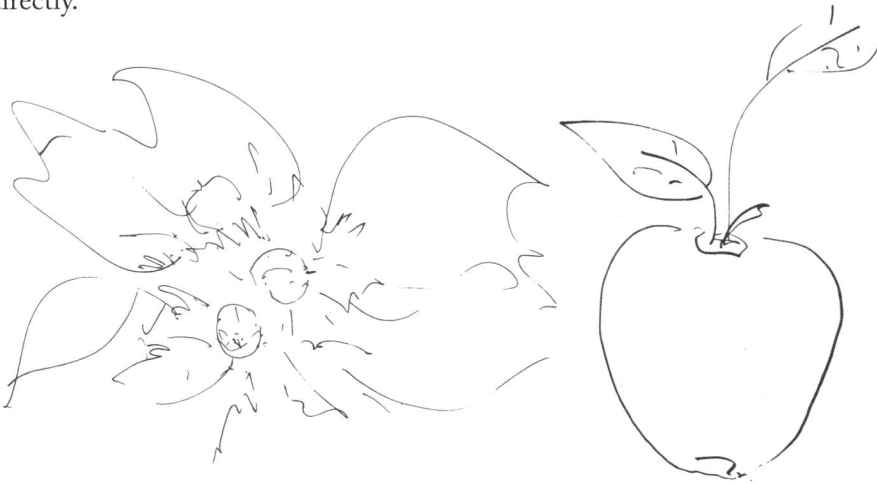

Starters 109

St Tola Irish Goat's Cheese & Warm Red Pepper Salad

Meg and Derrick Gordon started St Tola Goat's Cheese in the 1980s in Inagh, Co. Clare. Gerry Galvin of Drimcong, Galway first introduced me to their cheese. He was a terrific chef and I was fortunate to do a great course in Drimcong. Every Monday when in The Lime Tree, three logs were posted to me, beautifully packaged with great care. The cheese was astounding, it came out of the oven like a soufflé! Siobhán Ní Gháirbhith, who took over business in the late 1990s, shared the same passion as the Gordons and has developed it into one of the finest farmhouse goat's cheese in Ireland. Serve with beetroot, apple and toasted almonds, hazelnuts or pine nuts as an alternative to the peppers.

Ingredients

Serves 4

Red Pepper Mixture:

- 3 tbsp olive oil
- 4 red peppers, cored, seeded and sliced into batons
- 6 large fresh purple garlic cloves, peeled and finely chopped
- 2 tsp fresh thyme, basil or rosemary leaves
- 1 tbsp red wine vinegar

Goat's Cheese Salad:

- 4 portions of stewed red pepper mixture
- 4 slices of St Tola Irish Goat's Cheese Original Log (about 2cm/¾in)
- 4 handfuls of organic leaves
- Bunch of fresh basil leaves
- 4 tbsp citrus vinaigrette (p381)

Serving suggestions:

4 tbsp reduced balsamic (p131, omit ginger)

Method

Heat the oil in a large stainless steel saucepan, then add the peppers, garlic, thyme and vinegar. Reduce the heat and stew for approximately 10-12 minutes. Do not allow to brown. These can be kept in the fridge sealed in a jar for up to a week and taken out and warmed when needed. These form the base for the salad.

Preheat the oven to fan 200°C / fan 400°F / gas mark 7 or preheat the grill to medium. If the peppers were prepared in advance, warm them first in a saucepan. Place the warm peppers, divided into 4 portions, in a suitable dish for the oven or grill. Place a slice of goat's cheese on top of each pepper portion. Bake in the oven for about 5-7 minutes or grill for 3-4 minutes or until the cheese is lightly golden at the edges.

To serve, use a fish slice to place each serving of peppers and goat's cheese in the centre of each plate. Spoon the reduced balsamic around the peppers and goat's cheese. Dress the leaves in a bowl; serve on the side or separately.

Salad of Summer Fruits with St Tola Divine Irish Goat's Cheese

The combination of the fruit and the smooth and lightly whipped texture of St Tola Divine is delicious. As a variation to this salad, you could use chopped smoked ham or smoked chicken instead of the cheese. You can play around with this salad as you would like, grains are also a healthy addition.

Ingredients

Serves 4

- 4 tbsp simple citrus dressing (p383) or extra if desired
- 250g / 9oz Irish strawberries, quartered or halved if large, or whole if small
- 100g / 3½oz raspberries, whole
- 2 ripe nectarines, sliced
- 4 handfuls of mixed organic leaves
- 1 tbsp of fresh oregano or basil leaves
- 4 tbsp of St Tola Divine, or a similar soft goat's cheese
- 2 tbsp flaked almonds, toasted

Method

In a bowl, toss the fruit in half the dressing. In a separate bowl, toss the leaves and herbs in the remaining dressing. Divide the leaves across the four plates, intersperse the fruit and crumble the goat's cheese. Scatter the nuts over.

Starters 113

Rocket, Pear & Blue Cheese Salad with Toasted Walnuts and Apple & Walnut Oil Dressing

This is a delicious combination. Lovely on its own with homemade brown bread (p46) or a crusty country loaf.

Ingredients

Serves 4

- 3 ripe pears, peeled, quartered, cored and sliced (not over-ripe)
- 55g / 2oz walnuts, shelled and broken a little
- 170g / 6oz Cashel Blue, Crozier or Kerry Blue
- 75g / 2½oz rocket leaves and watercress or any organic salad leaves
- 4 tbsp of apple & walnut oil dressing (p380), more or less to taste

Method

Preheat the oven to fan 160°C / fan 325°F / gas mark 4. Spread the nuts on a baking tray and toast in the oven for about 7-10 minutes until browned and fragrant. Move around occasionally and check frequently to ensure they don't burn. Alternatively, you can place them in a dry pan on a low heat for 6-8 minutes, tossing them around and ensuring they don't burn. Allow to cool.

In a bowl, toss the pears, cooled walnuts and leaves in the dressing. Portion between 4 plates, crumble or scatter the cheese over each salad.

Serve immediately.

Salad Suggestions

Salads are very personal and can be adapted and played around with to your own individual tastes. It is essential to use good organic leaves. Below is a list of combinations that I regularly use in my salads for some ideas that can be dressed with any dressing of your choice. My favourite is the citrus vinaigrette (p381) in the summer and a balsamic dressing is nice in the winter time. The shallot vinaigrette (p382) is marvellous with smoked fish.

- Roasted or boiled beetroot and orange segments

- Roasted or boiled beetroot, cheese of your choice and apple

- Nectarines, cheese of your choice or baked ham with toasted nuts

- Smoked chicken with summer fruit

- Raw courgettes sliced finely with a mandolin, shavings of Parmigiano Reggiano, a squeeze of lemon and a drizzle of extra virgin olive oil

- Grains of your choice such as couscous or bulgur wheat with pomegranate seeds, toasted nuts, chopped dates and herbs such as chopped mint, flat leaf parsley and coriander

Starters 115

Crab Cakes with Tartare Sauce

Served at The Lime Tree and Packie's, these have been a staple on the menu at both restaurants. There are a few stages in preparation for the final crab cakes, but with all your elements laid out and prepared, the process is simple and the final result comes with ease. The curry powder adds a subtle flavour. The crab mixture can be prepared in advance, and the cakes freshly made when required.

Ingredients

Makes about 12 (around 8x5x2cm / 3x2x¾in when cooked)

- 45g / 1½oz butter
- 45g / 1½oz plain white flour
- 285ml / ½ pint whole milk
- 1 level tsp medium good quality curry powder (e.g. Green Saffron)
- Sea salt and cracked black pepper
- 2 eggs, lightly beaten
- 450g / 1lb white crab meat
- 110g / 4oz fresh soft white breadcrumbs
- 3-4 tbsp clarified butter, to fry

Serving suggestions:

Tartare sauce (p354), wedge of lime and a few organic leaves with dressing of your choice

Method

Melt the butter in a small saucepan over a low heat. Add the flour and cook for a further 2 minutes, continuing to stir with a whisk. Turn up to a medium heat and gradually pour in the milk, then sprinkle in the curry powder and continue to stir and cook for at least 6 minutes until the sauce is a very thick consistency (like choux pastry). Season to taste. Turn down to a low heat and add the eggs slowly, stirring vigorously to blend and ensure a smooth consistency. Remove from the heat. Add the sauce to a stainless steel or glass bowl and very gently fold in the crab meat, being careful to keep the crab in generous chunks. Cover and chill the mixture for at least 2 hours in the fridge. The mixture can be made the day before and chilled overnight.

Preheat the oven to fan 200°C / fan 400°F / gas mark 7.

When you want to cook the cakes, place the breadcrumbs on a large platter or tray nearby, take a heaped tablespoon of the crab mixture and place in the breadcrumbs and coat, not pressing or handling too much. They are fragile. Repeat with the remaining mixture.

Heat the clarified butter in an ovenproof frying pan over a medium heat. Cook the crab cakes in batches until golden (around 2-3 minutes either side). Finish the crab cakes in the oven for 5 minutes to puff up and lighten.

Serve warm with the homemade tartare sauce, a wedge of lime and a few organic leaves tossed in a dressing of your choice. Serve two each as a starter, or three each as a main course served with potato wedges and seasonal greens or a salad.

Crab & Coriander Bundles

These filo bundles make great canapés or starters. We served two cigar bundles with a little dressed green salad, a sprig of coriander and a wedge of lime. The pastry needs to be crispy.

Ingredients

Makes 18 if using Theo's Filo Pastry (30x34cm / 11¾x13½in per sheet). Number of parcels will vary depending on filo used.

- 55g / 2oz butter
- 4 banana shallots, peeled and finely chopped
- ½ tsp medium curry powder
- ½ tsp caster sugar
- 450g / 1lb white crab meat, cooked
- 2-3 tbsp coriander, stalks and leaves, chopped
- 6 sheets filo pastry (e.g. Theo's brand if possible)
- 110g / 4oz clarified butter, melted
- Sea salt and cracked black pepper

Method

Preheat the oven to fan 200°C / fan 400°F / gas mark 7 and line a baking tray ready for the rolled filo bundles.

Melt the butter in a small saucepan over a medium heat. Add the shallots to the pan and stir. Cover with a lid and sweat for 5 minutes. Remove the lid, add the curry powder and sugar and stir well. Mix in the crab meat until well combined, then lastly add the coriander. Season to taste. Transfer the crab mixture to a clean bowl to cool.

To prepare the bundles (like a spring roll), have the melted clarified butter and pastry at hand, keeping the filo pastry well covered in clingfilm to prevent it from drying out. Further cover with a damp tea towel to prevent it from crumbling, but do not allow the damp tea towel to touch the pastry directly.

Lay out one sheet of filo and brush with butter, ensuring the sheet is entirely coated with butter right out to the edges. Lay a second sheet carefully on top for a double layer and immediately brush with butter.

Using a sharp knife, cut the pastry into six equal sized rectangles. Place the crab mixture in the middle of the pastry lengthways along the pastry. Fold the two smaller sides first, brush with butter and then roll the pastry into a bundle or spring roll shape. Brush over butter once more. Repeat with the remaining filo and filling to make 18 bundles in total.

Bake the bundles in the oven for 10-15 minutes or until golden brown all over.

Serve warm with a little green salad as a starter or on their own as canapé.

Prawn & Spinach Pastry with Mousseline Sauce

These could never go off my menu! The succulent Atlantic prawns are the essential ingredient. Aim for the best quality ingredients for these pastries, it truly makes all the difference. If you can't source these prawns, you can use mussels instead, and if doing so, add garlic to your wilted spinach. People travelled and continue to travel to Packie's especially for this starter – these pastries are renowned.

Ingredients

Makes 8 pastries if using Theo's Filo Pastry (30x34cm / 11¾x13½in per sheet). Number of parcels will vary depending on filo used.

Pastries:

- 285ml / ½ pint of cold water with just a pinch of sea salt
- 500g / 1lb 2oz raw Atlantic prawns, already shelled
- 500g / 1lb 2oz fresh spinach
- 55g / 2oz butter, melted
- 8 sheets filo pastry
- 200g / 7oz clarified butter, melted and cooled
- Sea salt and cracked black pepper

Noilly Prat Sauce:

- Prawn poaching liquid
- 55g / 2oz butter
- 30g / 1oz plain white flour
- 140ml ¼ pint cream
- 4 tbsp Noilly Prat
- Sea salt and cracked black pepper

Mousseline Sauce:

- 6 tbsp hollandaise sauce (p342)
- 1 tbsp cream, whipped
- Juice of lemon, to taste

Serving suggestions:

A few sprigs of fennel, to garnish

Method

Preheat the oven to fan 200°C / fan 400°F / gas mark 7 with a baking tray inside.

To make the prawn and spinach filling, bring the water to the boil with a pinch of salt in a wide saucepan. Add the prawns and turn off the heat immediately, leaving them to rest in the poaching liquid for 2 minutes or until just cooked. Transfer the prawns to a plate, cover and allow to cool. Reserve the poaching liquid for the sauce.

Bring another saucepan of water with a pinch of salt to the boil, plunge in the spinach and stir for 30 seconds or until bright green. Drain and refresh in ice-cold water. Once cold, squeeze out the liquid from the spinach and toss in the melted butter with sea salt and cracked black pepper to taste.

To make the Noilly Prat sauce, return the prawn poaching liquid to the heat and reduce by two-thirds. Once reduced, melt the butter in a small saucepan over a low heat, then stir in the flour for 3-4 minutes to make a roux. Gradually stir in the reduced poaching liquid, cream and Noilly Prat to a smooth sauce. Season to taste.

To prepare the pastries, have the melted butter and pastry at hand, keeping the filo pastry well covered in clingfilm. Further cover with a damp tea towel to prevent it from crumbling, but do not allow the tea towel to touch the pastry directly.

Lay out one sheet of filo and brush with butter, ensuring the sheet is entirely coated with butter right out to the edges. Lay a second sheet carefully on top for a double layer and brush with butter.

Using a sharp knife, cut the pastry lengthways down the centre and then again across to quarter the pastry, which will give you two good sized parcels. Take a heaped spoonful of spinach and place in the centre of the pastry, with a heaped teaspoon of the Noilly Prat sauce on top. Add 3-4 prawns followed by another teaspoon of the Noilly Prat sauce. Fold the long part first from the bottom over the filling. Brush with butter again, then fold down from the top part. Butter, then fold under the outer sides and butter. Repeat with the remaining filo and filling to make eight parcels in total.

Place the folded filo parcels on the preheated oven tray and bake for about 12-15 minutes or until golden all over. Baking time will depend on your oven.

Make the mousseline sauce by folding the whipped cream into the hollandaise, then add lemon juice to taste.

Serve the pastries with the mousseline sauce and a sprig of fennel to garnish.

Seafood Mousse or Sausage with Beurre Blanc

Adapted from Michel Guérards' cookbook *Cuisine Gourmande*, this seafood mousse was served at The Lime Tree (when mousses were fashionable in the 1980s) and as sausages at Packie's – you can choose your preference. A small sprinkle of dillisk, a wild Irish seaweed, can be added to the beurre blanc and blanched samphire with the sausage. The seafood mousse I served at The Lime Tree was sometimes served with oysters and julienned leeks, which was utterly delicious. It was one of my French customer's favourite dishes. The sausages should be prepared the day before serving.

Ingredients

Serves 6

Mousse or Sausage:

- 380g / 13¼oz scallops (in season September to April)

or

- 310g / 11oz fresh raw salmon (in season May to October)
- 1 tsp sea salt
- ½ tsp freshly cracked black pepper
- 1 whole egg
- 1 egg white
- 640ml / 23fl oz cream

Sauce:

- 110g / 4oz fresh shelled cooked prawns (for sauce) when using salmon

or

- 12 oysters, shelled and shucked (2 per portion) when using scallops
- 1 leek, cut off top and bottom, green leaf julienned and rinsed

Serving suggestion:

Beurre blanc (p346)

Method

For the base of both the mousse and seafood sausage, blend the scallops or salmon with the sea salt and cracked black pepper in a food processor until smooth, approximately 2 minutes. Add the egg and egg white and blend for a further minute. Detach the food processor bowl with the mixture and place in the freezer for 15 minutes or 45 minutes in the fridge. This firms the mixture.

Re-attach the bowl to the food processor base and gradually add the cream, blending until smooth and creamy – this should only take a few seconds.

For the mousse, preheat the oven to fan 180°C / fan 350°F / gas mark 6. Line six ramekins with clingfilm and fill with the mixture. Place the ramekins in a deep baking tray and fill with boiling water until it reaches halfway up the ramekins to create a bain marie. Cover the tray with foil and bake in the oven for 15 minutes or until firm.

For the sausage:

Lay out 6 x A4 size sheets of foil, dull side up, and place a layer of clingfilm on top of each of the foil sheets for the six sausages. Place 2 tbsp of the mixture, side by side, in the middle of each, wrap the foil and clingfilm around the mixture and twist in opposite directions to form a sausage shape (around 2-4cm / 1-1½in in diameter and 8-10cm / 3-4in in length). Refrigerate overnight.

In a wide flat-based large pot, fill with water to about 60% full, add a pinch of salt and bring to the boil over a high heat. You may need two pots depending on the size to poach the sausages. Place the sausages into the boiling water. Bring the water back to the boil and then turn the heat down to low-medium and gently poach for 10 minutes. Remove from the water and allow to rest for 3-4 minutes. Remove the foil when slightly cooled.

To serve, slice the sausage diagonally in the middle.

If using scallops in the mousse or sausage, blanch the leeks for 2-3 minutes in a pot of boiling water with pinch of salt, then immediately refresh them in ice-cold water. Strain and gently press with some kitchen paper to dry. Add the leeks and freshly shucked oysters to the beurre blanc sauce to warm. Spoon over the mousse or sausage.

If using salmon and prawns in the mousse or sausage, just before serving, add the prawns to the beurre blanc sauce for 1-2 minutes to warm, not any longer. Spoon over the mousse or sausage.

Soused Mackerel

This is a lovely summer lunch dish or light supper. When the mackerel is prepared in this way, the oily content of the fish is more balanced and is easier to digest. The dish should be prepared the day before serving to allow the fish to marinate.

Ingredients

Serves 3

- 3 mackerel, gutted with heads removed but tails left on
- 2 onions, thinly sliced into rings
- 6 small bay leaves
- ½ tsp fresh thyme leaves, stems removed
- 12 whole black peppercorns
- 1½ tsp sea salt
- 200ml / 7fl oz white wine vinegar
- 200ml / 7fl oz cold water
- 2 tbsp fresh lemon juice
- 1 tsp caster sugar

Serving suggestions:

Green leaf salad with chopped apple and Purple Heather vinaigrette (p384); flat leaf parsley, to garnish

Method

Preheat the oven to fan 160°C / fan 325°F / gas mark 4.

Wash the inside of the mackerel under cold running water to ensure no blood remains (blood would add a bitter flavour), then pat dry with kitchen paper.

Lay the fish side by side in a small deep roasting tray or casserole dish just large enough to hold them comfortably. Strew the onion rings and bay leaves evenly over the fish, and sprinkle over the thyme leaves, peppercorns and salt. Mix the vinegar, water, lemon juice and sugar and pour over the fish.

On the stove top, bring the tray to a boil over a high heat, then bake uncovered in the oven for 15 minutes or until the fish is firm to touch, basting two or three times with the liquid.

Let the fish cool to room temperature and cover tightly with clingfilm. Chill in the fridge overnight to allow the fish to marinate. The liquid will form a gel which can also be served with the mackerel.

Remove the onions and bay leaves from the fish. Place the fish on a large platter and debone the mackerel for presentation, gently lifting the top fillet and removing the bone.

Serve the whole mackerel per portion with some of the chopped gel, the cooked onion rings and bay leaves and a dressed green salad with chopped apple.

Starters 125

Smoked Cod Cakes

These cod cakes can be made in advance and frozen for up to one month, making them ideal to be served at any time of day, be that breakfast, lunch or a light supper. The cakes can also be deep-fried for a crispier result in a canapé or starter size. To do so, shape the mixture into small balls (golf ball size) and deep fry in hot oil until golden brown. Serve about two per starter portion.

Ingredients

Makes around 15-20 cakes

- 450g / 1lb undyed smoked cod
- 285ml / ½ pint cold milk, for poaching
- 285ml / ½ pint water, for poaching
- 45g / 1½oz butter
- 45g / 1½oz plain white flour
- 285ml / ½ pint whole milk
- Sea salt and cracked black pepper
- 2 eggs, lightly beaten
- 55g / 2oz freshly grated Parmigiano Reggiano or mature Coolea gouda cheese
- 115g / 4oz fresh soft white breadcrumbs
- Oil and clarified butter (p376) to shallow fry, or oil for deep fat frying

Serving suggestions:

Tartare sauce (p354), lemon wedges and a green salad or chips

Method

Place the cod in a medium saucepan and cover with the milk and water. Bring to a boil over a medium heat, then reduce to a low heat to gently poach for 5 minutes or until the cod flakes easily. Remove the cod from the poaching liquid and flake into chunky pieces, removing any bones, sinew or skin.

In a small saucepan, melt the butter over a low heat. Add the flour and cook for a further 2 minutes, continuing to stir with a whisk. Turn up to a medium heat and gradually pour in the milk, continuing to stir and cook for at least 6 minutes until the sauce is a very thick consistency (like choux pastry). Season to taste. Turn down to a low heat and add the eggs slowly, stirring vigorously to blend and ensure a smooth consistency. Stir in the cheese. Remove from the heat.

Gently mix in the fish, being careful to keep the fish in generous chunks. With the breadcrumbs in a bowl nearby, take heaped tablespoons of the cod mixture and gently coat in the breadcrumbs, not pressing or handling too much. If shallow frying, make small little cakes. If deep fat frying, shape into small round balls (golf ball size).

Place on a tray and chill for 30 minutes in the fridge before frying, not covering to avoid soggy breadcrumbs.

Heat enough clarified butter and oil in a wide frying pan to cover the base, then shallow fry for 3 minutes either side until golden brown. Repeat in batches until all the cakes are cooked. Alternatively, deep fry in batches until golden brown.

Smoked Cod Mousse

A very old recipe first served in The Purple Heather in the 1960s. It was shared by a friend who was living in Kinsale with the recipe originating from Hedli MacNiece from the famous Spinnaker. Make the day before you're planning to serve, although the mousse will keep in the fridge for up to a week.

Ingredients

Serves 4

- 285g / 10oz undyed smoked cod, trimmed, boned and skinned
- 285ml / ½ pint cold milk, for poaching
- 285ml / ½ pint water, for poaching
- 4g / ⅛oz gelatine leaves
- 285ml / ½ pint Baxter's beef consommé
- 150g / 5¼oz mayonnaise
- Juice of ½ lemon
- 140ml / 5fl oz cream
- Sea salt and cracked black pepper

Serving suggestions:

Fingers of hot toast and a simple green salad

Method

Prepare four ramekins or a small terrine dish by lining them with clingfilm.

Place the cod in a saucepan and cover with the milk and water. Bring to a boil over a medium heat, then reduce to a low heat to gently poach for 10 minutes or until the cod flakes easily. Remove the cod from the poaching liquid and flake into small pieces. Allow to cool.

Soak the gelatine in cold water for 10 minutes. Meanwhile, warm 3 tbsp of the consommé in a small saucepan. Remove from the heat. Remove the gelatine leaves from the water and stir into the hot consommé to dissolve. (Note that gelatine must never boil as it will lose its setting properties.) Allow to cool, then stir in the remaining consommé.

Place the cooled flaked fish, mayonnaise and lemon juice into a food processor and pulse. Add the consommé and pulse again until smooth. Transfer the mixture to a bowl and chill in the fridge until it begins to gel.

Whip the cream to stiff peaks, then gently fold through the fish mayonnaise mixture and season to taste. Spoon the mousse into the each of the four ramekins and smooth the tops. Chill in the fridge overnight to set.

Serve with hot toast fingers and a green salad.

Smoked Bacon and Bread Stuffing Rolls

Accompanied by buttered greens, such as spinach or savoy cabbage, this would be a pleasing supper. It's also great as an accompaniment to roast duck, pheasant or chicken. We often serve the rolls as party finger food, just with a touch less filling, and they are devoured!

Ingredients

Makes 12 bacon rolls

- **Butter, softened to grease**
- **12 tbsp cold or fresh bread stuffing (below)**
- **12 dry cured smoked bacon rashers**
- **Cumberland sauce, warmed (p358)**

Bread Stuffing:

- **55g / 2oz unsalted butter**
- **2 shallots or 1 medium onion, peeled and finely chopped**
- **2 tsp fresh thyme leaves**
- **225g / 8oz fresh white breadcrumbs**
- **Sea salt and cracked black pepper**

Serving suggestions:

Buttered greens or colcannon (p262) with roasted chicken, duck or pheasant

Method

Preheat the oven to fan 200°C / fan 400°F / gas mark 7. Grease a large baking tray with butter across the base.

To make the stuffing, melt the butter in a saucepan over a low heat, add the onions or shallots and sweat covered for 10-15 minutes, stirring to make sure there is no colouring. Stir in the thyme leaves. Place the breadcrumbs in a bowl and pour over the herb onion mixture. Stir together with a fork to retain lightness. Season to taste.

Lay out the bacon rashers on a board and place the bread stuffing on the meaty or wide side of the bacon rasher. Roll the bacon up from the meaty end to the tail end. Keep the tail end on top as there is more fat for self-basting (the bacon roll can be held in place with a wooden toothpick if need be).

Place the bacon rolls on the greased baking tray and roast in the oven for 12-20 minutes or until golden.

Serve on a plate either by themselves with Cumberland sauce poured over, greens and colcannon or with roasted chicken, duck or pheasant.

Confit Duck Leg with Pear & Ginger Salad

Ingredients

Serves 2

- 2 confit duck legs (p222)

Balsamic Reduction:

- 250ml / 9fl oz good quality balsamic vinegar
- 2.5cm / 1in piece fresh ginger, peeled and julienned
- 2 tsp honey

Pear & Ginger Salad:

- 1 pear, peeled and julienned with a squeeze of lemon
- 2 handfuls of micro salad leaves, optional
- 1 tbsp olive oil, for the leaves (optional)
- Sea salt and cracked black pepper

Method

Preheat the oven to fan 200°C / fan 400°F / gas mark 7.

Place the vinegar, ginger and honey in a saucepan over a medium-low heat and reduce to around 125ml / 4¼fl oz. After 5 minutes remove the ginger with a slotted spoon, drain well and set aside.

Lightly grease the roasting tray with butter. Place the duck skin side up on the roasting tray and roast for about 10 minutes or until golden brown.

Toss the ginger and pear together with a drizzle of the balsamic reduction. If using salad leaves, lightly dress them in olive oil.

Serve the duck with the salad and leaves, if using, with a spoonful of balsamic reduction over the duck and more swirled on the plate if desired.

Chicken Mousseline with Carrots & Citrus Sauce

This simple starter can be made a day in advance and baked just before serving.

Ingredients

Makes 4 small ramekins

Mousseline:

- 150g / 5oz chicken breast, skin and sinew removed, cut into small pieces
- Egg white from 1 small egg
- 250ml / 9fl oz cold cream
- Sea salt and cracked black pepper

Carrots:

- 2 tsp butter
- 1 tbsp water
- 1 tsp sugar
- 140g / 5oz carrots, peeled and julienned

Citrus Sauce:

- Juice of 2 lemons
- 1 tbsp of water
- 40g / 1½oz sugar
- Juice of 1 orange
- Juice of 1 extra lemon
- 150ml / 5fl oz cold cream

Serving suggestion:

Tarragon leaves, to garnish

Method

Preheat the oven to fan 140°C / fan 275°F / gas mark 3. In a food processor, purée the chicken for 1 minute. Add the egg white and purée for a further minute. Remove the blender bowl, cover and place in the freezer for 10-15 minutes. Remove from the freezer and blend again for 1 minute. Very slowly pour in 150ml / 5¼fl oz of cream using the pulse button intermittently. Stop to scrape down the sides, then turn the blender on and add the remaining cream. Turn off and season generously.

Line four ramekins with clingfilm, allowing sufficient overhang at the sides. Divide the mousseline between the 4 ramekins and cover. Place in a roasting tin filled halfway up with boiling water. Cover the tin with foil and cook in the oven for 15 minutes or until slightly firm to touch.

To prepare the carrots, melt the butter in a heavy saucepan with the water over a low heat. Add the sugar and the carrots. Cook slowly over a low heat for the carrots to gently caramelise. Cover and keep warm.

For the citrus sauce, place the sugar, water and juice of 2 lemons into a saucepan and stir over a medium heat until the sugar has dissolved. Once dissolved, stop stirring and cook until lightly caramelised. Remove from the heat and pour in the juice of 1 orange and lemon, returning to a medium-low heat; swirl or tilt the saucepan to incorporate the caramel, do not stir. Add the cream, being careful as it will splutter, and cook until coating consistency. Taste and add more lemon juice if needed. Season to taste.

To serve, arrange a bed of carrots on the plates and turn out the mousseline on top. Pour over the citrus sauce.

Chicken Liver Pâté with Cumberland Sauce

Served at The Purple Heather since the 1970s, this pâté has been a permanent favourite. Serve as a starter or a light lunch with toast fingers and a green salad.

Ingredients

Makes 450g / 1lb loaf tin

Pâté:

- **1 tbsp sunflower oil**
- **500g / 1lb 2oz streaky bacon, diced**
- **85g / 3oz butter**
- **45g / 1½oz shallots, diced**
- **3 garlic cloves, sliced**
- **675g / 1½lb chicken livers with sinews removed, prepared by a butcher**
- **200ml / 7fl oz cream**
- **85ml / 3fl oz port**
- **85ml / 3fl oz brandy**
- **225g / 8oz clarified butter, melted**

Serving suggestion:

Cumberland sauce (p358)

Method

Line a loaf tin, Pyrex or ceramic terrine dish with clingfilm, keeping it flush to the sides and leaving a slight overhang over the edges.

In a frying pan, heat the oil over a medium-high heat and add the bacon. Cook until golden and crispy, then remove from the pan and drain on kitchen paper.

Melt the butter in a deep frying pan over a medium heat. Sauté the shallots and garlic until soft and translucent. Remove the onions and garlic and set aside. Increase the heat of the pan to high and add the livers. Sauté quickly for 2 minutes; the livers should still be pink inside. Add the cream, port, brandy and cooked bacon to the pan and bring gently to a boil then simmer for 3 minutes. Set aside to cool.

Place all the pan ingredients into a blender and blitz until smooth. Pour into the prepared lined tin or dish and seal with a thin layer of the clarified butter. Once completely cooled, remove from the tin or terrine dish, wrap well in clingfilm and foil and keep in the fridge for up to 5 days. Also suitable for freezing.

Serve a slice with the Cumberland sauce (p358).

Irish Black Pudding, Caramelised Apples & Citrus Vinaigrette Salad

Choose the type of black pudding you love best. For a more detailed discussion on black pudding, see the introduction note in the 'Breakfast' section.

Serve about four slices of round pudding or about two slices of the baked loaf style pudding per person, both around 3cm / ¾in thickness.

Ingredients

Makes 4

- 2 tbsp butter
- 2 eating apples, peeled and sliced into segments
- 1 tbsp demerara sugar
- 16 slices of round Irish black pudding of your choice
- 4 large handfuls of organic leaves
- 4 tbsp citrus herb vinaigrette or shallot vinaigrette (p381)

Method

Heat 1 tbsp butter in a non-stick frying pan. In a heavy-based saucepan, sauté the apples over a medium heat and toss them around, cooking for about 2 minutes. Sprinkle the sugar over the apples; turn them over to coat and then cook until the apples are golden brown with a bit of glaze – the sugar will help the caramelising. They will burn in a flash, so take care. This is a very quick process so stand by the pan.

Heat 1 tbsp butter in a frying pan and add the black pudding. Cook on a medium heat for 1½-2 minutes either side or until cooked to your liking; this depends on thickness. If you have them thicker, allow a little longer on each side. Keep them warm.

Dress your leaves. Using a warm plate, place the salad on the side of plate, the pudding in the centre and place the warm apples on top. Pour some extra vinaigrette over the pudding and apple for extra depth.

Cyril's boat at Coornagillagh Pier, Tuosist

Fish

Sole

Dover Sole Meunière	154
Dover Sole Stuffed with Atlantic Prawns & Brandy Cream Sauce	156
Dover Sole Stuffed with Atlantic Prawns & Garlic Butter	156
Dover Sole Stuffed with Spinach, Mushrooms & Noilly Prat Sauce	156
Lemon Sole with Tomato & Caper Salsa	160
Lemon Sole with Toasted Almonds, Lemon Butter & Parsley	160

Monkfish and Sea bass

Monkfish in a Garlic & Ginger Crust with Thai Dipping Sauce	162
Roast Monkfish with Red Pepper Relish	164
Roast Monkfish with Sweet & Sour Aubergine Relish	164
Roast Wild Sea Bass with Wholegrain Mustard Sauce	166

Cod

Roast Cod with Herb Crust	167
Roast Cod Mornay with Coolea Matured Cheese	168
Roast Cod with Chilli, Garlic & Rosemary Oil	169
Cod Provençale	170

Mackerel

Pan-Fried Mackerel in an Oatmeal Crust with Salsa Verde	174
Pan-Fried Mackerel in an Oatmeal Crust with Caper Salsa	174

John Dory and Brill

Fillet of John Dory or Brill with Pears, Leeks and Noilly Prat Sauce	176

Salmon

Baked Fillet of Wild Salmon with Lime & Coriander Butter	177
Baked Fillet of Wild Salmon with Gooseberry, Elderflower & Lime Sauce	178
Baked Fillet of Wild Salmon with Wild Sorrel Hollandaise	178

Turbot
Baked Fillet of Turbot en Papillote with Noilly Prat and Basil Orange   181
Baked Fillet of Turbot en Papillote with Salsify and Red Wine Sauce   182

Scallops
Seared Scallops with Curried Vermicelli   183
Scallops with Noilly Prat & Mushroom Sauce   185
Crumbed Scallops with Garlic Butter   186

Prawns
Cyril's Atlantic Prawns Roasted with Garlic Butter or Béarnaise Sauce   187
Brochette de Fruits de Mer with Sauce Choron   190

Lobster
Lobster Thermidor   191
Baked Stuffed Lobster   193

Mussels
Moules Marinière   194
Stuffed Baked Garlic Mussels   197

Fish

Fish is my real love. My love for cooking fish developed gradually. We are lucky with Kenmare being situated on the Atlantic in the south west of Ireland as the cold water fish and shellfish have a magical sweetness and flavour which I believe you do not get from warm water fish.

When I was a young girl, there was no fish shop in Kenmare. A lady from Castletownbere (a nearby town and one of Ireland's major fishing ports) would travel to Kenmare weekly and she sold fresh fish on Henry Street from the boot of her car. In those days people's attitude to fish was different. It was associated with penance and was eaten only on a Friday – the day meat was not allowed – for the main meal, generally at lunch time. We used to say, "why didn't our Lord have 12 butchers instead of 12 fishermen?" Needless to say, there were not any major queues for fresh fish but she did sell it.

People generally ate smoked fish such as cod or haddock, or salted fish such as ling. At that time, smoking and salting were the major preservation methods of food in Ireland. When my mother Agnes and I first opened The Purple Heather in 1961, we rented from Gerald O'Shea and operated as a tea and cake shop. We then moved across the street in 1963 to where The Purple Heather is located today, and at first continued with the tea and cake shop, but it soon evolved into a restaurant. Agnes looked after the front of house and I did the cooking. I loved cooking and being in the kitchen.

The main reason The Purple Heather became a restaurant was as a result of the fish I received from a friend, Kevin Cooper. Kevin, who grew up in London, spent a lot of his holidays in Kenmare, as his stepfather owned Dinish Island at the time. He had a love of Kenmare Bay and in the early 1960s bought a small trawler. He fished daily and because we were good friends he came in each evening and gave us his catch. The catch included a huge variety of fish including cod, haddock and all kinds of sole. He also caught whiting which was known as the chicken of the sea – a delicate fish that people loved just like they loved chicken. This was amazing produce and required a few subtle sauces to make superb dishes. With this excellent supply of fresh fish, I started cooking more in the evenings.

Scallops at that time were plentiful and we got them from Coornagillagh and Ardgroom on the Beara Peninsula side and from Blackwater and Tahilla on the opposite side of Kenmare Bay.

At that time, Lucy's of Waterville were exporting large amounts of lobster to Paris and another export that started was purple sea urchins. Diving for purple sea urchins off the coast of Kerry, including Kenmare Bay, grew to be a huge business with all the produce being exported mainly to Paris and very few eaten in Kenmare! Only part of the urchin is eaten, the gonads or sex organs which run along the inside of the shell. I didn't cook with them myself, but my good friend Colin O'Daly served them in the Park Hotel in the 1980s with scrambled eggs in their shells and the gonads on top. Unfortunately there are very few, if any, left in the area now.

By the mid to late 1960s The Purple Heather restaurant was thriving. Kevin's business also expanded, and he was joined by Ken Besson as director and they formed Kenmare Fisheries in April 1969. They employed a lot of people and ran a great business for years. They developed smoked salmon which was wild oak smoked salmon, and my cousin James McCarthy was the first person to smoke salmon in Kenmare Fisheries followed by Noel Bambury, Tom's son. They used a Dory kiln that came from Hull in England which smoked on the flat, dry salted and not brined like the mackerel. As well as smoking salmon, they smoked kippers, haddock, cod and coley (black pollock) used mostly for flavouring soup and chowders. For smoking eels, they used a different system: dipping the eels in a vat of boiling water to loosen the skins and hang them downwards, and they were then smoked in the kiln. The main market for the eels was in Germany. The eels were often caught under Roughty Bridge near where we built our family home.

In the early 1970s, we had a seafood festival in Kenmare called Les Fruits De Mer. It was a tremendous success. There were two main events: a seafood buffet competition, with chefs from the top hotels around the country and Europe each preparing a seafood display of all kinds of fish and shellfish with spectacular butter carvings as the centrepiece (p143), and the seafood banquette which was the finale. The banquette was held in the Silver Slipper Ballroom with the catering provided by the Great Southern Kenmare, always followed by dancing with a big showband. The festival raised the profile of Kenmare at a national and international level, with supporters including Charles Heidsieck who sponsored the champagne reception each year. The town was alive with activity and people returned especially for the festival – there was even a horse racing event held in Dunkerron on the O'Sullivan's farm. All the bars and restaurants participated; the bars provided free mussels and periwinkles on their counters. With the growth of the festival, one of the years the seafood banquette was held in different venues across Kenmare including The Purple Heather. I catered for about 50 guests including Theodora FitzGibbon, who became a good friend – she particularly enjoyed my avocado mousse which I served as a starter with crab.

The festival and its success got a lot of national and international press and it helped our tourism and food business grow even further in the town. In The Purple Heather, I had special menus which I handmade (p18). Starters were 1-6 to 7-6 of old Irish money at the time. 1-6 was one shilling and six pence so one could have had almost 12 bowls of mussel soup for one old Irish pound. I prepared and served an abundance of Brochettes de Fruits de Mer (p190) during the festival. The brochettes became a staple on our menu as they were so popular. They are a seafood heaven with a very simple cooking process.

Later, my major fish supplier was Michael Spillane. I was lucky as Michael and his brother Ned were friends of ours and we knew the family well. Michael ran Spillane Seafoods providing excellent quality fish. It is now run by his son Paudie, very successfully, with great service and he continues to provide quality fish. Paudie delivers fresh fish to me every few days now for Shelburne Lodge, and for the restaurant it was on a daily basis. Ted Brown, based in Dingle, started a fish company in early 1980s and he also supplied us with his high quality produce for the restaurants.

We are lucky in Kenmare as there are a number of great fish suppliers who create substantial local employment, including the renowned Star Seafoods by Danny McCarthy who supplies all over Ireland and abroad and also Gulf Stream Fish Products who supply locally and nationally.

Included in this chapter are many of my fish and seafood recipes and provided here are a few finer details and stories on fish.

Sole
There are three main types of sole: white, black and lemon. Dover, or black as it is known in Ireland, is my favourite and for me is the king of fish. Lemon sole is a lovely tasting fish but the flesh is not as firm as black sole. White sole is watery and not in the same league. Unlike most fish such as turbot, cod, trout, salmon, plaice, brill or lemon sole which are best straight out of the water, Dover sole must be left for 48 hours before cooking. If you eat it when it is caught the texture is tough, so it is best left to settle. Dover sole is the fish used in many of the classic French dishes, mainly because it arrived at the Paris kitchens a few days after it was caught so the quality was not impaired. Sole is best cooked on the bone which helps to retain the flavour and keep the fish succulent. I have included several Dover sole recipes (p154–156) and also a lemon sole recipe with a tomato and caper salsa or with toasted almonds and a lemon parsley butter (p160).

Monkfish
In Ireland, monkfish didn't appear on menus until the early 1970s. Very few people, if any, ate or had heard of monkfish. My family first encountered it at my sister Grainne's 21st birthday on the menu at the Waterville Lake Hotel, where The Lodge at Hogs Head is now located. It was a very memorable experience. Monkfish was initially regarded as a very ugly, poor quality fish and people didn't bother catching it. The texture was similar to prawns and some people used it for scampi as it was inexpensive; the small tails were mostly used for that purpose. Now it is a high end fish, very meaty and capable of handling strong robust flavours as an accompaniment. The monkfish in a garlic and ginger crust with Thai dipping sauce (p162) suits the texture of this fish as it is a spicy shallow fry.

displayed in The Purple Heather, featuring a seafood buffet competition entry from Jac Mention, head chef at Killarney's Hotel Europe; the magnificent seagull is a butter sculpture, exemplifying the rare and highly specialised chef skill of butter carving

Fish

Cod

Cod is a wonderful fish. It is moving more north now, but when I first started cooking fish cod was in abundance. It is a prime fish and is now very sought after and is getting more expensive. Deep fried cod with a great batter is the ultimate. My preference is for a medium-sized cod where you can obtain beautiful cod fillets suitable for roasting rather than the smaller codling. I have included in this section several cod recipes.

Salmon

Our own family home is located on the banks of the Roughty River and for many years our neighbour Jerry Mac or Jerry McCarthy fished for beautiful wild salmon on the river. Jerry first supplied me with wild salmon in the 1960s and continued to do so for several decades. When Jerry passed away, Raymond Bambury, son of Tom whom I mentioned in my artichoke recipe (p102), continued the fishing with Jerry's sons John and Jimmy for many years. We have such lovely memories of the boys heading out on their wooden fishing boat across from our home, the magical metronomic sound of the oars and watching the salmon leap! The spring salmon were always my favourite for cooking as they have much higher oil content than the later fish. Fresh wild salmon is a real treat. Sadly, the wild salmon are now scarce and no longer in abundance. Wild salmon with hollandaise was one of our best sellers in The Purple Heather. I have included this wonderful recipe on page 178.

Turbot

Turbot is a superb fish and must be very fresh. The ultimate way to cook turbot is on the bone. Many people, however, prefer a fillet off the bone. I have included two recipes for turbot in this section, baking the fillets in sealed little packets 'en papillote' to protect the fish when it is off the bone (p181). Sometimes brill (which is of the same family as turbot) is passed off as turbot. The skin of the turbot is bumpy whereas the brill has a smoother skin. When cooked, turbot has a larger flaky texture and a more robust flavour than brill. I personally prefer brill for its finer texture and more delicate flavour. Brill is also less expensive than turbot and for the recipes included you can use brill instead of turbot if you wish.

Scallops

Scallops are a winter and spring shellfish in Ireland like the native oyster. When there is an 'R' in the month shellfish are generally in season. We bought them whole from local fishermen when they were in season and we used to shell and beard hundreds of scallops which was mostly done by my father. Then we would seal, pack and freeze them so we could serve the scallops for the summer months. In later years, our fish supplier prepped them for us. In Ireland and Britain, we generally cook with the coral (orange tongue) on, however in America the coral is generally used for fish soups or scallop butter. If you are shelling your own scallops the shell must be closed to ensure the scallop is still alive.

A good fish supplier will shell them for you and prepare them for use in cooking. I have included an old recipe from The Purple Heather which was one of our most popular dishes – Scallops in Noilly Prat & Mushroom Sauce (p185).

Atlantic Prawns
The North Atlantic prawns (also known as langoustines or Dublin Bay prawns) are deliciously succulent and the beauty of these prawns is their sweetness. In the summer, Cyril – a chef who worked with me for years at The Lime Tree and Packie's and who is now a fisherman – supplies me with delicious whole Atlantic prawns of the very best quality. I have included a delicious recipe for these prawns on page 187. I like to keep it very simple to allow for the succulent sweet Atlantic prawns to speak for themselves.

Lobster
The Irish word for lobster is 'glíomach', which means the devil when directly translated because of its fierce appearance! People were afraid to fish for it and they didn't eat it traditionally. During Les Fruits De Mer festival in the early 1970s I did a special menu for the festival. Lobster American was on as a main course for 20 shillings (about 1 pound in old Irish money or over 1 euro). When we had the fish bar in The Purple Heather from 1975, lobster was not expensive. We had moved the restaurant upstairs for a few years and when I came back from Kenya where my husband Tom was working, I opened a fish bar downstairs again and closed the upstairs. Lobster was a big seller.

The best size lobsters are 450g / 1lb to 675g / 1½lb. If they are any larger, they tend to have heavy shells, with less and tougher meat, however they do vary. Very large lobsters are not tender and have heavy shells with very little meat content. We use Atlantic lobster, which is beautifully sweet and succulent.

Cooking a lot of lobster (when it was more affordable to do so), we found the most humane way to cook a lobster was to put the lobster into a pot of cold sea water or tap water with salt (10g of salt to 1 litre) allowing the lobster to go to sleep, then increasing the temperature gently. In this way, they faint and die almost immediately. If they are plunged into boiling water the lobsters go into spasm and the meat becomes tough. Be brave with lobster, as cooked well it is an absolute treat.

Mussels
We are lucky to live on the Atlantic in the south west of Ireland where we have mussels in abundance and many local producers. There is no doubt that most of the visitors coming to Ireland seem to want bowls of steaming mussels. Present day production methods mean that mussels are now available all year round. They are traditional here with a good pint of Guinness.

Fish

Irish Native Oysters
The Irish native oysters are flat, round and in season from September until April. It is recommended that they are always eaten raw. They take five to seven years to grow, and reproduce during the summer which is why they are not eaten during this time. Oysters are considered aphrodisiacs and native oysters are a luxury in the league of caviar. Galway is host to the famous oyster festival with its unique atmosphere. There is a competition held at the festival on the skill shown by the oyster openers. In London, the place to swallow these beauties with your Chablis is Bentley's on Swallow Street near Piccadilly, run by my good friend and marvellous Irish chef Richard Corrigan.

Pauline Bewick, the incredible artist, has captured the magical pleasure experienced by the ladies swallowing oysters in her painting 'Four Oyster Eaters'. This painting was on one of Declan Ryan's menu covers in the splendid Arbutus Lodge in Cork, which was a Michelin-starred restaurant for many years in the 1970s and 1980s.

Native oysters are almost impossible to get now, available for a very short period of time, similar to wild salmon. Gigas Pacific or rock oysters are different from native Irish oysters in taste and shape. They are more fleshy and oval in shape. They are farmed and take three years to grow. They wouldn't be in the same league as our native oysters, however they are available all year round and lend themselves more suitably for cooking as Oysters Rockefeller or grilled oysters, for example.

Some Fish Tips

Buying Fish
- Find a good fish supplier, whom you can trust and ask for advice on what is best to buy at the time as it can vary throughout the year.
- Fresh fish should be slimy when the skin is on it and slippery to touch.
- The eyes should be bright if the heads are on.
- Dull, flabby-looking fish or ones that smell fishy are past their best.
- For plaice, the spots should be bright orange.
- Fresh mackerel or herring should be firm or stiff. If soft, then it is generally not as fresh.
- Slip soles are a smaller version of black or Dover sole, and a less expensive option.

Storing Fish
- Fish deteriorate quickly once caught unless they are kept on ice; eat as soon as possible.
- Never put ice directly on the flesh or skin of fish. Seal the ice and then put it over and under the fish. It will stay fresh in the fridge for 2-3 days with this method.
- Try to avoid freezing fish. If you do freeze, thaw it slowly overnight in the fridge.

Preparing Fish
- Gutting fish is a messy business – if possible, ask your fishmonger to do this for you.
- If you are preparing fish, ensure that you clean all the blood out as it has a bitter taste.
- The less fish comes into contact with water the better. If you do want to wash, do so briefly and only under running water – never soak it.
- Before cooking fish, pat dry thoroughly with kitchen paper (if it is wet when you dip in seasoned flour it will form a batter when cooking).

Cooking Fish
- Pan-frying is a great way to cook fish. For a lot of my recipes, I seal the fish in the pan and then roast in the oven. It is therefore best to have a heavy non-stick frying pan that is also suitable for the oven.
- Clarified butter (p376) is best used to pan-fry fish; it has a higher smoking point and can withstand higher heat than regular butter. It also has a longer shelf life.
- To get a crispy coating on your fish, only grease the pan lightly. When you are turning the fish you can then re-grease, but only just a little.
- Baking in a parcel or 'en papillote' is another great way to cook fish. Use foil as it does not soak up the juices and is easier to handle. Allow enough foil so there is both room for steaming and to allow you to seal the edges tightly. Add the cooking juices to your sauce.
- Fish cooks quickly, so you will need to watch it carefully. Being very precise about fish cooking times is rather impossible. The shape, texture and thickness of the fish are important factors in cooking times. I have provided cooking time guidance in the recipes. A good tip is to check the thickest part of the fish with a pointed knife and if the flesh parts easily or comes away from the bone easily then it is ready. If it is off the bone and the flesh separates easily then it is cooked. Opaque fish is undercooked.

Sauces for Fish
- Good fish just needs a little enhancing.
- The dry vermouth, Noilly Prat, is an excellent addition to a sauce, does not have to be cooked out, adds instant flavour to your sauces and goes exceptionally well with scallops, sole or any flat fish.
- Keep tasting when you are making sauces for your fish; you are cooking to please yourself, so it must be something you like. If it is sour, add more sweetness (a tiny pinch of sugar); if it is sweet, add more acidity; if it is flat, a little squeeze of lemon juice can work wonders.

Dover Sole Meunière

This is without doubt my favourite fish, cooked simply, pan-fried and served with a light lemon butter. Always served on the bone, unless requested by a customer to remove it, it is delicate and delicious. In the old days in the top restaurants, the waiters would debone the fish at the table with great skill and panache – like the flambéing of meat or crêpes suzette at the table. Just magic.

Ingredients

Serves 1

- 1 black sole or Dover sole, trimmed, skinned and scissors used to remove head and all side bones (a fishmonger can do this)
- 1 tbsp plain white flour, seasoned with sea salt and cracked black pepper
- ½ tbsp clarified butter (just enough to coat the pan)

Lemon Butter:

- 15g / ½oz butter
- 1 tbsp lemon juice
- Lemon wedge and sprig of flat leaf parsley, to serve

Serving suggestions:

Colcannon (p262), new baby carrots (p257, omit coriander), buttered cabbage (p278, omit ginger), purple sprouting broccoli (p272), carrot purée (p258), rainbow chard (p271), wilted fresh spinach (p278), salad according to the season

Method

On a large plate, lightly coat the fish in the seasoned flour and shake off any excess to leave a light dusting. Melt the clarified butter in a non-stick frying pan over a medium heat. Place the fish in the pan top side down and cook for 3-4 minutes over a medium-high heat. Turn the fish over and cook for a further 3-4 minutes or until the fish comes away easily from the bone when checked with a knife at the thickest part of the fish. Cooking time will depend on the thickness of the fish.

Make the lemon butter in a small saucepan by melting together the butter and juice over a medium heat for around 30 seconds to amalgamate.

Spoon the warm lemon butter over the fish and serve with lemon wedges and a garnish of parsley.

To debone if one prefers:

Remove the fish from the pan and transfer to a large plate. Cut a slit down the centre of the sole and gently fold back the fillets on either side of the bone from the middle outwards. Carefully remove the bone from top to tail, not taking any of the flesh with it and fold back the fillets.

Dover Sole Stuffed with Atlantic Prawns & Brandy Cream Sauce or Garlic Butter or with Spinach, Mushrooms & Noilly Prat Sauce

Dover sole, also known as black sole in Ireland, for me is the king of fish. Hugh O'Neill wrote an *Irish Times* article in the 1980s about my 'Stuffed Sole on the Bone', stuffed with Atlantic prawns, cream and brandy. He enlightened me to its correct name which is 'Sole Hermitage'. I actually first started serving the stuffed sole with prawns and brandy in the late 1960s for 18 shillings and 6 pence in old Irish money, equivalent to just over 1 euro today! Testament to time, it is one of the dishes that must be on the menu to the present day. The key to this dish is that the sole is cooked on the bone which helps to retain the flavour and keep the fish succulent.

Once the sole is cooked, it is then deboned and filled with the stuffing of your choice below. Enjoy.

Ingredients

Serves 1

Basic Dover Sole for Stuffing:

- 1 tbsp plain white flour, seasoned with sea salt and cracked black pepper
- 1 medium black sole, trimmed, skinned and scissors used to remove head and all side bones (a fishmonger can do this)
- ½ tbsp clarified butter (just enough to coat the pan)

Atlantic Prawns and Brandy Cream Sauce:

- 30g / 1oz butter
- 1 tbsp cold water
- 85g / 3oz medium raw chilled shelled Atlantic prawns
- 1 tbsp brandy
- 2 tbsp whipped cream
- 1-2 tsp cornflour mixture (¼ tsp cornflour mixed with 1 tbsp cold water)
- Sprig of fennel or whole cooked prawn when in season, to garnish

Atlantic Prawns & Garlic Butter:

- 55g / 2oz garlic butter (p376)
- 1 tbsp cold water
- 85g / 3oz medium raw chilled shelled Atlantic prawns
- Sprig of flat leaf parsley, to garnish

Spinach, Mushrooms & Noilly Prat Sauce:

- Good handful of spinach
- 30g / 1oz butter
- 2 flat mushrooms (not too large and must be fresh), sliced
- 60-70ml / 2-2½fl oz Noilly Prat sauce (p176, omit leeks)

Serving suggestions:

Colcannon (p262), new baby carrots (p257, omit coriander), purple sprouting broccoli (p272), carrot purée (p258), rainbow chard (p271), wilted fresh spinach (p278), salad according to the season

Method

Preparing the Dover Sole:

Preheat the oven to fan 200°C / fan 400°F / gas mark 7.

On a large plate, lightly coat the fish in the seasoned flour and shake off any excess to leave a light dusting. In a large non-stick frying pan, melt the clarified butter over a medium heat. Place the fish in the pan and cook for 3 minutes over a medium-high heat. Turn the fish over and cook for a further minute. Move the pan into the oven and cook for 3-4 minutes or until the fish comes away easily from the bone when checked with a knife at the thickest part of the fish. Cooking time will depend on the thickness of the fish.

Remove the fish from the pan and transfer to a board or plate. To debone the fish, cut a slit down the centre of the sole and gently fold back the fillets on either side of the bone from the middle outwards. Carefully remove the bone from top to tail, not taking any of the flesh with it.

Atlantic Prawns & Brandy Cream Sauce:

In a small saucepan, melt the butter with the water. Add the prawns and toss to cook for a maximum of 2 minutes over a gentle heat. Remove the prawns from the pan, retaining the juice from the prawns and butter in the saucepan. Cover the prawns to keep warm. Add the brandy to the saucepan and increase the heat to high for 1 minute to cook out the alcohol. Turn down the heat to medium and stir in the whipped cream. The whipped cream gives the sauce a mousse-like consistency. Add 1-2 tsp of the cornflour mixture, just enough to thicken the sauce very slightly if needed. Remove from the heat, add the prawns and any juice from the prawns to the sauce and season to taste. Spoon the prawns and sauce into the opened sole and loosely fold back the fillets on top. Garnish with a sprig of fennel. When in season, garnish with a whole cooked prawn as optional.

Atlantic Prawns & Garlic Butter:

In a small saucepan, melt the garlic butter with the water over a medium heat. Add the prawns and cook for 2 minutes or until just cooked. Spoon the garlic prawns into the opened sole and loosely fold back the fillets on top. Garnish with a sprig of flat leaf parsley.

Spinach, Mushrooms & Noilly Prat Sauce:

In a saucepan of boiling water with a pinch of salt, blanch the spinach for 30 seconds and immediately refresh in ice-cold water. Drain and squeeze out the liquid. In another saucepan, melt the butter and sauté the mushrooms until soft. Stir in the spinach and season to taste. Spoon the spinach and mushroom filling into the opened sole and loosely fold back the fillets on top. To finish, spoon over the Noilly Prat sauce.

Fish 159

Lemon Sole with Tomato & Caper Salsa or Toasted Almonds with Lemon Butter & Parsley

Lemon sole is less expensive than Dover sole, with a softer flesh and a delicate flavour. It is delightful with the lemon butter and the crunchiness of the almonds enhances this simple fish.

Ingredients

Serves 2

- 2 x 340g / 12oz lemon soles, on the bone with skins removed
- 1 tbsp white flour, seasoned with sea salt and cracked black pepper
- 1 tbsp clarified butter or olive oil

Toasted Almonds with Lemon Butter & Parsley:

- 55g / 2oz flaked almonds
- 30g / 1oz butter
- Juice of ½ a lemon
- ½ tbsp chopped flat leaf parsley
- Lemon wedges, to serve

Tomato & Caper Salsa, p356

Serving suggestions:

Colcannon (p262), new baby carrots (p257, omit coriander), purple sprouting broccoli (p272), carrot purée (p258), rainbow chard (p271), wilted fresh spinach (p278), salad according to the season

Method

Preheat the oven to fan 200°C / fan 400°F / gas mark 7.

Gently pat the fish dry and lightly coat in the seasoned flour, shaking off any excess. In an ovenproof frying pan, melt the clarified butter over a medium-high heat. Add the fish and cook for 3 minutes, then turn over and cook for a further 2 minutes. Move the pan into the oven to finish cooking the fish for 4-6 minutes, or until the fish comes away easily from the bone when checked with a knife at the thickest part of the fish. Cooking time will depend on the thickness of the fish.

Toasted Almonds with Lemon Butter:

Preheat the oven to fan 140°C / fan 275°F / gas mark 3. Toast the almonds in a dry roasting pan in the oven for 15-20 minutes until golden brown, tossing halfway through. In a small saucepan, melt the butter over a medium heat, then add the almonds and lemon juice and warm through for 1 minute. To serve, spoon the sauce over the fish, sprinkle with chopped parsley and serve with lemon wedges.

Monkfish in a Ginger & Garlic Crust with Thai Dipping Sauce

I first made the ginger and garlic paste in this recipe as part of a complicated Indian curry dish and subsequently discovered that the paste makes a wonderful coating for fish, chicken or tempura vegetables. It worked particularly well with monkfish which has a great texture for shallow frying and roasting, so I introduced it as a new dish when I opened Packie's in 1993. It hasn't gone off the menu since and it is still a top seller in Packie's. The Thai dipping sauce is served cold with the fish and is a fantastically light and versatile sauce. It is best made in large quantities and stored in the fridge for up to 1 month; it can be added to tomato sauce, soups or red peppers to jazz up the dish.

Ingredients

Serves 4

Monkfish:

- 1kg / 2lb 3oz medium thick monkfish, tails trimmed and bone removed (your fishmonger will supply this way)

- 120g / 4¼oz fresh ginger, peeled and roughly chopped

- 60g / 2oz garlic cloves, peeled

- 1-2 tbsp olive oil or sunflower oil

- 3 tbsp plain white flour, mixed with ½ tsp sea salt and ½ tsp cracked black pepper

- 2 tbsp sunflower oil or clarified butter, for frying

Thai Dipping Sauce:

- 300ml / 10½fl oz good quality red wine vinegar

- 2 tbsp caster sugar

- 2 garlic cloves, peeled and finely chopped

- 3 large red chillies, deseeded and finely chopped

Per portion:
(served in small individual bowls)

- 2 tbsp Thai Dipping Sauce

- 1 tsp snipped coriander leaves, added to Thai dipping sauce just before serving (it will discolour if added earlier)

Serving suggestions:

Roast fennel (p270), purple sprouting broccoli (p272), roast vegetables (p261) or roast potato wedges (p266)

Method

Thai dipping sauce:

To make the Thai dipping sauce, place the vinegar and sugar in a small stainless steel saucepan. Bring to the boil, then simmer until the vinegar has reduced by half. Add the garlic and chilli then remove from the heat. Set aside to cool.

Monkfish:

Preheat the oven to fan 200°C / fan 400°F / gas mark 7.

Cut the monkfish into rounds/medallions (approximately 5-7cm / 2-2¾in wide and 2.5-4cm / 1-1½in thick). In a food processor, blitz the ginger and garlic until finely chopped, then add 1-2 tbsp of oil to form a smooth paste. Coat the fish in the garlic ginger paste, then dip in the seasoned flour to lightly dust.

Heat an ovenproof frying pan with the sunflower oil or clarified butter over a high heat until it reaches smoking point. Shallow fry the monkfish for 3 minutes or until golden brown either side. Place the pan in the oven and roast for 3-5 minutes, or until cooked depending on the thickness.

Serve the monkfish with a small dish of Thai dipping sauce on the plate with freshly snipped coriander over it, lime wedges and a sprig of coriander to garnish.

Roast Monkfish with Red Pepper Relish or Sweet & Sour Aubergine Relish

This red pepper relish is wonderfully adaptable. Not only does it suit this roast monkfish, but also pasta, goat's cheese, chicken and an assortment of summer vegetables. The sweet and sour aubergine is almost like a chutney and can be used to accompany many dishes. Both relishes will keep in jars in the fridge for up to 1 month.

Ingredients

Serves 4-6

- 1kg / 2lb 3oz medium thick monkfish, tails trimmed
- Clarified butter (p376), for frying

Red Pepper Relish (makes around 750g / 26½oz):

- 4 tbsp olive oil
- 4 red onions, diced
- 3 garlic cloves, roughly chopped
- 3 red peppers, deseeded, stalk removed and diced
- 1 tsp caster sugar
- ½ tsp sea salt
- 75ml / 2¾fl oz Thai dipping sauce (p358)
- 100ml / 3½fl oz water
- Sea salt and cracked black pepper

Sweet & Sour Aubergine Relish (makes around 650g / 1lb 7oz):

- 4 tbsp olive oil, for frying
- 2 large onions, peeled and thinly sliced
- 1 tsp sugar
- 1 tsp sea salt
- 2 heaped tbsp raisins, soaked in boiling water for 15 minutes
- 1 tbsp red wine vinegar
- 2 large aubergines, cut into cubes
- 1 heaped tbsp chopped mint
- 1 heaped tbsp chopped flat leaf parsley
- Juice of 1 lemon
- 1 tsp honey
- Sea salt and cracked black pepper

Serving suggestions:

Roast fennel (p270) or seasonal greens of your choice; balsamic reduction (p131, omit ginger)

Method

Red Pepper Relish:

Heat 2 tbsp oil in a saucepan, then add the onions and garlic, cover and sweat over a low heat for 10 minutes, stirring regularly. Remove the lid and add the remaining oil with the peppers, then cover and continue to cook over a low heat to soften for 25-30 minutes. Add the sugar, salt, Thai dipping sauce and water and simmer for 10 minutes. Briefly pulse using a hand blender. Season to taste.

Sweet & Sour Aubergine Relish:

Heat 2 tbsp oil in a large frying pan over a low heat, then add the onions and cook until soft, stirring regularly. Add the sugar, ¼ tsp salt and increase the heat to caramelise the onions, taking care to not burn them. Add the raisins and vinegar and continue to cook until the liquid evaporates. Tip the onion mixture into a bowl and return the frying pan to the stove top. Heat the remaining oil in the pan and cook the aubergine with the remaining salt until coloured and well reduced (about 20-25 minutes). Mix the aubergines in with the onion raisin mixture and set aside to cool. Add the herbs, then add lemon juice and honey to taste. Season to taste.

Preheat the oven to fan 200°C / fan 400°F / gas mark 7.

Monkfish:

Cut the monkfish into rounds or medallions (approximately 5-7cm / 2-2¾in wide and 2.5-4cm / 1-1½in thick). Brush an ovenproof frying pan with the clarified butter and heat to smoking point. Add the monkfish and cook each side for 2-3 minutes or until golden brown, then move the pan into the oven and roast for 3-5 minutes or until cooked through depending on the thickness.

Serve the monkfish with relish and a drizzle of the balsamic reduction (p131, omit ginger).

Roast Sea Bass with Wholegrain Mustard Sauce

The first time I came across sea bass was with Sonia Stevenson in the Horn of Plenty in Devon. She got whole bass which we cleaned and scaled and one of the ways she cooked them was roasting them whole in sea salt. Sea bass is an oily textured fish and because of the oil it can be seared in a hot pan and then roasted in the oven with the skin side up and lends itself very well to this high roast. It can also take strong flavoured sauces such as this wholegrain mustard sauce. Like mackerel as an oily fish, it would also work well with salsa verde (p357) or tomato and caper salsa (p378) – these pickled-type sauces cut through the oiliness of the fish.

Ingredients

Serves 4

- 4 x 180-230g / 6¼-8oz sea bass fillets, skin on and descaled
- Olive oil, to fry
- Sea salt and cracked black pepper
- 2 tbsp simple wholegrain mustard cream sauce (p349) per portion

Serving suggestions:

Roast beetroot & orange (p277) or seasonal greens

Method

Preheat the oven to fan 200°C / fan 400°F / gas mark 7.

Brush the sea bass fillets with the oil and season. Heat an ovenproof frying pan over a medium-high heat and place the fish skin side up and sear for 2 minutes. Move the pan to the oven, still with the skin side up and roast for 5-7 minutes or until the skin peels away easily from the fish. Cooking time will depend on the thickness of the fillet.

Serve the sea bass skin side down with the simple wholegrain mustard sauce on the side.

Roast Cod with Herb Crust

This is a very simple dish and the fresh thyme and crispy breadcrumbs are delicious with the texture of the roast cod.

Ingredients

Serves 4

Fish:

- 4 cod fillets (not codling), around 250g / 8¾oz per fillet, with skin on

- Clarified butter (p376), to grease

Herb Crust:

- 200g / 7oz fresh soft white breadcrumbs

- 100g / 3¾oz butter, melted

- 1 tbsp fresh thyme leaves

- 1 tbsp chopped flat leaf parsley

Serving suggestions:

Creamed leeks (p268), wilted fresh spinach (p278), purple sprouting broccoli (p272), chard or kale (p271); lemon wedges, to serve

Method

Preheat the oven to fan 200°C / fan 400°F / gas mark 7.

Prepare the herb crust by combining the breadcrumbs, butter and herbs.

Heat a large ovenproof frying pan, greased with clarified butter, over a low heat. Turn the heat to high and add the fish fillets, flesh side down, to the pan. Cook for 2-3 minutes to seal. Turn the fillets to be flesh side up and cover with the herb crust. Cook in the oven for 10-15 minutes or until the fish is cooked and flakes easily. Cooking time will depend on the thickness of the fillets; it may take even longer for a very thick fillet.

Serve with lemon wedges.

Roast Cod Mornay with Coolea Matured Cheese

The Coolea Matured is a mature gouda like cheese made by a Dutch family, the Willems, in the nearby Coolea Gaeltacht area and is very suitable for a Mornay or cheese sauce. A well flavoured mature cheese is key to a good cheese sauce packed with flavour. Alternatively a mature cheddar cheese can be used. The addition of the small amount of Parmigiano Reggiano gives the cheese sauce an extra oomph and is worth it. Other fish such as hake or haddock could also be used. The Mornay sauce is also delicious with vegetarian dishes.

Ingredients

Serves 4

Fish:

- 4 cod fillets (not codling), around 250g / 8¾oz per fillet, with skin on
- 125g / 4½oz fresh soft white breadcrumbs
- 55g / 2oz butter, melted
- Clarified butter (p376), to grease

Mornay Sauce:

- 55g / 2oz butter
- 30g / 1oz plain white flour
- 425ml / 15fl oz whole milk
- 140ml / 5fl oz cream
- 55g / 2oz Coolea Matured (or a mature cheddar cheese), grated
- 30g / 1oz Parmigiano Reggiano, freshly grated
- Sea salt and cracked black pepper

Method

To make the sauce, melt the butter in a saucepan over a low heat. Add the flour and stir for 2-3 minutes. Gradually pour in the milk, continuing to stir until you have a smooth consistency. Continue to cook gently for 15 minutes, stirring continuously, until the sauce has thickened. Add the cream and stir until the sauce has a thick coating consistency. Add the cheese, stirring until melted. Remove from the heat. Season to taste.

Preheat the oven to fan 200°C / fan 400°F / gas mark 7.

Prepare the crumb by combining the breadcrumbs and butter.

Heat a large ovenproof frying pan, greased with clarified butter, over a low heat. Turn the heat to high and place the fish fillets flesh side down in the pan. Cook for 2-3 minutes to seal. Turn the fillets to be flesh side up and spoon the sauce on top of the fish (flesh side), followed by the crumb. Move the pan to the oven and cook for 10-15 minutes or until the fish is cooked and flakes easily. Cooking time will depend on the thickness of the fillets; it may take even longer for a very thick fillet.

Serving suggestions:

Wilted spinach (p278), colcannon (p262) or seasonal greens

Roast Cod with Chilli, Garlic & Rosemary Oil

This oil is a gift. It is versatile and super drizzled over seared vegetables, fish and chicken. It is gorgeous drizzled over bread, pizza or soups. Store sealed in the fridge for up to 2 weeks.

Ingredients

Serves 4

Fish:

- 4 cod fillets (not codling), around 250g / 8¾oz per fillet, with skin on
- Olive oil, to grease
- Sea salt and cracked black pepper

Chilli, Garlic & Rosemary Oil:

- 250ml / 8½fl oz extra virgin olive oil
- 2 red chillies, deseeded and finely chopped
- 4 garlic cloves, finely chopped
- 1 tbsp rosemary leaves, chopped
- Lemon wedges, to serve

Serving suggestions:

Roast fennel (p270), braised chicory in orange or sweet wine (p271) or new baby carrots (p257, omit coriander)

Method

Preheat the oven to fan 200°C / fan 400°F / gas mark 7.

Make the oil by mixing all the ingredients together in a bowl.

Brush both sides of the fish with olive oil and season with sea salt and cracked black pepper. Heat a large ovenproof frying pan over a high heat and add the fish fillets to the pan skin side up. Cook for 2-3 minutes to seal, then move the pan to the oven, still with skin side up, and roast for 10-15 minutes or until the fish is cooked and flakes easily. Cooking time will depend on the thickness of the fillets; it may take even longer for a very thick fillet.

Serve the cod skin side down and 1-2 tbsp of the chilli, garlic & rosemary oil spooned over the hot fish.

Cod Provençale

This a lovely Mediterranean-style dish. The slow cooking of the sauce gives it a sweet flavour. If you are unable to get good quality Italian tomatoes, it is better to use good tinned tomatoes, rather than tomatoes which completely lack flavour. I have added one chilli; if a plain sauce is desired, omit the chilli, and if a hot sauce is desired add more.

The sauce can be made in advance and a large quantity can be made in the summer if there is an abundance of good tomatoes. It keeps in the fridge for up to 1 week and can be stored for up to 2 months in the freezer. It works well with many dishes, including pasta.

Ingredients

Serves 2

Fish:

- 4 cod fillets (not codling), around 250g / 8¾oz per fillet, with skin on
- 125g / 4½oz fresh soft white breadcrumbs
- 55g / 2oz melted butter, or 4 tbsp olive oil
- 2 garlic cloves, peeled and finely chopped
- Clarified butter (p376), to grease

Tomato Sauce:

- 1 tbsp olive oil
- 6 shallots, finely chopped
- 3 garlic cloves, crushed
- 600g / 1lb 5oz fresh ripe tomatoes, seeded and chopped or good quality tinned tomatoes
- 3 tsp tomato purée
- 200ml / 7fl oz apple juice
- 1 mild red chilli, split, deseeded and finely chopped
- Sea salt and cracked black pepper

Serving suggestion:

Pan-fried courgettes (p272), roast fennel (p270) or wilted spinach (p278)

Method

Preheat the oven to fan 200°C / fan 400°F / gas mark 7.

To make the sauce, add the oil to a small saucepan and gently sweat the shallots and garlic with a pinch of salt for 10 minutes over a low heat. Remove the lid, then add the tomatoes, purée and apple juice and simmer for at least 45 minutes, stirring occasionally otherwise it could stick and brown. Season to taste.

Prepare the crumb by combining the breadcrumbs, melted butter (or olive oil if you prefer) and garlic.

Heat a large ovenproof frying pan, greased with clarified butter, over a low heat. Turn the heat to high and place the fish fillets skin side up in the pan. Cook for 2-3 minutes to seal. Turn the fillets to be flesh side up and spoon the sauce on top of the fish (flesh side), followed by the garlic crumb. Move the pan to the oven and cook for 10-15 minutes or until the fish is cooked and flakes easily. Cooking time will depend on the thickness of the fillets; it may take even longer for a very thick fillet.

Fresh mackerel from Kenmare Bay

Pan-Fried Mackerel in an Oatmeal Crust with Salsa Verde or Caper Salsa

This is an old recipe and a traditional way to cook mackerel in Ireland. The fillets have a naturally oily flesh, and the crunchy oat crust adds a pleasant contrast. As well as serving the fish with the salsa verde or caper salsa, the gooseberry and elderflower sauce (p178) also works well. The salsa goes well with a variety of smoked fish including salmon, mackerel or eel. It's best made early to allow the vinegar to start pickling the onion for a sweeter salsa. It is very suitable for a substantial breakfast.

Ingredients

Serves 4

Fish:

- 4 mackerel, cleaned, with skin on, deboned leaving the two fillets still attached to the tail fanned out
- 3 tbsp melted butter
- 55g / 2oz organic porridge oats
- 4 tbsp olive oil or sunflower oil
- Sea salt and cracked black pepper

Salsa Verde:

- 2 tbsp finely chopped flat leaf parsley
- 2 tbsp finely chopped mint leaves
- 2 tbsp finely sliced basil leaves
- 2 garlic cloves, finely chopped
- 2 tbsp small capers, strained, leave whole
- 8 gherkins, finely chopped
- 1 tbsp Dijon mustard
- 1 tbsp red wine vinegar
- Zest of 2 limes and 2 tbsp lime juice
- 4 tbsp good quality extra virgin olive oil
- A pinch of sugar (optional)

Red Onion & Caper Salsa:

- 2 small red onions, finely diced
- 2 tbsp small capers, strained, leave whole
- 2 tbsp chopped flat leaf parsley
- ½ tbsp grated fresh horseradish or 1 tbsp horseradish sauce
- 2-3 tbsp extra virgin olive oil
- A little squeeze of lemon juice
- Sea salt and cracked black pepper

Method

Lay out the fillets skin side down on a plate. Spoon over the melted butter to evenly coat, then season. Dip the buttered flesh in the oats to coat generously on the flesh side.

Heat the oil in a large frying pan over a medium heat and gently fry the mackerel skin side up (oats down in the pan) for 2-3 minutes or until golden. Turn the fillets and cook for a further 2 minutes or until cooked through. Serve from the pan with either the salsa verde or caper salsa.

Salsa Verde:

In a bowl, mix together the herbs with the garlic, capers and gherkins. In a small bowl, combine the mustard, red wine vinegar, lime juice and zest, then stir into the herb mixture. Mix in the olive oil and taste. Add more oil if desired. If too bitter, stir in a pinch of sugar. Season to taste.

Red Onion & Caper Salsa:

In a bowl, mix together the onions, capers, parsley and horseradish. Stir in the olive oil and lemon juice, then season to taste, adding more lemon juice if necessary.

Fillet of John Dory or Brill with Pears, Leeks and Noilly Prat Sauce

John Dory is a rather ugly looking fish with its spines and huge head but it is a prime fish with a firm texture and excellent flavour. It is known as St Pierre in France for the dark circle mark on its side, which is said to be the thumb mark of St Peter, even though they are not to be found in the sea of Galilee!

After Dover sole, brill is next on my list of favourite fish. Brill in my view is a most underrated fish. Brill is closely related to turbot and has a delicate flavour and a fine texture. Brill could also be served with a herb beurre blanc (p346) or béarnaise (p344), both having enough flavour to enhance the fish.

Ingredients

Serves 4

Fish:

- 4 John Dory or brill fillets each weighing about 170-200g/6-7oz, with skin on
- 55g / 2oz butter
- 90g / 3oz leeks, julienned
- 2 pears, cored and cut into batons with lime juice to prevent oxidation
- 4 tbsp Noilly Prat

Noilly Prat Sauce:

- 30g / 1oz butter
- 55g / 2oz shallots, finely chopped
- 55g / 2oz leeks, white part only, finely chopped
- 100ml / 3½fl oz fish stock
- 60ml / 2fl oz Noilly Prat
- 100ml / 3½fl oz cream
- 30ml / 1fl oz port

Serving suggestion:

New baby carrots (p257, omit coriander)

Method

To make the sauce, melt the butter in a saucepan then add the shallots and leeks, cover and sweat for 10 minutes over a gentle heat, stirring occasionally. Add the fish stock and Noilly Prat and bring to the boil over a high heat, then turn down to a medium heat and reduce by half. Remove from the heat. Using a hand blender, blitz the liquid until the shallots and leeks are smooth. Return to the heat, add the cream and port and bring to the boil over a high heat, stirring continuously. Turn down to a medium heat and gently simmer the sauce to a coating consistency. Season to taste and set aside.

Bring a small saucepan of water to the boil and blanch the julienned leeks for 1 minute, then immediately remove and refresh in ice-cold water.

Preheat the oven to fan 200°C / fan 400°F / gas mark 7. Lay out four large square pieces of foil and place each fillet on a sheet, skin side down. Season with salt and pepper and then dot over the butter on each fillet and arrange the pears and leeks on top. Pour 1 tbsp Noilly Prat over the pears and leeks for each fillet. Fold up the sides of each foil square and loosely wrap and seal. Bake in the oven for about 10 minutes depending on the thickness of the fillets or until starting to flake with pressure.

Open the foil parcels and pour off the juices into the Noilly Prat sauce. Stir and warm the sauce over a gentle heat. Serve the fish with the pear, leeks, new baby carrots and a generous spoonful of the Noilly Prat sauce.

Baked Fillet of Wild Salmon with Lime & Coriander Butter

The flavour of coriander with lime and butter is a stunning accompaniment to the richness of the salmon.

Ingredients

Serves 4

- 4 wild salmon fillets
- 90g / 3oz cold butter, cut into small pieces
- Juice of 2 limes
- 30g / 1oz butter
- 2-3 tbsp finely snipped fresh coriander leaves
- Sea salt and cracked black pepper

Serving suggestions:

Colcannon (p262), purple sprouting broccoli (p272), sugar snaps with fresh mint (p274), new baby carrots with coriander (p257)

Method

Preheat the oven to fan 200°C / fan 400°F / gas mark 7. Lay out 4 large square pieces of foil and place each fillet on a sheet, skin side down. Season with salt and pepper then dot butter over each fillet. Fold up the sides of each foil square and loosely wrap and seal. Bake in the oven for 8-10 minutes or until cooked to liking.

Open the foil parcels and pour off the juices into a small saucepan. Combine the juices with the lime juice and butter over a medium heat, adding the coriander to the sauce just before serving over the salmon fillets.

Serve with a sprig of fennel.

Baked Fillet of Wild Salmon with Gooseberry, Elderflower & Lime Sauce or Wild Sorrel Hollandaise

If you can, use spring wild salmon. They are oilier than summer wild salmon, and more robust and flavoursome by nature. With elderflowers in abundance from mid-May to June, this is the best time to showcase them in this fragrant sauce.

Wild salmon is delicious on its own with a simple hollandaise. I served it in abundance in the 1960s. I used to stand over the stove, whisking the cold butter into my egg to get an emulsion, sometimes making a few batches a day. I spent over 20 years making it in the traditional classic fashion! Thankfully in the mid 1980s Sonia Stephenson taught me the swift way to make hollandaise (p342) with melted butter, which is just as light and delightful.

Ingredients

Serves 4

- 4 wild salmon fillets

- 55g / 2oz cold butter, cut into small pieces

- Sea salt and cracked black pepper

Gooseberry, Elderflower & Lime Sauce:

- 450g / 1lb gooseberries, topped and tailed

- 4 large elderflower heads, cut into separate heads and stems

- 4 tbsp water

- Zest and juice of 1 lime

- Demerara sugar, to taste

- Sea salt and cracked black pepper

Or

Wild Sorrel Hollandaise:

- 1 quantity of swift hollandaise sauce (p342)

- Handful wild sorrel leaves, washed and dried

Serving suggestions:

Colcannon (p262), roast fennel (p270), fresh wilted spinach (p278), sugar snaps (p274, omit mint)

Method

Preheat the oven to fan 200°C / fan 400°F / gas mark 7. Lay out four large square pieces of foil and place each fillet on a sheet, skin side down. Season with salt and pepper then dot butter over each fillet. Fold up the sides of each foil square and loosely wrap and seal. Bake in the oven for 8-10 minutes or until cooked to liking.

Serve with one of the following sauces.

Gooseberry, Elderflower & Lime Sauce:

Add the gooseberries, elderflowers (both stems and heads), water, lime zest and juice to a medium saucepan. Bring to a simmer over a medium heat, stirring occasionally for 20 minutes, or until the gooseberries are soft. Remove the elderflower stems from the pan, then blitz the sauce with a hand blender – it won't be completely smooth. Add sugar to taste, aiming to heighten the sauce's sweet and sour characteristics. Season to taste.

Wild Sorrel Hollandaise:

Make your hollandaise (p342). When the hollandaise is complete, add a handful of wild sorrel to the blender and blitz until it is blended – it will take only 10-20 seconds. This is also delicious with hollandaise on its own with the salmon.

Serve with a sprig of fennel.

180 Fish

Baked Fillet of Turbot en Papillote with Noilly Prat and Basil Orange Sauce

Cooking the turbot en papillote (French for 'in parchment') seals in the flavours, juices and gently steams the fish for a very delicate result. The sauce is beautiful. Without adding the fish juice at the end, it can be used for pasta and chicken. It could also be served as a side sauce for a vegetarian tart. Brill would also work very successfully in this recipe.

Ingredients

Serves 4

- 1kg / 2lb 3oz turbot, divided into 4 fillets
- 1 tbsp butter
- 4 tbsp Noilly Prat
- Sea salt

Basil Orange Sauce:

- Juice of 1 lemon
- 30g / 1oz granulated sugar
- 1 tbsp water
- Juice of 2 medium oranges
- 55ml / 2fl oz cream
- Juice of cooked fish
- 8 basil leaves, shredded (just before adding to sauce)

Serving suggestions:

Roast potato wedges (p266), braised chicory and orange (p271), roast fennel (p270), wilted fresh spinach (p278) or seasonal greens of your choice

Method

Preheat the oven to fan 220°C / fan 425°F / gas mark 9.

Lay out four sheets of foil dull side up (large enough for each fillet to be covered) on a baking tray. Place the four fillets skin side down on the foil, dot over small nuts of the butter, season with a small pinch of salt then pour over the Noilly Prat. Cover the fish with foil by folding it over and pinching to seal. Bake in the oven for about 10 minutes or until cooked to liking. Cooking time will depend on the thickness of the fish.

To make the sauce, add the lemon juice, sugar and water to a medium saucepan and stir over a medium heat until the sugar is dissolved, then stop stirring. Allow the sugar to caramelise and reach a light golden colour. Add the orange juice and cream, stir and cook until the sauce is thick enough to coat the back of a spoon. Pour the cooked fish juice into the sauce (omit for a non-fish dish). Continue to reduce the sauce to a coating consistency again. Stir the basil leaves into the sauce just before serving so they don't lose their colour.

Serve the turbot with a generous spoonful of the basil orange sauce on the side.

Baked Fillet of Turbot En Papillote with Salsify and Red Wine Sauce

Salsify are an overlooked vegetable in my opinion, primarily due to their appearance! They have a delicate flavour and a smooth, soft texture similar in taste to a globe artichoke. They work well in this recipe with the turbot and red wine sauce – if you wish to try something different then give it a go.

Ingredients

Serves 4

Salsify:

- 285g / 10oz salsify, unpeeled and whole
- 570ml / 1 pint water
- ½ lemon cut into slices (to acidulate the water)

Fish:

- 1kg / 2lb 3oz turbot, divided into 4 fillets
- 1 tbsp butter
- Sea salt and cracked black pepper

Red Wine Fish Sauce:

- 200ml / 7fl oz fish stock
- 150ml / ¼ pint red wine
- 100ml / 4fl oz ruby port
- 2 shallots, finely chopped, sweated and softened in butter
- 100mls / 4fl oz cream
- 50-75g / 2-3oz butter, chilled and cut into cubes

Method

Bring the water and lemon to the boil over a high heat in a wide-based saucepan of sufficient size to fit the whole salsify. Add the salsify, turn down to a medium heat and simmer for about 15 minutes. Take out the salsify and remove the skins completely once they have cooled a little. Trim, top and tail and cut into approximately 5cm / 2in batons for serving.

To cook the fish, preheat the oven to fan 220°C / fan 425°F / gas mark 9. Lay out four sheets of foil dull side up (large enough to cover each fillet) on a baking tray. Place the four fillets skin side down on the foil, dot over small nuts of the butter and season with a small pinch of sea salt and cracked black pepper. Cover the fish with foil by folding it over and pinching to seal. Bake in the oven for about 10-15 minutes. Cooking time will depend on the thickness of the fish. Any juice collected in the parcels from the fish should be added to the sauce when adding the cream.

To make the red wine fish sauce, in a medium saucepan reduce the fish stock, wine, port and shallots until it has reduced by three-quarters. Add the cream and any juice from the fish parcels, bring to the boil, then turn down the heat to medium and reduce until it reaches a coating consistency. Remove the pan from the heat, then stir in the cubes of butter gradually, stirring continuously until it is fully amalgamated and has a glossy finish.

Serving suggestions:

Roast fennel (p270), purple sprouting broccoli (p272) or seasonal greens of your choice

Seared Scallops with Curried Vermicelli

This dish is inspired by a wonderful dinner Grainne and I had in Paris at Lucas Carton when Alain Senderens was the head chef in the late 1980s. Served there as curried noodles with prawns, my version serves the seared scallops with curried vermicelli which do not take from the flavour of the scallops, they just enhance them. A thin pasta such as angel hair (capellini) or vermicelli or a thin noodle should be used for this dish. Their textures are not too cloying or heavy, as the intention of the dish is to be light.

The scallops are seared over a high heat to seal them quickly to retain the moisture. Two large heavy pans will be needed for this quantity to allow enough room for the scallops to sear and not stew.

Ingredients

Serves 4

Curry Cream:

- 150ml / 5fl oz cream
- 1 tsp curry powder
- Sea salt and cracked black pepper
- Pinch of light brown sugar

Scallops with Vermicelli:

- 100g / 3½oz vermicelli
- 16 scallops, sliced in half horizontally if they are very large (if preparing yourself, prize open the shell and remove beard and muscle)
- Olive oil, for brushing
- Sea salt and cracked black pepper
- Fresh coriander and lime wedges, to serve

Serving suggestions:

Delicious on its own or with carrot purée (p258)

Method

Place the cream and curry powder in a medium saucepan and bring to the boil. Turn down the heat and reduce to a coating consistency, then season with sea salt, crack black pepper and a pinch of sugar.

Bring a saucepan of water with a pinch of sea salt to the boil and cook the noodles according to the packet instructions. Strain and keep warm in a covered pan.

Brush the scallops very lightly with olive oil and season. Heat two large heavy-based frying pans over a medium-high heat. Once the pans are hot, add the scallops, being careful not to crowd the pans so they have enough space to sear. If the scallops are halved, sear on each side for 1 minute; if whole, sear for 1½ minutes either side. The scallops should be golden and cooked in the middle. Ensure you do not overcook, or they will toughen.

Add the curry sauce to the warm noodles, using just enough to coat. Serve the noodles in the centre and surround with the scallops, a garnish of fresh coriander and a wedge of lime.

Scallops with Noilly Prat & Mushroom Sauce

This is an old recipe from The Purple Heather that I first started serving in the 1960s and was one of our most popular scallop dishes. John B. Keane, the famous Kerry playwright, was a regular customer of ours and came especially from Listowel for the scallops with Noilly Prat!

Ingredients

Serves 3

- 18 large scallops

Noilly Prat Sauce:

- 30g / 1oz butter
- 120g / 4¼oz shallots, finely chopped
- 2 garlic cloves, peeled and finely diced
- 100g / 3½oz white mushrooms, finely chopped
- 1 large fresh flat mushroom, finely chopped
- 100ml / 3½fl oz fish stock
- 60ml / 2fl oz Noilly Prat
- 100ml / 3½fl oz cream
- 30g / 1fl oz port
- Sea salt and cracked black pepper

Serving suggestions:

Roast fennel (p270), buttered cabbage (p278, omit ginger), roast vegetables (p261), colcannon (p262) or creamed potatoes (p264)

Method

If preparing the scallops yourself, cut off both the beard and muscle. If pre-prepared by your fishmonger, just halve any large scallops horizontally.

To make the sauce, melt the butter in a saucepan over a gentle heat, add the shallots and garlic then cover and sweat for 10 minutes, stirring occasionally. Remove the lid, add the mushrooms and stir until cooked for a few minutes over a medium heat. Add the fish stock, cream and port and turn up to a high heat, bringing to the boil, then turn down to a medium heat. Add in the Noilly Prat and reduce to a coating consistency. Season to taste. The sauce can be prepared to this point the day before if you wish, for example for a dinner party. Before serving, add scallops to the hot sauce and cook gently for 3-4 minutes.

Serve six full scallops per person on hot plates and garnish with fennel, dill or sweet cicely.

Crumbed Scallops with Garlic Butter

This scallop dish is so simple yet very delicious. The crunchiness of the coating is a great contrast to the sweet flavour of the scallop. We do not use milk in the recipe, which makes the crumb soggy.

Ingredients

Serves 4

- 100g / 3½oz plain white flour
- 4 eggs, beaten
- 155g / 5½oz fresh soft white breadcrumbs
- 16 scallops, shelled and bearded or prepared by your fishmonger
- 2 tbsp olive or sunflower oil, for frying
- 1 tbsp butter
- Sea salt and cracked black pepper
- 4 tbsp garlic butter (p376), at room temperature

Serving suggestions:

New baby carrots with coriander (p257), roast fennel (p270), roast vegetables (p261), colcannon (p262) or seasonal vegetables of your choice; garlic butter (p376) and lemon wedges, to serve

Method

In a shallow bowl, add the flour and season. In another shallow bowl, beat the eggs. Place the breadcrumbs in a third shallow bowl. Lay them out in this order.

Dip the scallops in the seasoned flour, then into the eggs, then coat the scallops with the crumbs on both sides. To keep the lightness, do not press in the crumbs.

In a large frying pan, heat the oil and butter over a medium-high heat. Add the scallops to the pan and fry for 2-3 minutes per side, depending on the size of the scallops (less time if the scallops are small). Allow plenty of space between the scallops and do not overcrowd the pan. Cook in batches if necessary.

Serve with lemon wedges and garlic butter at room temperature, a nut dotted over each scallop.

Cyril's Atlantic Prawns Roasted with Garlic Butter or Béarnaise Sauce

Living in Kenmare I can get my prawns from Cyril, who was one of my great chefs. Because of his love of the sea and understanding of the Kenmare Bay he turned to fishing. His prawns are exquisite. Cold water fish and shellfish have a magical sweetness that you don't get from warm water fish. It just doesn't have the same flavour! You can serve these on a large platter for a party, or 3-4 per person as a starter and about 6-8 per person for a main course, depending on the size of the prawns. Again, the quality of the prawn is the magic ingredient.

Ingredients

Serves 8-9 as a starter or 4-5 as a main, depending on size

- 2kg / 4lb 6½oz fresh Atlantic prawns (generally about 19-20 whole prawns per kg)
- 300g / 10½oz garlic butter (p376) or 250ml / 8½fl oz béarnaise sauce (p344), to serve

Serving suggestions for a main:

Colcannon (p262), chips, new baby carrots (p257, omit coriander), purple sprouting broccoli (p272) and a large green salad

Method

Preheat the oven to fan 200°C / fan 400°F / gas mark 7.

Wash and clean the prawns with a brush under cold running water. Bring a large pot of water with a pinch of sea salt to the boil, making sure there is enough water to fully immerse the prawns. Plunge the prawns into the boiling water and put on a timer for 3 minutes, leaving the prawns in the pot over the heat. Remove from the stove and drain – the liquid can be reserved and used for preparing stock if not too salty.

When the prawns are cool enough to handle, ensure you keep the head intact, remove the fan at the end of tail and pull out the intestine. Split the tail of the prawn and dot the flesh with garlic butter or béarnaise. Roast in the hot oven for 2 minutes and serve immediately.

Brochettes de Fruits de Mer with Sauce Choron

I put these on the menu in The Purple Heather originally for Les Fruits De Mer Festival in Kenmare. They then became a staple on our menu as they were so popular. It is a simple dish, now in the luxury class, served with a wonderful béarnaise-type sauce with the addition of tomatoes. It is a superb combination.

Ingredients

Makes 4 skewers

- 2 x 450g / 1lb poached lobster (use Thermidor method opposite), flesh removed and claws cracked to remove meat
- 8 scallops (oven ready, shelled, bearded and muscle removed)
- 12 large prawns, shelled
- 100g / 4oz butter, melted
- 2 tbsp Sauce Choron per skewer (p344), to serve

Serving suggestions:

Creamed potatoes (p264), green salad or rice

Method

Preheat the oven to fan 200°C / fan 400°F / gas mark 7.

Thread each skewer alternatively with prawn, lobster and scallops, using 3 prawns, 2 pieces of lobster and 2 scallops per skewer. Brush the fish with the melted butter on both sides and place in a roasting pan. Roast in the oven for 6 minutes, turning the skewers halfway. Pour any juices from pan into the sauce choron.

To serve, spoon the sauce over each skewer and flash under a hot grill for 30 seconds.

Serve immediately.

Fish

Lobster Thermidor

This is a classic dish. Some people do not think it is necessary to have all the different flavours with the lobster but we had regular customers for it at The Lime Tree who would ring beforehand to ensure they could have Lobster Thermidor for their meal! Lobster over about 1kg / 2½lb are not prime and can sometimes have less meat. I use Atlantic Irish lobster, they are sweet and succulent and I think they have no competition!

Ingredients

Serves 2

- 2 lobsters, around 450-680g / 1-1lb ½oz each
- 45g / 1½oz butter
- Sea salt
- Fennel sprigs or dill, to garnish

Sauce:

- 30g / 1oz butter
- 30g / 1oz plain white flour
- 330ml / 11¾fl oz whole milk
- 3 tbsp dry sherry
- 5 tbsp cream
- 1 tbsp Dijon mustard
- 65g / 2oz Parmigiano Reggiano, freshly grated

Serving suggestions:

Creamed potatoes (p264), colcannon (p262) or roast potato wedges (p266)

Method

Fill a large saucepan with cold water, adding 10g / ¼oz of salt per litre of water. Add the lobsters to the saucepan and very slowly bring to the boil then turn down to a simmer. Cook for 15 minutes or until the shells have turned a pale orange colour; at this point we are not cooking the lobsters all the way through. Remove the lobsters from the pan, drain and cool. With a sharp knife, cut them in half down the spine, removing any waste parts (stomach sac). Take out the meat and cut into bite-sized pieces and set aside. Keep the shells.

To make the sauce, melt the butter in a medium saucepan, then add the flour and stir over a medium heat for 2 minutes. Gradually add the milk, stirring continuously, to form a smooth white sauce. Stir in the sherry and cook for 4 minutes. Lastly, stir in the cream, mustard and 40g / 1¼oz of the cheese. Cover and set aside.

Preheat the oven to fan 200°C / fan 400°F / gas mark 7. Place the lobster shells on a baking tray and warm in the oven for 5 minutes. Arrange the meat into the shells, spoon over the sauce and sprinkle over the remaining Parmigiana Reggiano. Bake in the oven for 5-10 minutes depending on size of the lobster; the top should be a little bit golden.

Baked Stuffed Lobster

The best season in Ireland for lobsters is generally late spring to October. This recipe was given to me at The Purple Heather by a man called Jim Hendersen who worked in the Great Southern, now Park Hotel. He came in the mid 1960s from Maine in America from a seafood restaurant family background where lobster was their specialty. (This is the reason for the Ritz crackers.) When we had the piano bar, he often entertained us with his party piece from the Wizard of Oz!

If you are using Ritz crackers, then use all unsalted butter as they are a salty cracker. Alternatively, if using breadcrumbs use salted butter.

Ingredients

Serves 4

- 2 lobsters, poached as in Thermidor method (p191)
- 4 tbsp unsalted butter, melted

Stuffing:

- 55g / 2oz unsalted butter, melted
- ½ tbsp fresh thyme leaves
- 1 garlic clove, finely chopped
- 100g / 3½oz cracker crumbs (ideally Ritz Original crackers) or fresh white soft breadcrumbs (use salted butter)

Serving suggestions:

Roast fennel (p270), purple sprouting broccoli (p272), creamed leeks (p268), chips, roast potato wedges (p266), colcannon (p262) or a green salad; serve with wedges of lemon or lime.

Method

Poach the lobsters as described in the Lobster Thermidor method (p191).

Use a sharp knife to split the lobsters in two, from the head to the tail, following the line of the body. Remove all the flesh from the shells. Using the back of the knife or a hammer, crack the claws and remove the claw flesh. Cut all the lobster into bite sized pieces. Add the lobster to a bowl, pour over the melted butter and combine. Keep the shells.

Preheat the oven to fan 200°C / fan 400°F / gas mark 7.

To make the stuffing, combine the butter, thyme leaves, garlic and crumbled crackers in a bowl.

To assemble, place the four shells on a baking tray smooth side down. Place a thin layer of stuffing in the base of the four shells. Place the lobster on top of the stuffing. Sprinkle over the remaining stuffing on top to protect the lobster. Bake in the hot oven for approximately 10 minutes.

Moules Marinière

In the old days we only ate mussels and oysters when there was an 'R' in the month, so from September until the end of April. However, with present day methods they are available throughout the year. It is important to clean the mussels under cold running water.

This is a classic dish, done simply with garlic, butter, wine and shallots. They are best enjoyed with a pint of Guinness as is tradition in Ireland. Enjoy.

Ingredients

Serves 6-8

- 2 ½ kg / 88oz mussels (1kg = 80-100 mussels)
- 60g / 2oz butter, plus extra to finish
- 2 large onions or equivalent weight in shallots, finely chopped
- 4 garlic cloves, finely chopped
- 300ml / 10½fl oz dry white wine
- 2 tbsp chopped flat leaf parsley leaves, plus extra to serve

Serving suggestions:

Pint of Guinness and good crusty bread

Method

Clean the mussels thoroughly under cold running water, using your hands or a clean scrubbing brush to scrape off any barnacles or seaweed and removing the fibrous beard that protrudes between the shell. To check any open mussels, squeeze them between your index finger and thumb; if they close again they can be used, if not, discard them along with any cracked mussels.

In a large saucepan wide enough for the mussels to not overcrowd, melt the butter over a medium heat. Add the onions and garlic and cook for 2-3 minutes, stirring.

Add the wine and bring to the boil. Add the mussels and parsley, cover with a lid and bring back to the boil, shaking the pan periodically to move the mussels around so they all cook evenly and steam open – this will take around 5 minutes. Discard any that don't open.

Serve in a bowl hot from the pan, with extra melted butter and chopped flat leaf parsley to garnish and good crusty bread.

Baked Stuffed Garlic Mussels

This is a simple and easy dish, the mussels can be prepared in advance and baked in the oven before serving.

Ingredients

Serves 6-8

- 1kg / 2lb 3¼oz mussels
- 120g / 4¼oz fresh soft white breadcrumbs
- 60g / 2oz garlic butter, melted (p376)

Serving suggestions:

Green salad, colcannon (p262), chips or roast potato wedges (p266)

Method

Preheat the oven to fan 200°C / fan 400°F / gas mark 7.

Clean the mussels thoroughly under cold running water, using your hand or a clean scrubbing brush to scrape off any barnacles or seaweed and removing the fibrous beard that protrudes between the shell. To check any open mussels, squeeze them between your index finger and thumb; if they close again, they can be used, if not, discard them along with any cracked mussels.

In a large saucepan over a high heat, add the mussels, cover with a lid and shake the pan periodically to move the mussels around so they cook evenly and steam open – this will take around 3-5 minutes. This may need to be done in batches so as not to crowd the pan. Discard any mussels that don't open.

Discard the empty upper shell of the mussels and lay out the other half containing the mussel on an oven tray. Mix the breadcrumbs into the melted garlic butter and top each mussel with the garlic breadcrumbs. Grill in the oven for 5 minutes or until golden brown.

Serve 10-15 per person with a wedge of lemon.

Meat

Chicken Vallée d'Auge with Caramelised Apples	207
Chicken in a Thyme & Mustard Crumb	209
Chicken or Vegetarian Java	210
Chicken with Coriander & Lime Butter	212
Chicken with Tarragon Cream Sauce	213
Chicken Coconut with Pineapple or Mango Salsa	215
Chicken with Lime & Lemongrass	217
Roast Chicken with Fresh Thyme & Honey Jus	218
Duck Casserole with Red Wine & Prunes	220
Confit of Duck	222
Roast Confit of Duck Breast, Thyme Bread Stuffing, Apple Sauce and Red Wine Jus	224
Roast Confit of Duck Breast with Bacon, Thyme Bread Stuffing and a Spicy Plum Sauce	225
Roast Pheasant with Bread Sauce	226
Rack of Lamb with Puy Lentils and a Red Wine Sauce	229
Traditional Irish Stew	231
Maura's Steak	232
Beef & Guinness Casserole	235
Roast Beef with Yorkshire Pudding	236
Christmas Ham with a Honey & Mustard Glaze	241
Maura's Christmas Turkey with all the trimmings	242

Meat

For good quality meat it is important to have a butcher you can rely on. My sister Grainne and I are lucky because our cousin Jerry Hurley has a butcher shop in Kenmare. His father, Timmy, ran the shop in the early days for many years before Jerry took it over and they have supplied us with prime meat from day one. They have quality local meat. The beef comes from local farmers, the lamb is Kerry mountain lamb which feeds on lovely wild herbs and the chicken is free range and delicious.

Jerry's sister, Therese, was my right-hand woman at The Lime Tree where we cooked together for many years. We had great fun, especially when Annie Goulding was with us. The Hurleys grew up over the butcher shop on Henry Street where, in the late 1940s, I spent several months living with my aunt Kathleen and family. Kathleen also followed my grandmother's footsteps into food when she started The Wander Inn in the 1950s. She ran the hotel for many years as a family business, and it is still called The Wander Inn today. In the late 1940s, I spent several months living with my aunt and family over the butcher shop.

At present in the town of Kenmare we have three great family butchers, which must be unique for a town of its size: Hurley's on Henry Street, Roger O'Sullivan in the Square and Randles' on Main Street.

The best end of lamb is used for the rack of lamb. It is a very simple dish and the cook has very little to do once the quality of the lamb is excellent. It can be enhanced with a good sauce (p229). If we are having a roast chicken dish I would generally get my chicken breasts with the bone attached. Free range chicken generally provides great flavour. Chicken is a great base because it lends itself to so many flavours, it is versatile and has endless cooking possibilities. I have included a diverse range of tasty chicken dishes in this chapter.

In Kenmare we are in the heart of the countryside while also having the advantage of being beside the sea. We have a good winter tourism trade, including a market for game shooting. There are very knowledgeable families here who guide mostly French tourists for shooting wild birds. Woodcock is the most prized for the French and can be shot from November through to January. It is only hung for one day or so and it is always cooked whole. The entrails or insides are not drawn, and the little bird is considered a great delicacy.

Pheasant is also shot at this time and the female is particularly plump and delicious. I have included a recipe for roast pheasant with bread sauce and game chips in this chapter (p226). The young birds are best for roasting whereas the older birds are more suitable for casseroles or braising.

"Pheasant is like a person really," says Maura Foley of Packie's restaurant in Co. Kerry. "When it gets old, its feet get sharp and pointed. So look to see if it's young. Look to see how it's shot. Look out for too much lead."

Extract from *The Irish Times*, November 1993 – John McKenna

We had guests in Shelburne Lodge for many years who would stay for a week in January to shoot game in Lauragh on the Beara Peninsula. They prepared 'bullshot' in their flasks every morning in my kitchen, which was an old shooting party tradition. Inside the flask was consommé soup topped up with vodka. They drank this for their 'elevenses' or mid-morning break. I prepared dinner for them in Shelburne Lodge in the evening and there were always great stories about their shoot.

There are plenty of wild duck in Kenmare but it doesn't appear to be as sought after as the woodcock. I source my duck from Skeaghanore in West Cork. The Hickeys have been supplying me since The Lime Tree and provide me with good quality duck and geese.

I have included a few confit duck dishes in this chapter, breast of duck (p224–225) and also a delicious duck casserole (p220). I love it in the winter time and it is a great dish to have for a large group. Fat can be expensive to buy so whenever I roast duck or goose, I keep the fat and store it in the freezer in a sealed container so I can take it out as needed for confit dishes. You could also use it for roast potatoes.

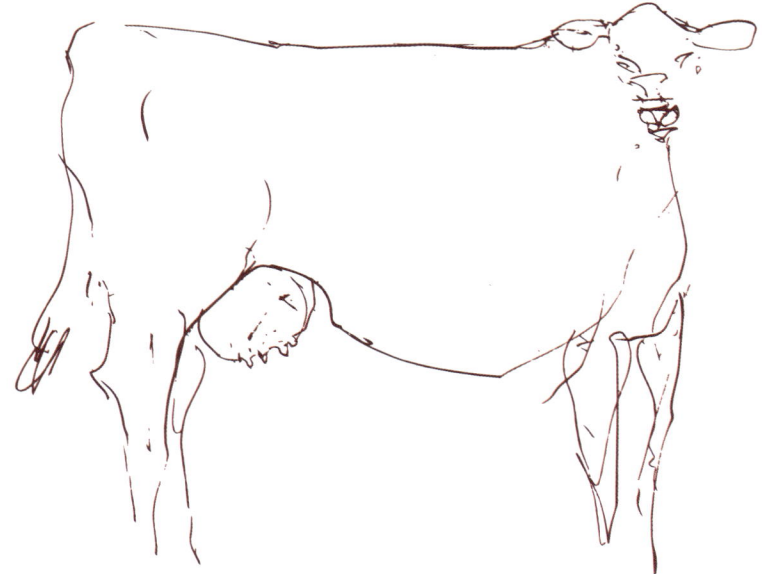

Chicken Vallée d'Auge with Caramelised Apples

It was during a *stage* at the famous Arbutus, a Michelin restaurant in Cork under chef Declan Ryan, that I learnt about this scrumptious chicken dish. Declan is a brilliant chef who trained at the prestigious Russell Hotel in Dublin under Pierre Rolland. The Arbutus Lodge featured in the first publication of the UK and Ireland Michelin Guide under its current format in 1974.

The dish utilises the best ingredients of Normandy: apples and calvados. My husband Tom is a cousin of Jane O'Callaghan of Longueville House in the Blackwater Valley in County Cork. Michael O'Callaghan was one of the first people in Ireland to plant a vineyard and bottle his own wine. The family continue the tradition and are making great apple brandy and cider from their orchards. I now use Longueville House Irish Apple Brandy for all my recipes that include calvados, plus a little nip for myself as a good pick me up! The cream reduction sauce gives this recipe great depth of flavour but I have also included a simpler alternative.

Ingredients

Serves 4

Chicken:

- 4 chicken breasts, skinned with the bone on
- 2 tbsp plain white flour, seasoned with sea salt and cracked black pepper
- 55g / 2oz clarified butter (p376)
- 2½ tbsp Longueville House Irish apple brandy
- 200ml / 7fl oz basic cream reduction sauce (p347), preferably made with chicken stock (alternatively, use 150ml cream and add 50ml of Irish dry cider and 1 tbsp brandy if desired when adding the apple brandy)
- Sea salt and cracked black pepper

Caramelised Apples:

- 1 tbsp butter, melted
- 2 eating apples (e.g. Cox's), peeled, cored and each cut into 8 pieces
- 1 tsp light brown or demerara sugar
- A little lemon juice, as needed

Serving suggestions:

Purple sprouting broccoli (p272), fresh spinach (p278) or other seasonal greens, depending on the time of year

Method

Preheat the oven to fan 200°C / fan 400°F / gas mark 7.

Lightly coat the chicken in the seasoned flour, shaking off any excess. Melt the clarified butter in an ovenproof frying pan over a medium-high heat. Add the chicken to the pan, breast side down, and cook for 3-5 minutes, then turn and cook for another 3-5 minutes or until golden brown. Move the pan into the oven and continue to cook for 10-15 minutes or until cooked through, depending on the thickness of your chicken.

Remove the chicken from the pan, cover to keep warm and set aside. Pour off any excess fat from the pan, then return to the stove over a low heat. Add the apple brandy to deglaze the pan for 2-3 minutes, scraping off all the residue from the base of the pan. (If using cream only, add the cider and optional apple brandy to deglaze and cook for 5-7 minutes.) Add the cream reduction sauce (or the cream, if opting for that simpler alternative), stir to combine, bring to the boil and gently simmer. Season to taste.

To make the caramelised apples, melt the butter in a small saucepan over a medium heat. Add the apples and sauté for a few minutes until the apples are starting to colour. Sprinkle over the sugar and toss them around to caramelise until just golden brown, not dark. Add a little lemon juice to taste as needed.

If there is any juice from the resting chicken, add this to the sauce and stir. To serve, the chicken breast can be kept whole or sliced at an angle. Spoon the sauce in the centre of the plate and place the chicken on top. Place a mound of the apples on one end of the chicken. Garnish with a sprig of rosemary.

Chicken in a Thyme & Mustard Crumb

This is a very tasty quick dish. The mustard and thyme can be omitted to make a nice dish for children.

Ingredients

Serves 4

Chicken:

- 4 chicken breasts, skinned and boneless
- 115g / 4oz clarified butter (p376)

Crumb:

- 3 eggs, beaten
- 4 tbsp wholegrain mustard
- 200g / 7oz fresh soft white breadcrumbs
- 1 tbsp fresh thyme leaves
- Sea salt and cracked black pepper
- Flat leaf parsley, to garnish
- Lemon wedges and a green salad, to serve

Serving suggestions:

Colcannon (p262) and a green salad on the side

Method

Place the chicken breasts on a board and use a sharp knife to slice into one side of the breast, starting at the thicker end and ending at the thin point – be careful not to cut all the way through to the other side. Open out to butterfly like an escalope. Place a sheet of clingfilm under and over the opened breast and gently bash with a rolling pin to create an even thickness.

In a large shallow bowl, combine the eggs and mustard. In another bowl, combine the breadcrumbs and thyme. Dip the chicken breasts first into the egg mustard mixture to lightly coat, then toss into the crumb mixture to cover. Press the crumbs in a little to ensure you have a good thick coating on both sides.

Heat a heavy-based frying pan with the clarified butter over a medium-high heat. Place the butterflied chicken in the pan and cook for 4-5 minutes either side or until golden brown and cooked through. Depending on the size of your pan, you may need to do this in batches; if so, wipe the pan clean between batches to remove any burnt breadcrumbs and adding more clarified butter before cooking more chicken.

Garnish the chicken with parsley and serve with lemon wedges.

Chicken or Vegetarian Java

This is a flavoursome, mildly spiced orange curry sauce. It is so versatile and works very well with chicken or simply on its own as a vegetarian option. The flavour permeates so it is best to make the sauce the day before serving. This is a dish that specifically requires tasting so you can adjust the flavours, as it can be quite different each time you make it. If you prefer more heat, add more curry powder. Add more sugar or mild honey if required, or for more piquancy add more lime juice. Always season at the last minute with sea salt and cracked black pepper.

Any extra sauce once cooled can be placed in an airtight container and stored in the freezer for up to one month. I have also provided a recipe for a quick Java sauce if you are short on time.

Ingredients

Serves 4-6

- 4 chicken breasts, skinned and boneless
- 2 tbsp plain white flour, seasoned with sea salt and cracked black pepper
- 55g / 2oz clarified butter

Java Sauce:

- 2 tbsp butter
- 8 shallots, finely chopped
- 8cm / 3in piece of fresh ginger, peeled and grated
- 3 garlic cloves, crushed
- 2 tsp coriander seeds, toasted and ground
- 3 tsp good quality curry powder (e.g. Green Saffron)
- 1 tbsp plain white flour
- 2 sticks of celery, roughly chopped
- Zest and juice of 2 oranges
- 1 tbsp apple chutney (p378), or similar chutney
- 570ml / 1 pint vegetable stock (p374) or water
- Juice of ½ lime
- 200ml / 7fl oz crème fraîche
- Sea salt and cracked black pepper

Serving suggestions:

Brown basmati rice, orange and lime wedges and organic whole natural yoghurt, to serve and snipped coriander leaves, to garnish

Method

Preheat the oven to fan 200°C / fan 400°F / gas mark 7.

Lightly coat the chicken in the seasoned flour, shaking off any excess. Melt the clarified butter in an ovenproof frying pan. Add the chicken to the pan, breast side down, and cook for 3-5 minutes over a medium heat, then turn and cook for another 3-5 minutes or until golden brown. Remove the chicken and pour off any excess fat from the pan. Slice the chicken into three pieces, then return to the pan in preparation for the oven.

To make the Java sauce, melt the butter in a small saucepan then add the shallots, cover and sweat for 5 minutes over a low heat. Add the ginger, garlic, coriander seeds, curry powder and flour. Cook for 5 minutes, while continuing to stir. Add the celery, orange zest and juice, chutney and stock. Bring to the boil, then reduce to a simmer and leave to gently bubble for 15-20 minutes. Add the lime juice and crème fraîche and stir to combine. Season to taste.

Pour the Java sauce on top of the chicken, coating well. Move the pan into the oven and bake for 10-15 minutes. If you prefer, you can leave out this step but ensure your chicken breasts are cooked through in the earlier frying process.

Garnish the chicken with snipped coriander leaves and serve with brown basmati rice, orange and lime wedges and a spoonful of yoghurt.

Quick Java Sauce:

In a small saucepan, melt 1 tbsp butter then add 2 sticks of finely chopped celery, a knob of grated ginger, the zest of 1 orange and 1 tbsp curry powder. Cook over a gentle heat for 10 minutes. Add the juice of 2 oranges and bring to a simmer. Add 200ml / 7fl oz cream or 3 tbsp crème fraîche and stir to combine. Add the juice of 1 lime and 1 tbsp apple chutney (p378) or similar, adding more or less to taste. Season with sea salt and cracked black pepper and serve as suggested opposite.

Chicken with Coriander & Lime Butter

This dish is quick, easy and bursting with flavour. The coriander and lime butter is simple to make and works well with chicken, a seared fillet of fresh wild salmon or vegetarian dishes.

Ingredients

Serves 4

Chicken:

- 4 chicken breasts, skinned with the bone on
- 2 tbsp plain white flour, seasoned with sea salt and cracked black pepper
- 55g / 2oz clarified butter

Coriander & Lime Butter:

- 115g / 4oz butter
- Juice of 4 limes
- Large bunch of fresh coriander, snipped
- Sea salt and cracked black pepper
- A dash of honey, to taste (optional)

Serving suggestions:

Serve with sugar snap peas (p274) and noodles of your choice

Method

Preheat the oven to fan 200°C / fan 400°F / gas mark 7.

Lightly coat the chicken in the seasoned flour, shaking off any excess. Melt the butter in an ovenproof frying pan over a medium-high heat. Add the chicken to the pan, breast side down, and cook for 3-5 minutes, then turn and cook for 3-5 minutes or until golden brown. Move the pan into the oven and cook for 10-15 minutes or until cooked through, depending on thickness of your chicken.

To make the butter, melt the butter in a small saucepan then add the lime juice and warm gently to coagulate – it should form a light emulsion. Season to taste. Add a dash of honey, if desired. Stir in the snipped coriander just before serving.

To serve, slice the chicken thinly at an angle. Serve on a warm plate and pour over the lime and coriander butter just before serving. Delicious served with noodles, and sugar snap peas (p274) which are sweet and work well with the tartness of the lime.

Chicken with Tarragon Cream Sauce

Summer is the time for tarragon in Ireland, so naturally this sauce works well with fresh or sautéed summer vegetables. The sauce also goes well with savoury tarts, pastries and pasta.

Ingredients

Serves 4

Chicken:

- 4 chicken breasts, skinned with the bone on
- 2 tbsp plain white flour, seasoned with sea salt and cracked black pepper
- 55g / 2oz clarified butter (p376)

Tarragon Cream Sauce:

- 1 tbsp butter
- 75g / 2½oz finely diced shallots (around 3 shallots, but will depend on size)
- 1 tbsp tarragon vinegar (p34)
- 200ml / 7fl oz cream reduction sauce (p347)
- 60g / 2oz fresh tarragon leaves
- Sea salt and cracked black pepper

Serving suggestions:

Summer vegetables such as pan-fried courgettes (p272), sugar snaps (p274, omit mint) or seasonal greens

Method

Preheat the oven to fan 200°C / fan 400°F / gas mark 7.

Lightly coat the chicken in the seasoned flour, shaking off any excess. Melt the butter in an ovenproof frying pan over a medium-high heat. Add the chicken to the pan, breast side down, and cook for 3-5 minutes, then turn and cook for another 3-5 minutes or until golden brown. Move the pan into the oven and continue to cook for 10-15 minutes or until cooked through, depending on the thickness of your chicken.

In a small saucepan, melt the butter over a low heat then add the shallots, cover and sweat for 10 minutes or until soft but not coloured, stirring occasionally. Add the vinegar and reduce for 5 minutes over a medium-high heat until the liquid has evaporated. Add the cream reduction sauce, bring to the boil, then turn down the heat and simmer for a few minutes. Blitz using a hand blender, or in a food processor. If using a food processor, return to the saucepan to heat through. Season to taste. Add the tarragon leaves to a sieve and plunge into a saucepan of boiling water for 1 minute. Remove the sieve with the leaves and refresh under cold running water. Pat the leaves dry with kitchen paper. Snip the leaves into the sauce and stir.

Serve the chicken with the tarragon cream sauce and a garnish of tarragon.

Chicken Coconut with Pineapple or Mango Salsa

This is an adaptation from the magical Nigel Slater's *30-Minute Cook*. The paste can be used as an addition to many curry sauces. There are people who go to Packie's especially for this dish, including one of my daughters. The key to this recipe is the creamed coconut. Ensure you do not use coconut milk. This versatile curry paste can be batch made and frozen, making this recipe even quicker.

Ingredients

Serves 2

Thai Green Curry Paste (makes around 285g / 10oz):

- 1 tsp cumin seeds
- 1 tsp coriander seeds
- 6 hot green chillies, around 5cm / 2in long, deseeded and chopped
- 4 lemongrass stalks, outer layers removed, chopped
- 3 tbsp chopped coriander, including stems
- 2 banana shallots, finely diced
- 3 garlic cloves
- 7.5cm / 3in piece of fresh ginger, peeled and roughly chopped
- ½ tsp crushed black peppercorns
- Zest and juice of 2 limes

Chicken and Creamed Coconut:

- 4 tbsp cream
- 4 tbsp creamed coconut
- 4 tbsp Thai green curry paste
- 2 chicken breasts, skinless with the bone on
- 2 tbsp plain white flour, seasoned with sea salt
- 1 tbsp clarified butter (p376)
- Sea salt, to season

Pineapple or Mango Salsa:

- 1 medium sweet pineapple, finely chopped, or 2 mangos, peeled and diced
- 50ml / 1¾fl oz Thai dipping sauce (p358)
- 1 tbsp coriander, roughly chopped

Serving suggestions:

Brown basmati rice, lime wedges and organic whole natural yoghurt to serve and snipped coriander leaves, to garnish

Method

Preheat the oven to fan 200°C / fan 400°F / gas mark 7.

In a dry frying pan, add the cumin and coriander seeds and toast over a medium heat until the spices become strongly aromatic. Remove from the pan and crush using a pestle and mortar. Tip the spices and the remaining curry paste ingredients into a blender and pulse to form a paste.

In a small saucepan, gently warm the cream. Pour the warm cream into a bowl and mix in the creamed coconut, followed by the curry paste and a pinch of salt. Add more cream if you prefer. Set aside.

Lightly coat the chicken in the seasoned flour, shaking off any excess. Melt the butter in an ovenproof frying pan over a medium-high heat. Add the chicken to the pan, breast side down, and cook for 3-5 minutes, then turn and cook for another 3-5 minutes or until a golden brown colour.

Move the pan to the oven and continue cooking for 10-15 minutes or until cooked through, depending on thickness of the chicken. Remove from the oven and slice the chicken diagonally into 3 pieces, then return to the ovenproof pan, spoon over the creamed coconut curry sauce and flash in the oven for 3-5 minutes.

To make the salsa, mix the fruit with the dipping sauce and add the coriander just before serving (it will lose its colour otherwise).

Serve the chicken with brown basmati rice on the side, salsa, a spoonful of organic whole natural yoghurt and a wedge of lime. Garnish with fresh coriander.

Chicken with Lime & Lemongrass

Ingredients

Serves 4

Chicken:

- 4 chicken breasts, skinned and boneless

- 2 tbsp plain white flour, seasoned with sea salt and cracked black pepper

- 55g / 2oz clarified butter (p376)

Marinade:

- 2 tbsp mint

- 2 tbsp coriander leaves

- Zest and juice of 2 limes

- 1½ birdseye chillies, halved and deseeded

- 2 tbsp olive oil

- 3 lemongrass stalks, trimmed and chopped (reserve trimmings and outer leaves)

- 5cm / 2in piece of fresh ginger, chopped

Lime Syrup:

- Zest and juice of 3-4 limes

- 55g / 2oz brown sugar

- 2 tbsp white wine vinegar

- Lemongrass trimmings

- Chopped mint and coriander leaves, to garnish

Serving suggestions:

Sugar snaps with mint (p274) or wilted fresh spinach (p278)

Method

In a food processor, blitz together all the marinade ingredients until well minced. Add the chicken breasts to a bowl and thoroughly coat in the marinade. Cover and chill in the fridge for 4 hours or overnight.

Preheat the oven to fan 180°C / fan 350°F / gas mark 6.

In a small saucepan, combine all the lime syrup ingredients and bring to a gentle simmer, then leave to continue simmering for 8-10 minutes or until the liquid has reached a syrupy consistency. Add more lime juice to taste if needed.

Lightly coat the chicken in the seasoned flour, shaking off any excess. Melt the clarified butter in an ovenproof frying pan over a medium-high heat. Add the chicken to the pan, breast side down, and cook for 3-5 minutes, then turn and cook for another 3-5 minutes or until golden brown.

Move the pan to the oven and cook for 10-15 minutes or until cooked through depending on the thickness the chicken. Turn the oven down to fan 160°C / fan 325°F / gas mark 4. Remove the pan from the oven and drizzle lime syrup over each of the breasts (around 1 tbsp per breast) and cook in the oven for a further 2 minutes. Remove the breasts from the pan.

With the frying pan on the stove over a medium heat, deglaze by pouring in the remaining lime syrup with an additional 2 tbsp water, scraping the base of the pan to release any extra flavour. Simmer for a few minutes until it reaches a coating consistency. Season to taste.

Serve the chicken with the sauce. Garnish with chopped mint and coriander.

Roast Chicken with Fresh Thyme & Honey Jus

This jus is an adaptation from my wonderfully talented friend Colin O'Daly, who won a Michelin star for the restaurant in the Park Hotel Kenmare in 1983. The jus, which I've shared here, is simply delicious. Add a little more honey if you would like it sweeter or a squeeze of lemon if it is too sweet for your taste. I roast my chicken breast side down to ensure that the joints are exposed to high heat earlier in the cooking process and the breasts are protected, which are the driest part. Use a skewer to check if the chicken is cooked as described below. I like my chicken well cooked and check by pushing the drumstick out a little from the body; if there is resistance, continue to cook the chicken for a little longer.

Ingredients

Serves 4

Roast Chicken:

- 1 organic whole chicken (2kg / 4½ lb)
- 100g / 3½oz butter
- Bunch of fresh thyme
- Cracked black pepper

Fresh Thyme & Honey Jus:

- 2 tbsp white wine vinegar
- 500ml / 17½fl oz chicken stock (p370)
- 2 tbsp Noilly Prat
- ½ tsp cornflour mixed with 1 tbsp water (optional)
- 1 tsp fresh thyme leaves
- 1-3 tsp honey
- Sea salt and cracked black pepper

Serving suggestions:

Colcannon (p262), roast vegetables (p261), purple sprouting broccoli (p272) or gratin of leeks (p268), depending on season

Method

Preheat the oven to fan 200°C / fan 400°F / gas mark 7.

Pat dry both the outside and inside of the chicken with kitchen paper. In a roasting pan, melt 70g / 2½oz of the butter on the stove or in the oven (ensure the butter does not burn) and use this to coat the entire chicken and season with black pepper as well (there is enough salt in the butter). Stuff the remaining 30g / 1oz butter into the cavity of the chicken with the thyme. Turn the chicken to be breast side down in the roasting tin and roast in the oven for 1 hour.

Turn the oven down to fan 170°C / fan 340°F / gas mark 5 and turn the chicken breast face up, baste well with the juices and roast for another 40 minutes basting a few more times. To check if cooked, pierce the thickest part of the thigh with a skewer and let the juices run out.

If they are clear then it is cooked, but if they still look pink, return to the oven for another 15 minutes. When cooked, remove the chicken from the roasting tray to rest for 15 minutes, covering with foil to keep warm.

Pour off any excess fat in the roasting tin, being careful not to lose any of the juices. To make the jus, firstly add the vinegar and cook for a few minutes until almost all evaporated, then add the stock and Noilly Prat to the roasting tin and scrape the residue from the base of the pan. Simmer on the stove top over a medium-high heat until the liquid has reduced by half to a coating consistency. If the sauce is too thin, whisk in the cornflour and water mixture to thicken. Add the thyme and honey to taste.

Carve the rested chicken and serve with a generous spoonful of the jus.

Meat

Duck Casserole with Red Wine & Prunes

This is an old French recipe, perfect in the winter or autumn for a large gathering. We have used Skeaghanore duck from Ballydehob for many years; the farm is owned by the Hickey family and is now in the second generation of production. Their ducks have great flavour and a succulent taste. We also cook one of their geese at Christmas which are beautifully plump. This recipe is enough for 12; when you make this dish, it is advisable to make this large quantity and freeze in portions as needed. You could use three whole ducks jointed by your butcher or 12 legs; ask your butcher a day earlier to reserve the duck livers. A good tip is to always keep the goose or duck fat for other uses such as roasting potatoes.

This casserole is deeply satisfying.

Ingredients

Serves 12

- 12 duck legs, or 3 ducks jointed by a butcher
- 55g / 2oz duck or goose fat
- 600g / 1lb 5oz onions, peeled, chopped and sliced
- 2 bottles / 1.5 litres full-bodied Rhône red wine or similar
- 1 bouquet garni (several springs of thyme, parsley stalks, celery leaves and one bay leaf tied with cotton twine)
- 6 garlic cloves, peeled and crushed
- 9 black peppercorns
- 300g / 10½oz smoked dry cured bacon, cut into lardons
- Approximately 36 large moist whole prunes, not pitted (3 per person)
- Port, to taste

For thickening:

- 3 duck livers (optional), well cleaned and trimmed of sinews
- 50ml / 1¾fl oz Armagnac or brandy
- 1 tbsp beurre manié (p394)
- Sprigs of thyme and rosemary, to garnish

Serving suggestions:

Buttered cabbage (p278, omit ginger), creamed potatoes (p264), turnip purée (p260) or roasted turnips

Method

Preheat the oven to fan 140°C / fan 275°F / gas mark 3.

Season the duck with sea salt and cracked black pepper. Heat a very large casserole dish with the fat over a medium heat until sizzling. Add the duck and fry until golden all over; this may need to be done in batches. Reduce the heat and add the onions to the pan, cooking gently for 10-15 minutes.

Pour off all the fat and keep for future use. Pour in the red wine, turn up to a medium heat and bring to the boil. Add the bouquet garni, garlic, peppercorns and lardons. Place the casserole pot (without the lid) in the oven and cook for 2-2½ hours or until the meat comes away easily from the bone. Add the prunes and cook for a further 10 minutes in the oven. Using a slotted spoon, remove the duck and prunes to a plate and keep warm. Skim off all the fat from the casserole liquid. Move the pot to the stove over a low heat with the lid off.

To thicken the sauce with the livers, pound the livers with the Armagnac or brandy in a pestle and mortar or food processor until smooth, then stir into the sauce. Cook for approximately 5 minutes, stirring continuously until smooth. (Alternatively, if not using the livers, take a small spoonful of the sauce and stir it into the beurre manié with the Armagnac or brandy until smooth, then stir back into the sauce. Cook for approximately 5 minutes, stirring continuously until smooth.) Reduce the sauce if required; it should be a coating consistency that is slightly thickened.

Season the sauce, adding port to taste. Add back the duck and prunes into the casserole and mix to coat.

Serve three prunes per duck portion and top with a garnish of thyme and rosemary.

Confit of Duck

Before refrigeration, people developed their own way of preserving food such as salting, pickling, smoking and drying. Storing slow cooked meat by complete immersion in fat is also a way of preserving. For this recipe, you will need the legs and breasts (with the little bone) from two ducks and some duck fat. The legs can be used for a starter and breasts for a main course. The French, of course, use all parts of the duck, and so does John Desmond of Island Cottage on Heir Island. He serves a delightful pâté from the duck livers and uses all the smaller trimmings for graisserons and the bones for flavouring stocks and sauces.

The traditional method to confit is to salt the duck the day before; however I don't do this, which makes the recipe a little simpler but still delicious. Once the confit ducks are ready, they can be served on the same day or stored in the fridge for a few weeks as they are preserved in the fat.

Ingredients

Serves 4

- 2 ducks, breasts and legs
- 1 large onion, cut into wedges
- 2 celery sticks, roughly chopped
- 1 carrot, roughly chopped
- 2 leeks, washed and roughly chopped
- 1 orange, skin on and cut into wedges
- 5cm / 2in piece of fresh ginger, peeled and chopped
- 6 garlic cloves, peeled
- 3 sprigs fresh thyme
- 3 sprigs rosemary
- 6 black peppercorns
- 2 litres / 3½ pints duck or goose fat, melted (amount needed will depend on size of ducks)

Method

Preheat the oven to fan 130°C / fan 265°F / gas mark 2. Place all the vegetables, orange wedges, aromatics and herbs into the base of a large deep roasting tin and spread out. Place the duck breast and legs skin side up on top of the vegetable mix and pour over enough fat to completely immerse the duck.

Bring to the boil on the stove over a medium heat, then transfer to the oven to cook for 2-2½ hours or until the flesh comes away from the bone of the legs. Remove from the oven and, if using immediately, allow to rest for at least 30 minutes.

To serve immediately:

Follow the recipe for Confit of Duck Legs (p131) and Roast Confit of Duck Breast (p224-225).

To store (can be kept for a few weeks in the fridge):

Once cooled, transfer the duck to a clean container and ladle over the cooled fat to cover the meat. Do not pack too tightly and the meat must be surrounded entirely by fat – be careful not to pour in any cooking juices or residue as these will interfere with preservation.

Note that if excess fat is available, pour this into a container along with the juices and refrigerate for up to a few weeks. The juices will then form a jelly at the base that can be used for sauces or stews.

Retaining duck fat:

When you have eaten the duck, don't throw out the fat it is immersed it. It is very valuable and can be used again for your next confit. Put it in a stainless steel pan and bring it to the boil, continue to cook for a few minutes, then turn off the heat. Allow it to cool a little, then pour the fat only (not the residue) into a sterile container. Once cooled, seal and refrigerate for up to 2 weeks or freeze for up to 6 months.

Roast Confit of Duck Breast, Thyme Bread Stuffing, Apple Sauce and a Red Wine Jus

Ingredients

Serves 4

- 4 confit duck breasts (p222)

Fresh Thyme Bread Stuffing:

- 55g / 2oz butter
- 3 shallots or 1 medium onion, peeled and finely chopped
- 225g / 8oz fresh soft white breadcrumbs
- 2 tsp fresh thyme leaves
- Sea salt and cracked black pepper
- 4-6 tbsp apple sauce (p364) and 8-10 tbsp red wine jus (p360), to serve

Serving suggestions:

Braised chicory in orange or sweet wine (p271), buttered cabbage (p278, omit ginger), turnip purée (p260) and roast potatoes (p266, omit garlic and rosemary)

Method

Preheat the oven to fan 200°C / fan 400°F / gas mark 7.

To make the stuffing, melt the butter in a saucepan then add the onions, cover and sweat for 10-15 minutes, stirring occasionally to make sure there is no colouring. Stir in the thyme leaves. Place the breadcrumbs in a bowl and pour over the herb onion mixture. Stir together with a fork to retain lightness. Season to taste.

Press the stuffing onto the flesh side of the duck (the underneath part) and place on a greased roasting tray. Roast skin side up for 12-15 minutes in the oven or until the skin is crisp and browned. Take up the duck and stuffing with a fish slice and serve on a plate with the apple sauce and spoon the jus around the base of the duck.

Serve the duck breast with apple sauce and red wine jus.

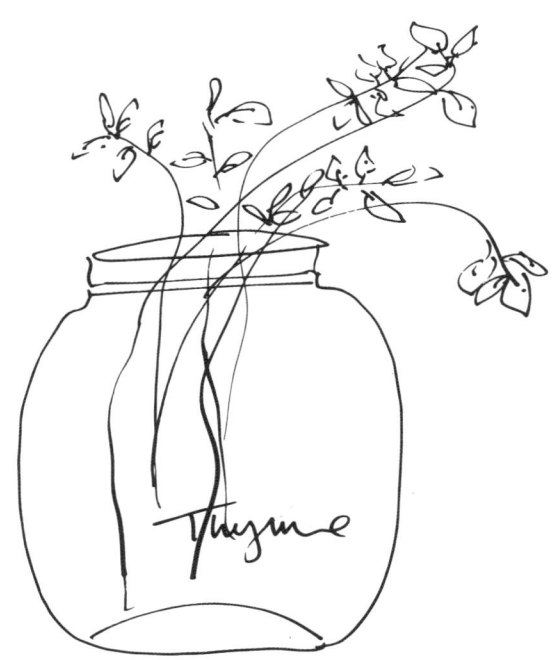

Roast Confit of Duck Breast with Bacon, Thyme Bread Stuffing and a Spicy Plum Sauce

This recipe makes a surplus of the spicy plum sauce; halve the quantity if you wish to have none leftover, but the extra works perfectly without puréeing as a breakfast compote or served as a side with crème brulée.

Ingredients

Serves 4

- 4 confit duck breasts (p222)
- 4 dry cured streaky smoky bacon strips

Spicy Plum Sauce:

- 200g / 7oz demerara sugar
- 200ml / 7fl oz cold water
- 200ml / 7fl oz red wine
- Zest and juice of 1 lemon
- Zest and juice of 1 orange
- 1kg / 2lb 4oz dark purple plums, halved and stones removed
- 12 cloves, in a muslin bag

Thyme Bread Stuffing (p224)

Serving suggestions:

Buttered cabbage (p278, omit ginger), turnip purée (p260), roast beetroot (p277, omit orange)

Method

To make the spicy plum sauce, place the sugar, water, wine, zests and juices into a medium stainless steel saucepan over a medium-high heat. Stir until the sugar dissolves. Add the plums and cloves then simmer over a medium heat for 30-40 minutes or until the fruit is soft. Remove the muslin bag of cloves. Purée the plum sauce using a hand blender or in a food processor.

Preheat the oven to fan 200°C / fan 400°F / gas mark 7.

Press the stuffing onto the flesh side of the duck breasts (the underneath part) and place strips of bacon over the stuffing (not over the skin side of the breast). Carefully place onto a roasting tray skin side up and roast for 10-12 minutes or until the skin is crisp and browned. Carefully remove the duck breasts with a fish slice, being careful to keep the bacon and stuffing in place.

Serve the duck breast with plum sauce and garnish with a sprig of rosemary.

Roast Pheasant with Bread Sauce

Pheasants are a game bird native to China and were introduced to Britain at a very early date, back to Elizabethan times. George Washington was supposed to have imported pheasants for his estate in 1789. However, Judge Denny, the consul general for the US in Shanghai, had a great number of pheasants transported from China to Oregon and they are now in almost every state. The Normans are believed to have brought them to Ireland. The cocks have beautiful plumage but are less tender than the females, which are plumper and sweeter. The young birds are best for roasting whereas the older birds are more suitable for casseroles or braising. The birds are hung from the neck for a number of days to allow the meat to become more tender. Some people like their game hung very high, almost rotting, but I like it hung for just a few days. They are in season from October to February, but they are at their best from November to January.

Because the wild bird is very active, the legs tend to be more tough and sinewy, so it is a good idea to cook them separately from the breast. They can be braised earlier in the day. The gravy and bread sauce can also be made in advance.

Ingredients

Serves 4

Roast Pheasant:

- 2 young female pheasants, plucked, drawn and cleaned (ask the butcher to do this for you), legs separate
- 255g / 9oz butter
- 400ml / 14fl oz red wine
- 400ml / 14fl oz chicken stock (p370)
- 4 shallots, diced
- 12-16 sprigs of thyme (for braising legs and for crowns)
- 8 smoked dry cured streaky bacon rashers (4 per crown)
- 4 tbsp thyme bread stuffing (p243)

Gravy:

- Braising juices from the legs
- 3 tbsp port
- 1 tbsp redcurrant jelly
- Roasting juices
- Sea salt and cracked black pepper
- 1 tsp beurre manié, if desired (p394)

Bread Sauce:

- 1 onion, peeled and halved
- 10 cloves
- 400ml / 14fl oz whole milk
- 100ml / 3½fl oz cream
- 100g / 3½oz fresh soft white breadcrumbs
- 30g / 1oz butter, softened
- Sea salt and cracked black pepper
- A pinch of grated nutmeg (optional)

Serving suggestions:

Serve with game chips (p265), roast winter root vegetables (p261) and winter greens

Method

Preheat the oven to fan 130°C / fan 265°F / gas mark 2.

Remove the legs from the carcasses with a sharp boning knife, being careful not to damage the breast skin. Pull the legs outwards from the carcasses and crack the joints. Cut off the legs from the carcasses, cutting against the bone, with breasts remaining on the carcass (crown). The butcher can do this for you if you prefer.

To braise the legs, melt 55g / 2oz of the butter in a small casserole pan and fry the pheasant legs skin side down for 5 minutes or until golden brown. Cook the other side for 1-2 minutes to seal. Cover the legs with the red wine and stock. Add the shallots and sprigs of thyme and bring to a simmer. Cover with a lid and braise in the oven for 2 hours.

To make a reduction for the gravy, put the braising liquid into a saucepan and reduce by half, then add the port and redcurrant jelly. Simmer for 5 minutes, then season to taste. It should be coating consistency. Set aside.

To sauté the breast sides of the crowns, preheat the oven to fan 200°C / fan 400°F / gas mark 7. Melt 85g / 3oz of the butter in a heavy roasting pan and sauté both breasts of the crowns until golden brown. Place the crowns breast side up and cover crossway with the streaky bacon (this prevents the meat from drying out). Fill each cavity with thyme and 30g / 1oz of the butter. Roast in the oven for 10 minutes, then cover with foil and roast for a further 20 minutes. Remove from the oven and take out the crowns from the roasting pan. Keep them covered in the foil and rest for 10 minutes to allow the juices to settle, then remove the breasts from the carcass.

To complete the gravy, skim off the fat from the roasting pan, then add the reduction to the roasting pan and deglaze over a medium heat, scraping all the residue. If you prefer a thicker consistency, add a little beurre manié. Season to taste.

To make the bread sauce, stud each of the onion halves with the cloves, then place in a saucepan with the milk and cream. Bring to the boil, then remove from the heat and leave to infuse for 30 minutes. Stir in the breadcrumbs and butter until well combined. Return to the hob and cook for 5 minutes over a very low heat. Remove the onion and season with sea salt, cracked black pepper and nutmeg to taste.

To complete the dish, preheat the oven to fan 220°C / 425°F / gas mark 9. Place 1 tbsp thyme bread stuffing under each breast and alongside each of the legs, then melt the remaining 55g / 2oz butter and use this to baste the meat. Roast for another 5 minutes in the oven.

Serve the pheasant with the crispy bacon, gravy, warm bread sauce and game chips.

Rack of Lamb with Puy Lentils and Red Wine Sauce

Our Kerry mountain lamb feeds on the beautiful wild mountain herbs giving it its distinct and special flavour. Kerry lamb is used in all good kitchens and Connemara lamb is equally fantastic.

In the restaurant, before we roasted the lamb, we would divide the best end into two allowing a rack of 4 cutlets per portion. We cooked the rack whole and sliced into 4 cutlets per portion before serving. Fat should be left on the meat to protect it and give it a greater flavour. In spring and early summer, paloise (p343) is a superb sauce to accompany the lamb – this is a béarnaise using mint instead of tarragon – or it can be served with a fast and easy red wine jus (p360) using the residue in the roasting pan. In late summer and autumn, a stronger flavoured rich red wine sauce can be used, enhanced with rosemary and garlic (p360).

Ingredients

Serves 4

- 2 best ends of lamb with fat on, French trimmed by your butcher (4 racks of 4 cutlets per person, each rack cooked whole)
- 20g / ¾oz butter, melted
- 250g / 9oz puy lentils (or dark speckled), washed under water until the liquid runs clear
- 55g / 2oz butter
- 3 shallots, finely diced
- 2 medium carrots, peeled and finely diced
- 1 tbsp fresh thyme leaves, chopped
- Sea salt and cracked black pepper
- Choice of sauces as mentioned above
- A few sprigs of rosemary, to garnish

Serving suggestions:

Buttered carrots (p257, omit coriander), colcannon (p262), roast beetroot (p277, omit orange), sugar snaps with mint (p274), garden peas

Method

Preheat the oven to fan 200°C / fan 400°F / gas mark 7.

Brush the meat with the melted butter on both sides. Heat an ovenproof pan over a medium-high heat. Add the lamb fat side down to seal for 2-3 minutes per side or until all the fat is golden brown.

Move the pan into the oven and cook for about 20 minutes for rare, 25 minutes for medium rare or longer depending on how well cooked you would like the lamb. Cooking time will depend on the meat. Remove the lamb from the pan and rest for 10 minutes.

To make the lentils, add the lentils to a small saucepan and cover with cold water. Bring to the boil, then reduce to a simmer and cook for 15-20 minutes or until the lentils have just a small bite to them. Drain and rinse well. In another small saucepan, melt the butter over a low-medium heat. Add the shallots, cover and sweat gently for 10 minutes or until very soft. Stir in the carrots and thyme and sweat for a further 5 minutes. Stir in the lentils and season to taste.

Serve 4 cutlets per person with the puy lentils and sauce.

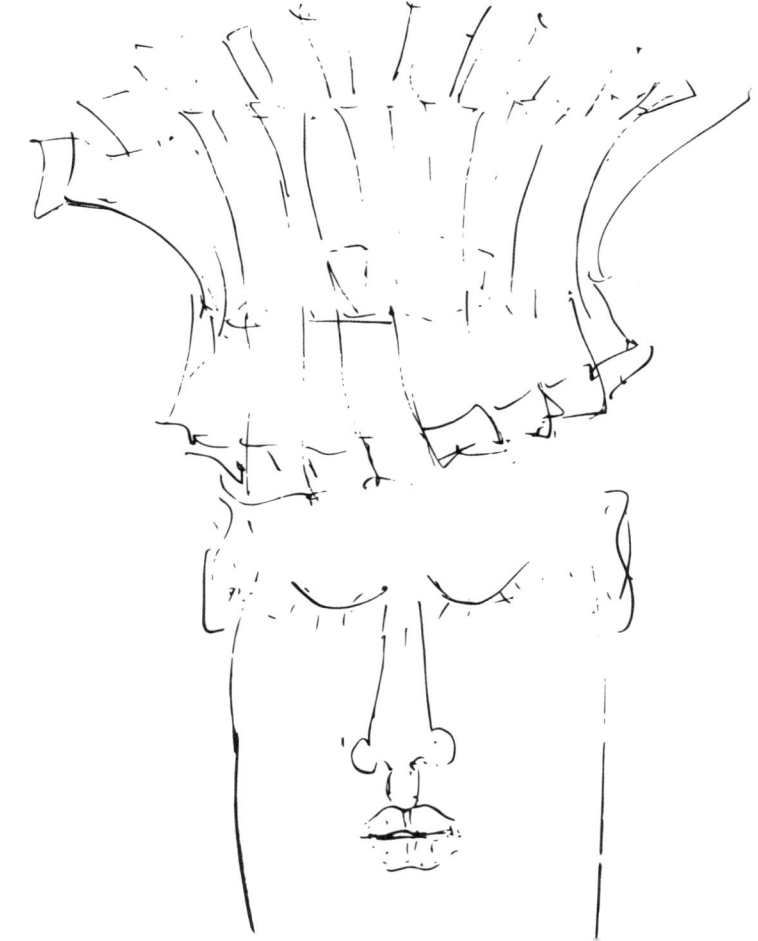

Traditional Irish Stew

In the old days in Ireland, when mutton and lamb were considered luxury, kid was used initially for an Irish stew. As time passed, mutton became more accessible, however it is now used much less due to its strong taste. Lamb is used more frequently as it has a more delicate flavour. A stewing lamb chop should be used for this dish, retaining the bone for added flavour. A waxy variety of potatoes should be used to avoid disintegration and mushiness as Irish stew is a broth with solids, like a bouillabaisse. Fresh thyme rather than dried thyme is an essential ingredient. In the old-fashioned method, it was cooked on the side of the open fire with hot coals on top of the lid to seal the stew. In my version, I use a thin layer of dough paste around the edge of the casserole with the lid on top to seal the stew and keep in the steam. There are many variations of traditional stews in Ireland. This is our mother Agnes' very simple traditional version using lamb.

Ingredients

Serves 6-8

- 2.5-3kg / 6lb waxy potatoes, peeled and sliced into 1cm / ½in thick rounds
- 8 onions or 16 shallots, sliced
- 3 tbsp fresh thyme leaves
- 12 black peppercorns
- 1.8kg / 4lb stewing lamb chops, trimmed of fat
- 2 tbsp plain white flour, mixed with 1 tsp sea salt
- 1.5 litres / 3 pints cold water

Sealing Paste:

- 255g / 9oz plain white flour
- 100ml / 3½fl oz water

Method

Preheat the oven to fan 150°C / fan 300°F / gas mark 3.

Cover the base of a 6 litre capacity casserole pot or saucepan with half of the sliced potatoes, sprinkle with a pinch of sea salt followed by a layer of half the onions then sprinkle over half of the thyme and peppercorns.

Toss the lamb in the seasoned flour to coat, shaking off any excess, and lay it evenly over the onions. Sprinkle over the remaining thyme, peppercorns and onions. Place over a final layer of the potatoes to cover the lamb completely, sprinkled with a pinch of salt, then pour over the water.

Make the sealing paste by placing the flour in a bowl, making a well in the centre and stirring in just enough water to make a slightly sticky soft paste; be careful not to beat the mixture. Roll the paste into a thin rope with your hands and place around the edge of the casserole dish, then fix the lid on top. This provides a tight seal for the stew.

Heat the casserole on the stove for 5 minutes over a medium heat, then place in the oven to cook for 3 hours.

Maura's Steak

In Ireland, steak is traditionally served with sautéed onions. A good thick T-bone was the ultimate – today, a fillet or sirloin are more popular. The most important person when it comes to quality meat is your butcher; find one you can rely on and who will not give you the meat when it is too fresh. Meat needs to be well hung otherwise it will be tough. Look for meat with good marbling and plenty of fat.

Allow the meat to reach room temperature before cooking. Salt should not be used on the steak before you cook it as it draws out the blood and dries the meat. Resting the meat after cooking is essential to let the meat relax and coagulate; it tenderises the meat and helps retain the moisture. If serving very rare, the blood will settle and should not run onto the plate when it is cut. Here are a number of sauce suggestions which are delicious with steak.

Serving suggestions:

Strong vegetables are best with steak; roast shallots, sautéed onions, colcannon (p262), chips, purple sprouting broccoli (p272), gratin of leeks (p268), creamed leeks (p268), celeriac purée (p259), roast turnip

Ingredients

Serves 4

- 4 x 225-285g / 8-10oz sirloin steak or 4 x 170-225g / 6-8oz fillet steak, at room temperature
- Butter, to grease pan
- Oil, to grease pan
- A tiny sprinkle of cracked black pepper
- Dijonnaise sauce (p361)
- Béarnaise (p344)
- Green peppercorn (p361)
- Port & Cashel Blue (p362)
- Garlic butter (p376)

Method

Tempering the steaks helps the meat cook more evenly. Remove the steaks from the fridge and allow to come to room temperature for 30-60 minutes.

Heat a large heavy-based griddle pan or frying pan over a high heat. Lightly brush with the butter and oil. When the pan is very hot, add the steaks. Ensure there is enough space for the steaks to sear rather than stew. Brown quickly to seal and then turn to seal the other side.

Cook the meat according to the required taste: rare is very red inside but brown on both sides, medium-rare is pink all through but brown on both sides, medium is mediumly pink all through but brown on both sides and well-done is no pink, just brown but brown on both sides (it tends to toughen the steak).

One should consider the thickness in relation to how they want their steak cooked. The press test is useful – the meat gets firmer the more it is cooked. You can use this as a guide. Rest the steak for 5 minutes and serve with your choice of sauce.

Beef & Guinness Casserole

This is the Irish version of beef bourguignon, using Guinness instead of red wine. A lovely winter warmer.

Ingredients

Serves 4-6

- 1¼ kg / 2lb 12oz stewing beef, trimmed and cut into around 4cm / 1½in pieces

- 2 tbsp plain white flour, seasoned with sea salt and cracked black pepper

- 1 tbsp olive or vegetable oil

- 4 tbsp butter

- 500ml / 17½fl oz beef stock (p372)

- 1 tbsp tomato purée

- 4 large onions, peeled and sliced

- 225g / 8oz carrots, peeled and sliced

- 225g / 8oz celery, roughly chopped

- 500ml / 17½fl oz Guinness

- 5 thyme sprigs

- A few springs of flat leaf parsley or a small bay leaf, to garnish

- Sea salt and cracked black pepper

Serving suggestions:

Creamed potatoes (p264) or colcannon (p262)

Method

Preheat the oven to fan 170°C / fan 340°F / gas mark 5.

Toss the beef in the seasoned flour to coat, shaking off any excess. In a large casserole dish, heat the oil and melt 3 tbsp of the butter over a high heat. Add the beef to the pan and quickly brown in batches. Be careful not to crowd the pan as the beef will stew instead of sear and caramelise. Remove the seared beef to a plate. Reduce the heat to low and add 100ml / 3½fl oz of the beef stock to deglaze, scraping the residue off the base to save the caramelised flavour. Stir in the tomato purée and then turn the heat off.

In a frying pan, melt the remaining butter over a medium heat. Add the onions and sauté for 10 minutes or until softened. Tip the onions out of the pan and set aside. To the same pan, add the carrots and celery and sauté for 5 minutes, stirring occasionally. Deglaze this pan with a little of the stock and add to the casserole.

Add the meat, onions, carrots and celery to the casserole dish with the Guinness and remaining stock. Add the thyme sprigs and stir all together to ensure everything is well distributed. Bring the casserole to the boil over a high heat, then cover and braise in the oven for 3 hours, checking periodically that it's not drying out and adding more stock (or water) if necessary. Check the meat with a skewer or knife to see if it's tender; it should be soft and easily come apart. Season to taste.

Roast Beef with Yorkshire Pudding

The choice of beef cut is very important for roasting. Traditionally rib roast is used as it is very succulent. A standing rib roasted gives more flavour as the bone acts as a conductor of heat inside the lean part of the joint. However, if you want it easier to carve, ask your butcher to bone and roll the rib.

The meat must be at room temperature for at least 1 hour before roasting. Salt should not be used on the meat before you cook it as it draws out the blood and dries the meat. It is also important that the meat is cooked in a higher oven temperature, initially at fan 220°C / fan 425°F / gas mark 9. Once cooked, allow the meat to rest 30 minutes before carving. This resting time is essential to let the meat relax and coagulate; it tenderises the meat and it will retain the moisture. If very rare the blood will settle and not run onto the plate when it is carved. When resting the meat, cover it loosely with foil and keep it in a warm place. The joint will retain its heat for a considerable length of time.

I call Yorkshire puddings 'the miracles'. Unlike a soufflé mix with whisked egg whites folded in, the pudding batter is a flat batter mix and it is the combination of the hot oven and the hot fat that miraculously helps them rise to be light and fluffy. My sister Grainne makes beautiful Yorkshire puddings using an electric beater. We use a muffin tray with muffin cups that have a diameter of 7cm / 2¾in. The batter can be pre-made in the morning and stored in the fridge. It must then be beaten for a good 5 minutes with the electric beater before pouring into the hot prepared tins. These Yorkshire puddings are suitable for vegetarians as we don't use any beef or goose fat. I have also included a quick version if short on time.

For a smooth running Sunday roast, here is a sequence that works well for timing:

The purée of turnip (p260) can be made the day before and put in a large ovenproof gratin dish and warmed in the oven when the Yorkshire puddings are cooking (make sure you do not open the oven door when the puddings are in). As mentioned above, you can prepare the Yorkshire pudding batter in the morning, beating before use. The potatoes can be par-boiled in the morning ready for roasting. Cabbage can be blanched and refreshed in the morning with excess water drained off. For serving, warm the cabbage, then toss in melted butter and season. The gravy can be made with the juices of the roast while the meat is resting.

Here is a guide to recognised cooking times for beef:

Rare: 15 minutes per 450g / 1 lb
Medium-rare: 15 minutes per 450g / 1lb + 15 minutes extra
Medium-well: 15 minutes per 450g / 1lb + 30 minutes extra

Ingredients

Serves 6-8

Roast:

- 100g / 3½oz butter, melted
- 1 tbsp oil
- 2.5 kg / 5lb 8oz rib of beef

Gravy:

- Juices from the roasting pan
- 1-2 tsp beurre manié (p394)
- 340ml / 12fl oz beef stock (p372) or water
- 60ml / 2fl oz port
- Sea salt and cracked black pepper

Yorkshire Puddings (makes 10):

- 215ml / 7½fl oz whole milk
- 2 eggs
- 115g / 4oz plain white flour
- ½ tsp sea salt
- 10 dessert spoons of sunflower oil
- 45g / 1½oz butter, chopped into 10 cubes (about 2x2cm / ¾x¾in) for the 10 individual muffin cups

Horseradish sauce, to serve

Serving suggestions:

Roast potatoes (p266, omit rosemary and garlic), turnip purée (p260), buttered cabbage (p278, omit ginger), celeriac purée (p259)

Grainne in the The Purple Heather

Meat 237

Method

Preheat the oven to fan 220°C / fan 425°F / gas mark 9.

Melt the butter and oil in a heavy deep roasting tray over a low heat on the hob. Place the beef on the tray with the fatty side up. Roast for 30 minutes in the oven, then turn the oven down to fan 170°C / fan 340°F / gas mark 5. Baste with the juices (if there is not enough juice, cover the beef for the last 15-30 minutes) and roast for another 1½ hours for medium-well. Baste the lean part of the meat at least 3 times during the entire cooking time; this will add more flavour and prevent the meat from drying out. Remove from the oven and rest for 30 minutes, covered in foil to keep warm.

To make the gravy, spoon off all the fat from the pan, ensuring to retain any juices. Add the stock or water and port and place over a medium heat. Mix well, scraping the precious sediment stuck to the pan. Transfer to a medium saucepan and continue to make your gravy. Bring to the boil then turn down the heat and simmer for about 5 minutes or to a coating consistency. If too thin, crumble in 1 tsp beurre manié and simmer for a few minutes. Season to taste.

To make the Yorkshire puddings, sieve the flour and salt into a bowl and mix. Beat the eggs with the milk to combine, then pour into the flour and briefly blend with a fork to bring the batter together. Use an electric mixer to beat the batter for 10 minutes. Transfer the batter to a jug and chill in the fridge for at least 1 hour.

To make the quick version of the Yorkshire pudding batter, add the ingredients to a food processor and blitz at high speed for 2-3 seconds. Turn off the machine, scrape down the sides of the food processor and blitz again for 2-3 minutes. Transfer to a jug and chill in the fridge for 1 hour.

Preheat the oven to fan 200°C / fan 400°F / gas mark 7.

Beat the batter with an electric mixer for 5 minutes. Put a dessert spoon of oil and a cube of butter into 10 muffin cups. Place the muffin tray in the preheated oven until the fat starts to splutter. Beat the batter lightly, then pour into the muffin cups, filling to about two-thirds full.

Cook in the centre of the oven for 15 minutes, then reduce heat to fan 180°C / fan 350°F / gas mark 6 and bake for another 10 minutes or until the puddings are golden and well risen. Do not open the oven during the cooking time as they may drop. Serve immediately so they don't lose their crispness. For that reason, plan the roast accordingly.

To serve, use a carving knife to slice from the fat part down against the grain. Serve with gravy and the Yorkshire pudding. Serve with horseradish sauce on the side, if you like. There are very good pre-made horseradish sauces available. You can grate your own horseradish into the sauce if you wish. Enjoy!

Christmas Ham with a Honey & Mustard Glaze

We prefer smoked gammon to green. When buying your gammon, ensure you have a pot large enough to fit it for cooking! My sister Grainne always cooks the gammon the day before Christmas Eve and finishes the ham in the oven with a beautiful glaze. A considerable amount of the ham is demolished by our family when they return from the traditional Christmas Eve celebrations in The Purple Heather!

Ingredients

- 1 raw smoked gammon joint
- 255ml / 8fl oz cider or cola (more or less depending on the size of your joint)

Glaze:

- 4-6 tbsp English mustard (depending on the size of joint)
- 4-6 tbsp local honey or demerara sugar (depending on the size of joint)
- Cloves (optional)

Method

Weigh the gammon or ask your butcher to weigh it; for reference see cooking times below. Place the gammon into a large pot and cover with cold water. Cover with a lid and bring to the boil over a high heat. Once boiled, drain the water from the saucepan. This allows the removal of excess salt. Add the cider or cola to the pot and enough fresh cold water to cover the gammon. Cover with the lid and bring to the boil. Reduce to a low heat and simmer for 20 minutes per 450g / 1lb, topping up with water when necessary to keep the liquid level above the gammon. The ham is ready when the bone at the knuckle end sticks out and starts to feel loose. Let it rest for about 30-60 minutes in the liquid in the pot.

Preheat the oven to fan 200°C / fan 400°F / gas mark 7. Remove the ham from the pot and transfer to a board when the ham is cool enough to handle. Pat dry with kitchen paper. Use a sharp knife and take care when removing the skin, being sure to leave an even layer of fat. Score the fat in a diamond/criss-cross pattern.

To glaze, spread the mustard then the honey all over the fat. If desired, stud each diamond with a clove. Place the ham in a large roasting tin lined with a sheet of foil and bake in the oven for 20-30 minutes or until the glaze caramelises, watching it to ensure the glaze doesn't burn. It should be a golden brown. Remove from the oven and set aside to rest for 15-20 minutes before slicing to serve.

On Christmas Day, wrap the slices of ham needed in foil and warm in the oven before serving.

Maura's Christmas Turkey with all the Trimmings

We live in the countryside and are surrounded by great neighbours. We are very fortunate to have the Lehane family nearby who have supplied us with our Christmas turkey over two generations. The turkeys are always plump, delicious and are true free range. Being in the hospitality industry all my life, Christmas is a very special family time. Our home is situated on a former part of Paddy O'Brien's farm, who was our closest neighbour, and he joined our family for Christmas Day for many years, regaling us with fascinating local stories.

I had a Maeve Binchy moment one Christmas. My routine on Christmas morning is to put the turkey in the oven before we head off to Mass. We came home and there was no lovely aroma coming out to meet us. I quickly discovered the turkey was in a cold oven! We had a good laugh with our friends who join us every year after Mass for a drink. Instead of Christmas lunch we had Christmas dinner! Another year, we forgot to make the bread sauce.

The rule of thumb for cooking a turkey is 13 minutes per pound or 450g. I normally use a 16lb / 7.25kg turkey, so the standard estimated cooking time would be around 3½ hours. However, I cook the crown unstuffed and with the legs off, so it reduces the cooking time considerably.

I think everyone worries about how to fit the turkey into their oven at Christmas time! The simple solution is to remove the legs from the carcass, debone, stuff and roast them separately. This means you have the crown of the turkey on the bone which should fit into most family ovens.

The process of deboning and stuffing the legs detailed below is quite descriptive. If the words don't make visual sense, one of my daughters advises that you can watch a good quality YouTube video on deboning the legs of a turkey. This will help you to grasp where to use the knife.

A note about vegetarian dishes. I have two daughters who are vegetarian and one of the dishes I prepare ahead of time (up to 2 weeks in advance and stored in the freezer) is the Moroccan Vegetable Parcels (p104) in the shape of Christmas crackers.

To simplify and enjoy Christmas Day, have as much prepping done as possible the day before. I make larger quantities of bread and potato stuffing than are needed on Christmas Day as these can be used post-Christmas. Recipes can be multiplied or divided to suit your needs.

Ingredients

Serves 12-16

Fresh thyme bread stuffing (prepare on Christmas Eve):

- 450g / 1lb butter
- 14 shallots or 6 medium onions, finely chopped
- 4 tbsp fresh thyme leaves (or 1 tbsp dried thyme if not available)
- 1.36kg / 3lb fresh soft white breadcrumbs
- Sea salt and cracked black pepper

Potato stuffing (prepare on Christmas Eve):

For mash:

- 5kg / 11lb of floury potatoes, washed, peeled and cut into even size if they are large
- 500g / 1lb 2 oz butter
- 600-750 ml / 21-26½fl oz whole milk (amount needed will depend on absorption of the potatoes)

For stuffing:

- 120g / 4¼oz butter
- 14 shallots or 6 medium onions, finely chopped
- 3 tbsp fresh thyme leaves

Bread Sauce (can be made on Christmas Eve):

- 1 onion, peeled and halved
- 10 cloves
- 400ml / 14fl oz whole milk
- 100ml / 3½fl oz cream
- 100g / 3½oz fresh soft white breadcrumbs
- 30g / 1oz butter, softened
- Sea salt and cracked black pepper
- A pinch of grated nutmeg (optional)

Turkey:

- 7.25kg / 16lb turkey (with legs separated)
- 560g / 1¼lb butter, at room temperature, plus extra for greasing
- 4 tbsp fresh thyme bread stuffing (2 tbsp for each leg)
- 3-4 tbsp olive oil
- 12 sprigs of fresh thyme

Gravy:

- Juices from the roasting pan
- Juices from the cavity of the roasted turkey
- 100ml / 3½fl oz port
- 1 tbsp redcurrant jelly
- 285ml / ½ pint chicken stock (p370)
- Thyme sprigs, reserved from the turkey cavity
- Beurre manié (p394)
- Sea salt and cracked black pepper

Grainne's Cranberry, Orange & Port Sauce:

- 285g / 10oz fresh cranberries
- 6 tbsp water
- 5 tbsp port
- Zest and juice of 1 orange
- 170g / 6oz demerara sugar

Brussels Sprouts:

- 500g / 17½oz Brussels sprouts
- 45g / 1½oz butter
- 3 tbsp water
- Cracked black pepper

Serving suggestions:

Celeriac purée (p259) (this can be made the day before and baked in the oven to warm on Christmas Day), purple sprouting broccoli (p272)

Meat 243

Method

Grainne's Cranberry, Orange & Port Sauce:

Grainne makes this every Christmas to accompany our turkey and it is delicious. Just the right amount of acidity and sweetness. This sauce can be made 2-3 days before Christmas Day and will keep in the fridge for 5 days.

To make the cranberry sauce, place the cranberries and water in a heavy stainless steel pot and bring to the boil, then continue to simmer until the skins start to split. Add the port, zest, juice and sugar and stir until the sugar has fully dissolved. Bring back to the boil, turn down the heat and simmer for about 10 minutes until thickened. Taste it to ensure you are happy with the balance. Add more sugar or juice if needed. Let it cool and store in an airtight container or jar in the fridge.

Fresh Thyme Bread Stuffing (prepare on Christmas Eve):

Grease a very large ovenproof dish (or two medium-sized dishes) with butter. Melt the butter in a saucepan then add the shallots or onions, cover and sweat for 10-15 minutes, stirring occasionally to make sure there is no colouring. Stir in the thyme leaves. Place the breadcrumbs in a bowl and pour over the herb onion mixture. Stir together with a fork to retain lightness. Season to taste. Use some of the stuffing for the turkey legs. Place the remaining stuffing in the ovenproof dish (or two dishes – one can be used in the days after Christmas Day), gently spreading out evenly to allow the stuffing to remain light and crumbly. Do not press, as otherwise it will become dense.

On Christmas Day, bake in the oven at fan 180°C / fan 350°F / gas mark 6 for 15 minutes or until golden brown.

Potato Stuffing (prepare on Christmas Eve):

To make the mash, bring a large saucepan (or two medium saucepans) of water with a pinch of sea salt to the boil over a high heat. Add the potatoes and simmer over a medium heat for 15 minutes or until soft – check with a knife or skewer. Drain, return to the pan and dry out briefly over a low heat and mash well. Add the butter and milk and mix well to combine; add more milk depending on the absorbency of the potatoes to make a nice fluffy mash. Season to taste. Set aside some of the mash for family or guests who may not want potato stuffing.

In a small saucepan, melt the butter over a low heat, add in the shallots or onions and cover to sweat for 10-15 minutes, stirring occasionally. Stir in the thyme. Mix in the mashed potatoes and place in large ovenproof dish (or two medium-sized dishes), spreading out evenly.

On Christmas Day, bake in the oven at fan 180°C / fan 350°F / gas mark 6 for 30-40 minutes until golden on top.

Brussels Sprouts
(can be prepared on Christmas Eve):

Look for fresh organic brussels sprouts. Wash the sprouts and trim slightly at the base, removing any unsightly leaves. Thinly slice from the top to the base to minimise the cooking time. At this stage, they can be added to a ziplock bag and stored in the fridge overnight.

On Christmas Day, just at the serving time, melt the butter in a medium stainless steel wide-based saucepan. Add the water and toss in the brussels sprouts and cook over a high heat for 3-4 minutes. Season with cracked black pepper.

Bread Sauce
(can be made on Christmas Eve):

To make the bread sauce, stud each of the onion halves with the cloves, then place in a saucepan with the milk and cream. Bring to the boil, then remove from the heat and leave to infuse for 30 minutes. Stir in the breadcrumbs and butter until well combined. Return to the hob and cook for 5 minutes over a very low heat. Remove the onion and season with sea salt, cracked black pepper and nutmeg to taste. On Christmas Day, warm before serving.

Preparing the Turkey
(on Christmas Eve):

Prepare both the turkey meats (legs and crown) on Christmas Eve, ready to cook on Christmas Day. To remove the legs, place your turkey on a tray, breast side up and press out the legs away from the breast. Cut the skin at the base (between the legs and breast) and, being careful not to damage the breast skin, cut against the lower carcass. Remove the legs from the carcass, being very careful to take the pearl with you at the base of the leg. Give it an extra push out and cut the remainder sinews to remove the legs completely from the carcass.

Preparing the crown:

Next, to prepare the crown, grease a large roasting tray with 3 tbsp oil and slice 340g / ¾lb butter around the tray evenly, ensuring there is a lot of butter in the centre where the breasts will lie. Brush the turkey breasts with oil, and place the turkey crown breast side down in the tray ensuring there is plenty of slices of butter under each breast. Place 225g / ½lb butter with the sprigs of fresh thyme into the cavity of the crown. Cover with foil or loosely with a damp tea towel and place in the fridge ready for roasting on Christmas Day.

Deboning and stuffing the legs to prepare two stuffed leg sausages:

The aim is to remove the bone without going right through and damaging the outside skin of the leg. Place the legs skin side down on a board. To debone, use a pointy boning knife to cut down from the centre joint against the bone down to the knuckle without damaging the skin on the opposite side. Then cut down the other side at the drumstick part, make an incision up to the knuckle joint, and crack it. Slit the centre of the leg, from the drumstick to the knuckle. In doing that you will be cutting through to the leg bone. You then scrap the flesh outwards from the centre exposing the bone. Slide the knife in under the bone and run up against the bone towards the knuckle to separate the flesh from the bone. Do the same on the fat thigh part.

Once both sides are cut and the flesh loosened from the bone, use one hand to bring the two bones together and squeeze them together like a scissor handle closing. This enables you to loosen the flesh and skin away from that joint while keeping the skin intact.

Lay each leg flat on a sheet of clingfilm, skin side down, press them out and flatten. Place another layer of clingfilm on top over the flesh, then gently bash to flatten with a rolling pin (like you would with an escalope). Remove the clingfilm. For each leg, place a large double layer of foil on a work surface with the unglazed side up (large enough to cover over the leg with extra foil to make a sausage). Brush the foil with a very thick layer of softened butter. Place the turkey leg skin side down onto the foil. Spread out 2 tbsp bread stuffing per leg. Lift the skin on both sides of the leg towards the centre and roll the leg into a sausage, then take the foil and fold it over the sausage into a long sausage shape. Twist the foil edges on either end in opposite directions, squeezing inwards. As you twist, push one end into the other to compact the sausage. Keep the two stuffed leg sausages overnight in the fridge, ready for roasting on Christmas Day. I generally roast the stuffed leg sausages (still wrapped in the foil) for 1 hour and put them in the same time as the crown for the first hour of roasting.

Roasting the Turkey on Christmas Day:

In the morning, preheat the oven to fan 200°C / fan 400°F / gas mark 7. Place the stuffed leg sausages (still wrapped in the foil) onto the roasting tray with the crown breast side down if there is enough space. Alternatively, roast the two sausages separately in a deep baking tray with 1 tbsp oil and roast for 1 hour.

Place the roasting tray with the crown and stuffed leg sausages into the oven uncovered for one hour. Remove the legs and let them rest in the foil – they are complete. Just before serving, unwrap and slice.

Turn the oven down to fan 170°C / fan 340°F / gas mark 5, cover the crown loosely with foil and cook for another hour. After this hour, remove the foil, turn the turkey breast side up, taking care not to damage the skin when turning and turn up the oven to fan 200°C / fan 400°F / gas mark 7 again. Baste with the juices, place back into the oven and roast for 15 minutes or until you have a golden glaze on top (it depends on your oven).

Remove the crown from the tray and rest on a large platter breast side up for 30 minutes, covering with tin foil to keep warm before carving.

Gravy:

Let the juices in the roasting tray settle. Skim or spoon off all the fat. Pour all the juices from the roasting pan into a medium-sized saucepan. Pour any juices from the cavity of the crown into the saucepan and add the thyme from the cavity of the turkey. Add the redcurrant jelly and stock to the saucepan.

Deglaze the roasting pan with the port, scraping off any precious sediment attached to the pan; this is an essential step to make a good gravy. Add this into the saucepan.

Over a medium heat, bring the gravy to the boil and then reduce to a simmer for 5 minutes. To thicken the gravy, add a little of the beurre manié at a time to get your desired thickness. People vary in preference from thin to syrupy gravy consistency (I like syrupy the best). Remove the thyme and season to taste. It should be a lovely rich deep brown gravy full of flavour.

Serve the sliced ham (p241), sliced turkey, including sliced turkey leg, on each plate with gravy and a good spoonful of bread stuffing. Serve potato stuffing and vegetable sides on the table in large serving platters, with the bread sauce and cranberry sauce in side dishes.

Meat

Vegetables

Billy and Matty Clifford pictured at their farm, White Thorn, in Kenmare

Vegetables | 251

Vegetables

New Baby Carrots with Coriander	257
Carrot Purée	258
Celeriac Purée	259
Turnip Purée	260
Roast Vegetables	261
Colcannon	262
Creamed Potatoes	264
Potato Stuffing	265
Game Chips	265
Garlic & Rosemary Roast Potatoes	266
Roast Wedge Potatoes	266
Gratin of Leeks or Creamed Leeks	268
Roast Fennel	270
Braised Chicory in Orange or Sweet Wine	271
Garlic Buttered Rainbow Chard or Kale	271
Purple Sprouting Broccoli	272
Pan-Fried Courgettes with Rosemary & Garlic	272
Sugar Snaps with Fresh Mint	274
Tempura Courgettes	275
Roast Beetroot & Orange	277
Wilted Fresh Spinach	278
Buttered Cabbage with Ginger	278

Vegetables

Vegetables can be so versatile. I have always believed in quality produce. If you feel the vegetables are not good enough, then don't use them. I was so lucky when we opened The Lime Tree in the 1980s that Billy Clifford had started an organic garden at his home in Kenmare. Initially, he wasn't operating on a commercial basis. I approached him to see if he would supply me for the restaurant, he agreed, and I was blessed.

Over the years he expanded his business, now called White Thorn Farm, and has been instrumental in providing our restaurants with diverse produce. He calls to me in Shelburne Lodge weekly with a seasonal box of fruit and vegetables and it is a such a pleasure to look into the boxes. Billy is passionate about his business and his son Matty continues to be as passionate. They will not sell any produce that they are not happy with themselves, ensuring the customer gets quality. Billy is always ahead of trends in the food business and his garden reflects the time and effort he has put into it. It is a revelation. I think if he were to offer tours, people would be queueing in droves!

At Billy's there is an abundance of choice. Wonderful seasonal fruits and vegetables and beautiful flowers. White Thorn Farm now supplies many of the hotels and restaurants in Kenmare with first class quality produce.

At Shelburne Lodge, we have a very beautiful old orchard, a simple herb garden and soft fruits including lovely blackcurrants. Tom and I have been heartbroken with the blackbirds sneaking in to eat them all! They even burrowed underneath when we tried to use nets. This past year they ate the whole first crop. They weren't bothered with the second crop. We also have our own wild blackberries. I am a wild flower lover, it gives me great delight to see the wild bluebells growing under our beech trees.

This chapter includes a small variety of seasonal vegetable side options. Using seasonal vegetables is important as they will be at their best. It also helps bring variety to what one eats at different times of the year. I hope this chapter offers you some inspiration when using vegetables.

New Baby Carrots with Coriander

This is one of my favourite vegetable dishes. A match made in heaven and utterly delicious. Billy, my organic supplier, often gives me wonderful delicious new baby carrots with their feathery greens on top. Serve alongside chicken, lamb or fish.

Ingredients

Serves 3-4

- **14-18 new baby carrots**
- **Bunch of fresh coriander, roughly chopped**
- **1 tbsp butter**
- **Sea salt and cracked black pepper**

Method

Wash the carrots well, snip off the long root and trim the green tops leaving a length of about 2.5cm / 1in. Bring a large saucepan of water with a pinch of sea salt to the boil over a high heat, then turn down to a medium heat, add the carrots and blanch for 4-6 minutes or until tender. Cooking time will depend on the thickness of the carrots.

Strain them; keep the water for vegetable stock if you can. Toss in butter and season. Pop in lots of fresh coriander just before serving.

Carrot Purée

Coriander seeds when roasted and crushed are delicious with carrots. The two flavours are very compatible.

Ingredients

Serves 4-6

- 1 kg / 2lb 2oz carrots, washed, peeled and chopped
- 2 tbsp butter
- 100-140ml / 3½-5¼fl oz cream (depending on size)
- 2 tsp coriander seeds, toasted and crushed with a pestle and mortar
- Fresh coriander, to garnish
- Sea salt and cracked black pepper

Method

Bring a medium saucepan of water with a pinch of salt to the boil over a high heat. Add the carrots, bring back to the boil over a medium heat then simmer for about 10 minutes or until they are nicely soft – check with a knife. Drain and return the carrots to the saucepan and, over a medium heat, add the butter and cream and allow to heat up to a bubble (this prevents it from getting sour, especially if you're keeping it in the fridge for later). Take off the heat and purée using a hand blender. Alternatively, purée in a food processor. To finish, stir in the crushed coriander. Season to taste.

Serve with a garnish of fresh coriander.

Celeriac Purée

In the winter months, celeriac purée makes regular appearances at my family dinners. It is comforting, soothing and has a delicious taste, despite its ugliness in its natural state! It is very important to have vegetables of different textures as it is more pleasing to the palate. I would also serve with some greens.

Ingredients

Serves 4-6

- 1 head of celeriac, peeled and chopped into small pieces
- 100-140ml / 3½-5¼fl oz cream (depending on size)
- 2 tbsp butter
- Sea salt and cracked black pepper
- Parsley and toasted pine nuts, to garnish

Method

Bring a large saucepan of water with a pinch of sea salt to the boil over a high heat. Add the celeriac, bring back to the boil over a medium heat, then simmer for 10 minutes or until they are nicely soft. Drain and return the celeriac to the saucepan and, over a medium heat, add the butter and cream and allow to heat up to a bubble (this prevents it from getting sour, especially if you're keeping it in the fridge for later). Take off heat and purée using a hand blender. Alternatively, purée in a food processor. Season to taste. Garnish with parsley and toasted pine nuts.

Turnip Purée

A delightful accompaniment for roast beef, steak, beef casseroles, beef burgers or any beef dish. Not suitable for fish, chicken or lamb.

Ingredients

Serves 4

- 2 small turnips, washed, peeled and chopped into small even pieces
- 2 tbsp butter
- 100-140ml / 3½-5¼fl oz cream (depending on size)
- ¼ tsp freshly grated nutmeg optional)
- Sea salt and cracked black pepper
- Brown sugar, if needed

Method

Bring a small saucepan of water with a pinch of sea salt to the boil over a high heat. Add the turnips, bring back to the boil over a medium heat then simmer for 10 minutes or until very soft. Drain and return the turnip to the saucepan and, over a medium heat, add the butter and cream and allow to heat up to a bubble (this prevents it from getting sour, especially if you're keeping it in the fridge for later). Take off heat and purée using a handheld blender. Alternatively, purée in a food processor. Grate over a few grinds of nutmeg (optional). Season to taste. Add a pinch of brown sugar, if needed, which works well with the turnip.

Roast Vegetables

Roasting vegetables in this way enhances the natural sweetness of the vegetables with very few nutrients being lost – great in autumn and winter. They are very versatile and will go with a lot of foods. This is a seasonal autumnal version. Celeriac works so well in a combination like this. Red peppers are also delicious, but they are best sweated a little before adding to the roasting dish. In my experience, one needs to be cautious of adding red pepper to your roast particularly if you are hosting a dinner party as a lot of people have an intolerance to peppers. However, they do work wonderfully in summer time, particularly roasted on their own as I do for my roast red pepper soup (p86).

Ingredients

Serves 4

- 100g / 3½oz butter
- 2 tsp olive oil
- 500g / 1lb 2oz carrots, peeled and cut into batons
- 500g / 1lb 2oz parsnips, peeled and cut into batons
- 6 banana shallots, halved and peeled, or 3 medium red onions, peeled and quartered
- Bunch of fresh thyme
- 2 tbsp farm pressed apple juice or water
- Sea salt and cracked black pepper

Method

Preheat the oven to fan 180°C / fan 350°F / gas mark 6.

Add the butter and oil to a roasting tray and heat in the oven for a few minutes. Take out and arrange the vegetables, shallots and thyme on the tray, tossing to coat them in the butter and oil. Pour in the apple juice/water and cover with foil. Steam in the oven for 10 minutes to soften initially, then remove the foil, move the vegetables around and season. Roast in the oven for a further 8-10 minutes or until caramelised to your liking.

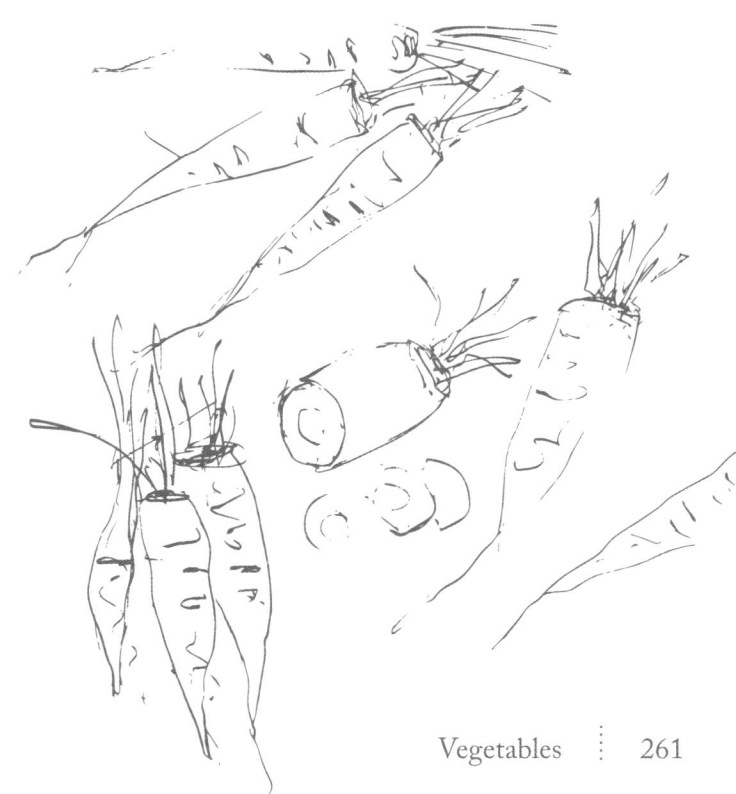

Vegetables

Colcannon

This is a traditional Irish potato dish with no exact recipe. Each area and household tends to have their own version hence there are numerous variations. I started using it as a side dish in The Lime Tree in the 1980s. If I didn't have it on, regulars were disappointed, so it very quickly became a permanent side dish and just had to be on the menu. It's a very balanced healthy dish and the potatoes are the key magic ingredient. The potatoes must be floury fluffy varieties and not waxy or soapy. Colcannon is versatile and a great side dish. Here is my version.

Ingredients

Serves 4-6

- 1kg / 2lb 4oz floury potatoes (e.g. Golden Wonder or Kerr's Pink), washed, peeled and cut into small even chunks
- 100g / 3½oz butter
- 2 medium onions, diced
- ½ head (around 450g / 1lb) seasonal cabbage (Savoy is best), washed and finely chopped
- 255ml / 9fl oz whole milk, plus extra if necessary (absorbency varies with the potatoes)
- Sea salt and cracked black pepper

Method

Bring a medium saucepan of water with a pinch of sea salt to the boil over a high heat. Add the potatoes and simmer over a medium heat for 15 minutes or until soft – check with a knife or skewer. Drain, then return to the pan to dry out briefly over a low heat and mash well. This is an important step; drying out the potatoes to get rid of excess water will result in a brilliant mash.

In a saucepan, melt the butter over a low heat, then add the onions, cover and sweat for 10-15 minutes, stirring occasionally and ensuring they do not colour.

Bring a medium saucepan of water with a pinch of sea salt to the boil. Add the cabbage and blanch for 3-4 minutes, strain, then refresh in a bowl of ice-cold water, allowing to cool completely before draining again. Squeeze out all the excess moisture from the cabbage.

Warm the milk in a saucepan over a medium heat, stirring while bringing to the boil. Mix the sweated onions into the mashed potato followed by the warm milk, stirring to combine. Lastly, add the cabbage. Mix and season to taste.

Creamed Potatoes

In Ireland, traditionally we don't do the creamed potato purée that they do in France. People love Irish mashed potatoes and it is a staple in Irish family homes. It is a less rich version and generally one mashes the potatoes without lumps and adds plenty of butter and milk or cream, seasoned with black pepper and sea salt. The potatoes should be very dry after boiling them – they need to be strained very well. If they are moist, then a good tip is to keep them on the heat for a few minutes, shaking them to ensure they don't brown or burn.

Ingredients

Serves 4-6

- 1kg / 2lb 4oz floury potatoes, washed, peeled and cut into even size if they are large
- 100g / 3½oz butter
- 150ml / 3½fl oz milk, plus extra if necessary (absorbency varies with the potatoes)
- Sea salt and cracked black pepper

Method

Bring a large saucepan of water with a pinch of sea salt to the boil over a high heat. Add the potatoes and simmer over a medium heat for 15 minutes or until soft – check with a knife or skewer. Drain, return to the pan and dry out briefly over a low heat and mash well. Add the butter and milk and mix well to combine, adding more milk depending on the consistency you like. Season to taste.

Potato Stuffing

My favourite is Irish potato stuffing, a variation of mashed potato where sweated onions, fresh thyme and milk are added to the creamed potatoes and baked with more nuts of butter on top. It is traditional at Christmas with roast turkey or goose.

Ingredients

Serves 6-8

- 120g / 4¼oz butter
- 12 shallots or 6-8 medium onions, finely chopped
- 4 tbsp thyme leaves
- 5kg / 11lb potatoes to make creamed potatoes (opposite)
- 50g / 1¾oz butter for scattering on top prior to baking

Method

Preheat the oven to fan 180°C / fan 350°F / gas mark 6.

Make the creamed potatoes following the method opposite. In a small saucepan, melt the butter over a low heat, add in the shallots or onions and cover to sweat for 10-15 minutes, stirring occasionally. Stir in the thyme. Mix in the creamed potatoes and place evenly in a good size Pyrex dish greased with butter. Add a few extra nuts of butter scattered on top. Bake in the oven for 30-40 minutes or until golden on top.

Game Chips

These are simple but delicious. They are traditionally served with roast wild game and with bread sauce on the side to give a contrast of textures.

Ingredients

Serves 4-6

- 4 medium potatoes, peeled and sliced raw with a mandolin
- Few grinds of sea salt
- Small deep fat fryer

Method

Preheat the deep fat fryer.

Dry the sliced potatoes well with kitchen paper. Batch fry in the deep fat fryer until golden. Do not overcrowd. Lift up the basket, let the fat drip a little and toss onto kitchen paper. Sprinkle with sea salt to keep them crisp.

Garlic & Rosemary Roast Potatoes

I love to use floury potatoes for roasting, they generally get a lovely crisp outer crust. I use olive oil and butter of course, and I always parboil them first as it thickens the crust even more by absorbing the fat. Personally, I don't use goose fat but only as I have a few vegetarians in my family. In summer, the Kerr's Pink potato variety works well and in autumn Golden Wonders. Every autumn I particularly look forward to the Golden Wonders when a good friend of ours kindly brings us a few big bags from their farm in West Cork. To me, roast potatoes are a great accompaniment to any roast and my favourite is with rosemary and garlic. The garlic and rosemary works well with lamb and chicken. The rosemary can be replaced with thyme and red onions or shallots added to the tray to accompany beef.

Roast Wedge Potatoes:
To make these, use the same method as opposite, cutting the potatoes into wedges instead and omitting the garlic and rosemary.

Ingredients

Serves 4-6

- 1kg / 2lb 4oz floury potatoes washed, peeled and cut into even size if they are large
- 100ml / 3½fl oz olive oil
- 100g / 3½oz butter, chopped
- 1 tbsp rosemary leaves, snipped
- Full head of garlic, cloves separated and skins on
- 1140ml / 2 pints water
- Sea salt and cracked black pepper

Method

Preheat the oven to fan 200°C / fan 400°F / gas mark 7.

Bring a large saucepan of water with a pinch of sea salt to the boil over a high heat. Add the potatoes to the saucepan and parboil over a medium heat for about 3-4 minutes, depending on the size. Drain and allow to steam dry for a few minutes. Place the oil, butter and snipped rosemary leaves in a large roasting tray and heat in the oven for a few minutes to melt the butter, being careful not to burn the butter. Take the tray out of the oven and add the potatoes, spreading them out and coating them well in the fat. Roast in the oven for 25-35 minutes or until crispy and golden, continuing to turn the potatoes to coat them in the fat a few times during the roast. Add the garlic halfway through roasting the potatoes.

Gratin of Leeks or Creamed Leeks

This gratin is just delicious! During the winter I make this regularly for family dinners. The first part of the recipe makes creamed leeks, a great accompaniment on its own with fish, chicken, lamb or roast beef. These creamed leeks can then be used to make a gratin with the simple addition of buttered crumbs on top, which is then baked to become crisp. If you want to make the dish even richer, add 40g / 1½oz of freshly grated Parmigiano Reggiano to both the cream and breadcrumbs.

Ingredients

Serves 4-6

- 6 medium leeks, topped and tailed, peeled and cut diagonally 1.5cm / ½in thick, washed to remove any sand or grit
- 200ml / 7fl oz cream
- 55g / 2oz butter
- 150g / 5¼oz fresh soft white breadcrumbs

Method

Creamed Leeks:

Bring a medium saucepan of water with a pinch of sea salt to the boil over a high heat. Add the leeks and blanch for 3-4 minutes. Drain the leeks, pressing to remove excess water. In a small saucepan, bring the cream to a boil, stirring continuously, then stir in the leeks with 15g / ½oz of the butter. Season to taste. The creamed leeks can be served as they are or can be made into the gratin.

Gratin of Leeks:

To make the gratin, preheat the oven to fan 180°C / fan 350°F / gas mark 6. In a small saucepan, melt the remaining butter and pour over the breadcrumbs, using a fork to mix together to retain the lightness. Spread the creamed leeks into the gratin dish or deep oven tray and sprinkle over the breadcrumbs. Bake in the oven for 15 minutes or until golden brown on top.

Vegetables : 269

Roast Fennel

A great accompaniment to many fish dishes including the turbot with basil and orange sauce (p181). Ensure you cut out the hard core in the centre of the fennel.

Ingredients

Serves 4

- 2 fennel bulbs, washed, trimmed and cut in half (quarter them if they are large)
- 2 tbsp olive oil
- Knob of soft butter, for brushing
- Sea salt and cracked black pepper

Method

Preheat the oven to fan 180°C / fan 350°F / gas mark 6.

Lay the fennel out on a roasting tray, drizzle over the olive oil with a few tbsp of water and season. Cover with foil and steam in the oven for 15 minutes. Remove the foil and brush the fennel with butter. Roast for another 15 minutes or until browned and tender.

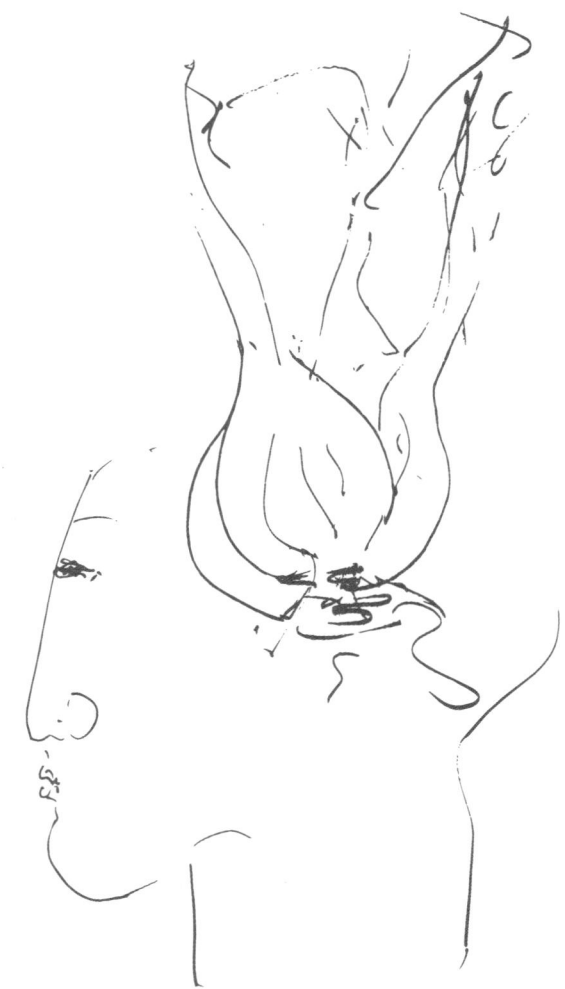

Braised Chicory in Orange or Sweet Wine

The orange juice can also be replaced with 6 tbsp of a sweet dessert wine for a more decadent option. It goes perfectly with roast duck or lamb.

Ingredients

Serves 3-6

- 3 heads of chicory, halved lengthways
- 2 tbsp butter, softened
- Zest and juice of 2 large oranges
- Sea salt

Method

Preheat the oven to fan 190°C / fan 375°F / gas mark 6. Use 1 tbsp of the butter to grease the base of a deep oven dish or roasting tray. Place the chicory in the dish cut side up, grate over the zest and pour over the juice. Season and cover with foil. Bake in the oven for 15 minutes, then remove the foil, add the remaining butter and roast for 10 minutes or until softened and slightly golden.

If accompanying with roast duck or lamb with a jus, you can add any cooking juices from the chicory to the meat jus to add extra flavour.

Garlic Buttered Rainbow Chard or Kale

While I find the stems of chard too strong for my liking and remove them in this recipe, if you do end up keeping the stalks or wanting to avoid waste, a great Dutch friend of mine would chop them and use them in a cheese sauce or as a part of a gratin with a cheese and butter crumb. Kale will work equally well in this recipe with ginger instead of the garlic.

Ingredients

Serves 4

- 500g / 1lb 2oz rainbow chard or kale, washed and stems removed
- 2 tbsp butter
- 1 garlic clove, finely chopped
- Lemon juice, to taste
- Cracked black pepper

Method

Bring a large saucepan of water with a pinch of sea salt to the boil over a high heat. Add the chard, blanch for 3-4 minutes then drain and press to remove excess water. In a large saucepan, melt the butter over a low heat, add the garlic and stir to infuse the butter. Add the chard and toss well to coat with butter and to warm the chard.

Season to taste.

Purple Sprouting Broccoli

My favourite vegetable, especially with hollandaise (p342).

Ingredients

Serves 4

- 500g / 1lb 2oz organic purple sprouting broccoli
- 2 tbsp butter or hollandaise (p342)
- Cracked black pepper

Method

If the broccoli has a thick stem, split the stem lengthways to allow even cooking. Bring a medium saucepan of water with a pinch of salt to the boil over a high heat. Add the broccoli to the water and blanch for 3-4 minutes or until tender. Drain immediately and refresh in ice-cold water.

Melt the butter in a frying pan over a low heat, toss in the broccoli, season and serve. Alternatively, serve the broccoli with hollandaise spooned on top.

Pan-Fried Courgettes with Rosemary & Garlic

This is a great fast summer side. Lovely with tomato sauce and pesto.

Ingredients

Serves 4

- 4-6 small courgettes, washed and cut at an angle, around ½cm / ¼in thick
- 2 tbsp butter or olive oil
- 1 garlic clove, peeled and finely chopped
- ½ tsp fresh rosemary leaves
- Sea salt and cracked black pepper

Method

Melt the butter in a large frying pan or wok over a medium heat. Increase the heat to high and add the courgettes, then sprinkle over the garlic and rosemary, tossing a few times to cook quickly. Season with a little sea salt and cracked black pepper.

Sugar Snaps with Fresh Mint

A delicious summer vegetable side with lamb, chicken or fish and super in a stir fry.

Ingredients

Serves 4

- **400g / 14oz sugar snaps, washed and trimmed**
- **1 tbsp butter**
- **2 tbsp fresh mint leaves, chopped**
- **Sea salt and cracked black pepper**

Method

Bring a medium saucepan of water with a pinch of sea salt to the boil over a high heat. Add the sugar snaps and blanch over a medium heat for 2-3 minutes or until tender but crisp. Drain immediately and refresh in ice-cold water.

Melt the butter in a small pan over a low heat and toss in the sugar snaps. Season and serve with fresh mint.

Alternatively, the sugar snaps can be stir-fried in butter over a high heat for 1-2 minutes. They add great texture and crunch to a stir fry.

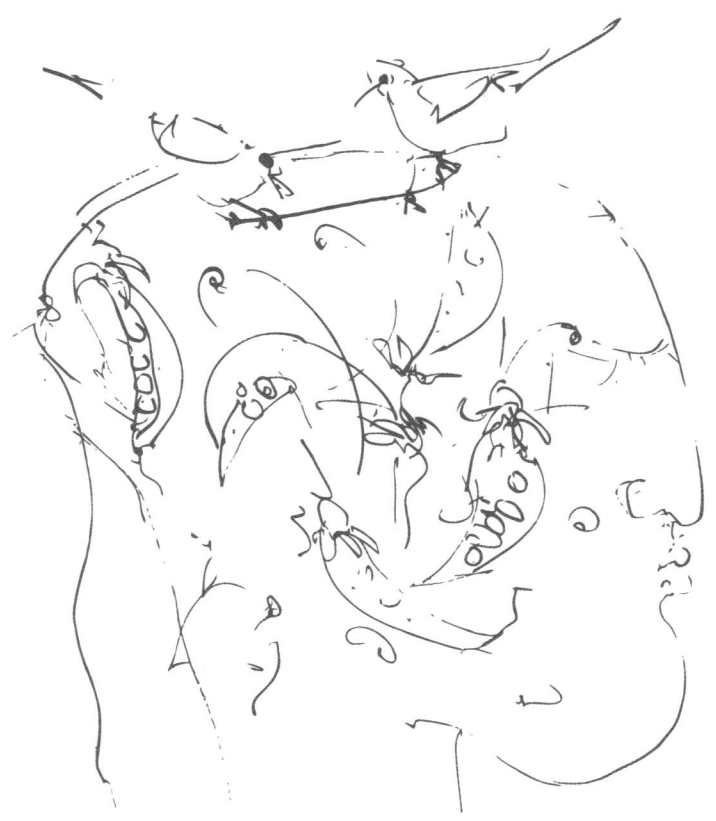

Tempura Courgettes

The batter here can be used to tempura many vegetables such as aubergines, lightly blanched cauliflower or broccoli. It is important that the vegetables are dry and to fry in small batches to ensure a light and crisp result. Tempura bananas are super and can be made with this same batter – lovely with pan-fried chicken or with ice-cream.

Ingredients

Serves 6-8

- 4-6 courgettes, cut into batons, around 5cm / 2in long, dried on kitchen paper

Tempura:

- 1 litre / 35fl oz vegetable oil, for frying, or a small deep fat fryer
- 240g / 8½oz plain white flour
- 2 egg yolks
- 285ml / ½ pint ice-cold water
- Pinch of sea salt

Serving suggestions:

Thai dipping sauce (p358)

Method

If you own a deep fat fryer, preheat to 175-180°C / 345-355°F. Alternatively, heat a deep heavy saucepan filled with around 1 litre of oil over a high heat, also bringing to 175-180°C / 345-355°F.

In a bowl, add the flour followed by the yolks, water and salt and whisk to combine until smooth. Dip the courgettes into the batter, shaking off a little of the excess, then quickly drop into the fryer or pan, being careful of the hot oil. Cook the courgettes in batches, being sure to bring the oil back up to temperature if using the pan and removing small pieces of the tempura batter.

Place the cooked courgettes on kitchen paper to drain off any excess oil.

Roast Beetroot & Orange

Roasting completely transforms beetroots, turning them rich, sweet and intensely ruby in colour. I mostly roast beetroot sealed in foil with thyme and olive oil; the skins peel off easily once cooked. Beetroot is wonderful with goat's cheese or chicken or it can be added to roast vegetables or used in any salad with nuts for added texture. Apples work beautifully with beetroot and a honey mustard dressing. Crumbled blue cheese also works well.

Another alternative is to pickle the beetroot after roasting; the instructions for this are below.

Ingredients

Serves 4-6

- 4 beetroot, around 500g / 1lb 2oz
- 3 tbsp olive oil
- Few sprigs of thyme
- 1 tbsp butter
- 1 orange, peeled and segmented
- Sea salt and cracked black pepper

Method

Preheat the oven to fan 160°C / fan 325°F / gas mark 4.

Trim just the beetroot stems, leaving around 2.5cm / 1in, and leave the root. Place all the beetroot on a large sheet of foil, drizzle over the olive oil and arrange the thyme sprigs on top. Wrap the foil around each beetroot, pressing to seal. Place on an oven tray and roast in the oven for 1½ hours or until the beetroots are tender and the skin peels off easily. Once cool enough to handle, peel and cut the beetroot into wedges.

In a saucepan, melt the butter and add the beetroot and orange segments (and any residual juice), mixing together over a low heat. Season to taste.

To Pickle (optional)

Add the chopped cooked beetroots to a large sterilised jar. In a small saucepan, bring 570ml / 1 pint of apple cider vinegar to the boil over a high heat, then add 4 tbsp of good quality honey and set aside to cool. Pour this liquid over the beetroot and seal with a lid. The pickle can keep in the fridge for up to 1 month.

Wilted Fresh Spinach

Good quality spinach is important; source well. It works well in savoury pastries, tarts and as a perfect accompaniment to fish, especially if there is a sauce.

Ingredients

Serves 4

- 500g / 1lb 2 oz organic spinach leaves
- 2 tbsp butter
- 2 tbsp water
- A little freshly grated nutmeg (optional)
- Sea salt and cracked black pepper

Method

Wash the spinach well, shaking off any excess water.

In a large saucepan, melt the butter over a medium heat, add the spinach to the pan and continue to stir while the spinach wilts.

Season to taste and grate over the nutmeg (optional).

Buttered Cabbage with Ginger

This is a perfect side for curries or spicy dishes. It is also brilliant with fish, duck and chicken. If you prefer, the cabbage can be swapped for kale. Buttered cabbage without the ginger is wonderful with roast beef or ham.

Ingredients

Serves 4

- 500g / 1lb 2oz any cabbage, washed and finely sliced
- 1 tbsp fresh ginger, peeled and finely chopped
- 2 tbsp butter
- Sea salt and cracked black pepper

Method

Bring a saucepan of water with a pinch of sea salt to the boil over a high heat. Blanch the cabbage for 2-3 minutes or until tender. Drain and refresh in ice-cold water. Press to remove excess water.

Melt the butter in a deep frying pan over a medium heat, add the ginger and cook for a few minutes to infuse the butter. Add the cabbage, toss well to coat with butter and to warm the cabbage. Season to taste.

Desserts & Baking

Desserts & Baking

Chocolate Cake   288
Chocolate Pots   289
Bitter Chocolate Praline Tart   290
Chocolate Coffee Meringue Gateau with Chocolate Ganache   294
Chocolate Marquise with Crème Anglaise and Brandied Kumquats   296
Porter Cake   300
Date, Orange & Sunflower Seed Loaf   301
Coffee & Walnut Cake   302
Delicious Gateau with Coffee Bean Sauce   304
Génoise Sponge Cake with Red Berries & Grand Marnier   305
Victoria Sandwich   306
Tunisian Orange Cake   308
Sticky Toffee Pudding   310
Irish Barmbrack & Butter Pudding   312
Spicy Apple Rum Pudding   313
Creamy Caramelised Apple Tart   314
Rum & Walnut Tart with Rum Butterscotch Sauce   316
Iced Coffee Parfait   318
Homemade Vanilla Ice-Cream   320
Vanilla & Praline Ice-Cream   321
Zabaglione Ice-Cream with a Rum Caramel Syrup   322
Tuilles   323
Thos' Lemon Posset with Shortbread   324
John Desmond's Island Cottage White Chocolate Mousse   328
Grainne's Christmas Pudding with Brandy Butter   330
Grainne's Wholemeal Shortbread Biscuits   332
Grainne's Oatmeal Biscuits   333

Desserts & Baking

Many people look forward to desserts when dining out and there is nothing more satisfying than a delicious treat to complete a meal.

My grandmother Nonie started to sell homemade ice-cream from her grocery store in 1929, which was hand churned in a vat using blocks of ice delivered by train. Today, of course, methods and flavours have evolved. A few years ago, Paul Flynn and his wife Máire, of the wonderful restaurant The Tannery, hosted Stephen Harris of The Sportsman for the West Waterford Food Festival. Stephen is one of my current food heroes along with Tom Kerridge – I was very excited. My husband Tom and I attended the very special dinner 'The Sportsman at the Tannery' and the best part was the superb dessert of cream cheese ice-cream, pear and gingerbread crumb – so simply described yet delectable. (The previous year, when the festival celebrated pioneering women in food, it was a great honour to be invited as a guest speaker. I was a guest of Eunice Power's and I had the pleasure of dining with other guests of the festival at Paul and Máire's restaurant.)

There is a recipe for vanilla and praline ice-cream (p321) and also a more indulgent zabaglione ice-cream (p322) included in this chapter. These are more classical in comparison to Stephen's version of a modern twist on ice-cream.

Naturally, my love of food started with pastries and making delicious cakes, which enabled me to start a life in food. In this chapter I have included a variety of recipes for cakes and desserts, some from my early days in baking and others from my restaurants.

Agnes O'Connell's recipe notes and my grandmother Nonie's ice-cream expenses

Chocolate Cake

This is a rich cake with a chocolate fudge filling and icing and a chocolate ganache. For sheer decadence, you can add, Bailey's, Cointreau or Grand Marnier.

Ingredients

Serves 6-8

Cake:

- 340g / ¾lb dark chocolate, at least 70%, broken into pieces
- 170g / 6oz ground almonds
- 85g / 3oz self-raising flour, sieved
- 5 eggs, separated
- 225g / ½lb butter
- 100g / 3½oz caster sugar

Chocolate Fudge Icing:

- 140ml / ¼ pint milk
- 170g / 6oz butter
- 55g / 2oz dark cocoa powder (e.g. Green & Black's)
- 500g / 1lb 2oz icing sugar, sieved
- 3 tbsp Bailey's, Cointreau or Grand Marnier, (if desired)

Chocolate Ganache:

- 75ml / 2½fl oz cream
- 55g / 2oz dark chocolate, at least 70%, broken into pieces
- 35g / 1½oz butter, softened
- 2 tbsp Bailey's, Cointreau or Grand Marnier, (if desired)

Equipment:

- 20cm / 8in round cake tin

Method

Preheat the oven to fan 160°C / fan 325°F / gas mark 4. Grease and line a 20cm / 8in springform cake tin.

Add the chocolate and butter to a heatproof bowl and melt over a saucepan of hot water (not simmering), with the base not touching the water. Once the chocolate has melted, mix and set aside to cool.

Combine the ground almonds and sieved flour. In a large bowl, use an electric mixer to beat together the egg yolks and sugar until pale and fluffy. Stir in the cooled chocolate mixture. Carefully fold in the ground almonds and flour.

In a separate bowl, use an electric mixer (ensuring the whisks are clean and dry) to beat the egg whites until stiff. Mix in one spoon of the egg white to loosen the chocolate mixture, then gently fold in the remaining egg white. Do not overmix as this will toughen the cake.

Add the mixture to the tin with a slight hollow in the centre. Bake in the oven for 45-50 minutes until the cake remains moist but baked. Do not overbake. Remove paper and allow to cool completely.

To make the fudge icing, place the milk and butter in a pan over a medium heat and stir. Add the cocoa powder and mix. Allow to cool. Sieve the icing sugar into a large bowl, add the chocolate mixture and beat well using an electric mixer. Mix in the liqueur of your choice if desired.

To make the chocolate ganache, place the cream in a pan and bring to the boil over a medium heat while stirring. Remove from heat, add the chocolate and butter and stir until the chocolate has melted and the ganache has thickened. When it has cooled a little, mix in the liqueur. Allow to cool. Once cool, split the cake then fill and cover with the icing. Pour over the cooled ganache; allow to set.

Chocolate Pots

In the early 1980s, there was a wonderful restaurant called Alastair Little's on Frith Street and for years it was our go-to place when in London along with Andrew Edmunds, also in Soho. Next stop was Ronnie Scott's for jazz which was nearby. Alastair kindly gave me his recipe which I have since adapted and served at The Lime Tree from 1985, then later at Packie's. These are almost foolproof to make and produce a lovely silky texture. It was another customer favourite.

These can be made in advance and stored in the fridge and then warmed in a preheated oven at fan 160°C / fan 325°F / gas mark 4 for about 4-5 minutes.

Ingredients

Makes 6

- 140ml / ¼ pint cream
- 110ml / 3¾fl oz whole milk
- 225g / 8oz dark chocolate, at least 70%, broken into chunks
- 2 egg yolks
- 45g / 1½oz caster sugar
- Pouring cream, to serve

Equipment:

- 6 ramekins

Method

Preheat the oven to fan 150°C / fan 300°F / gas mark 3.

In a saucepan, heat the cream and milk to boiling point, stirring continuously to avoid sticking and burning. Remove from the heat and mix in the chocolate.

In a separate bowl, beat together the egg yolks and sugar until pale and fluffy. Fold in the chocolate mixture, ensuring it is well combined.

Pour into 6 ramekins and place in a deep oven tray. Pour enough boiling water into the tray to come halfway up the ramekins to create a bain marie. Bake in the oven for 25-30 minutes until slightly risen.

Serve warm with pouring cream on the side.

Bitter Chocolate Praline Tart

The combination of caramelised nuts and chocolate, for me, is a marriage made in heaven. This is an immensely rich tart. I make the praline with toasted hazelnuts (not almonds) – a personal favourite.

For best results, make the pastry the day before. It is delicious served with plain vanilla ice-cream (p320). It can also be used to make praline ice-cream (p321).

Ingredients

Serves 10-12

Hazelnut Praline:

- Butter, to grease
- 120g / 4½oz caster sugar
- 40ml / 1½fl oz water
- ½ tsp lemon juice
- 85g / 3oz hazelnuts, toasted, skinned and roughly chopped

Pastry:

- 250g / 9oz plain white flour, sieved, plus extra
- 50g / 1¾oz icing sugar
- Pinch of sea salt
- 130g / 4½oz butter, softened
- 1 whole egg
- 2 yolks

Chocolate Filling:

- 360ml / 12½fl oz cream
- 140ml / ¼ pint whole milk
- Zest of 1 orange
- 400g / 14oz dark chocolate (e.g. Valrhona or similar), at least 70%, broken into small pieces
- Pinch of sea salt
- 6 egg yolks, lightly beaten
- 170g/ 6oz coarse praline

Equipment:

- 25cm / 10in tart tin with removable base
- Ceramic baking beans or dried pulses

Serving suggestion:

Vanilla ice-cream (p320) or cold whipped cream

Method

To make the praline, lightly grease a baking tray with butter. In a medium saucepan, combine the sugar, water and lemon juice. Over a medium-high heat, continuously stir until the sugar has dissolved and the liquid is clear. Stop stirring, turn the heat to high and bring the syrup to a boil, not stirring or the sugar will crystallise. Cook until the syrup turns a deep golden caramel, being very careful as the sugar can burn very quickly. Remove immediately from the heat, add the nuts and shake the pot to coat the nuts. Immediately pour the caramel and nuts onto the greased tray and allow to cool completely.

Once cooled, break up the praline by placing the praline between two sheets of non-stick baking paper and bashing it with a wooden rolling pin to a coarse crumb, or pulse in a food processor to a coarse crumb. If storing, keep in an airtight container in a dry place; the praline will keep for 1 month.

To make the pastry, put the flour, icing sugar, salt and butter into a food processor. Pulse to a breadcrumb-like texture. Lightly beat together the egg and yolks with a fork, then add to the food processor, pulsing again until the mixture starts to form a dough – be careful not to overwork it. The minute it comes together, stop pulsing. Wrap in clingfilm and chill for 1 hour in the fridge or preferably overnight.

Preheat the oven to fan 200°C / fan 400°F / gas mark 7. On a lightly floured surface, roll out the pastry to 3mm / 0.1in thick and gently lift and line a 25cm / 10in tart tin, pricking the base with a fork. Chill for at least 30 minutes in the fridge. Cover the pastry with baking paper, fill with ceramic baking beans or dried pulses and blind bake for 15 minutes. Remove the baking paper and beans or pulses. Reduce the oven heat to fan 150°C / fan 300°F / gas mark 3. Place the tart case back into the oven and bake for a further 10-15 minutes or until golden brown all over. Allow to cool. Reduce the oven to fan 130°C / fan 265°F / gas mark 2.

To make the chocolate filling, place the cream and milk in a saucepan and bring to a simmer over a medium heat, stirring frequently. As it just starts to simmer, remove the pan from the heat and add the orange zest, chocolate and sea salt. Let it sit for 1 minute, then gently stir until a smooth consistency. Mix the egg yolks with a fork and gently mix into the chocolate mixture, followed by the praline. Pour the chocolate filling into the tart case. Bake in the oven for 40-50 minutes or until the chocolate custard filling still has a slight wobble in the centre.

Allow to set for 30 minutes.

Serve the tart warm with a scoop of vanilla ice-cream or cold whipped cream.

Hazelnut praline (p290) with chocolate

Desserts & Baking 293

Chocolate Coffee Meringue Gateau with Chocolate Ganache

This three-layered gateau covered in a chocolate ganache makes a special and decadent dessert. It is adapted from a recipe I learnt during my stage at the Horn of Plenty in the 1980s, a restaurant that was owned and run by Sonia Stevenson who was the first British woman to win a Michelin star in 1974. For meringues, eggs must be at room temperature for the right consistency.

Ingredients

Serves 12-14

Meringues:

- 140g / 5oz caster sugar
- 140g / 5oz icing sugar
- 5 egg whites, at room temperature
- Pinch of sea salt

Filling:

- 3 tbsp extra strong espresso coffee
- 130g / 4½oz dark chocolate, chopped
- 1½ tbsp water
- 340g / 12oz butter

Chocolate Ganache:

- 300ml / 10fl oz cream
- 240g / 3½oz dark chocolate, 70%, broken into pieces
- 130g / 4½oz butter, softened

Equipment:

- 2 large baking trays

Serving suggestion:

Serve at room temperature with whipped cream

Method

Preheat the oven to fan 110°C / 230°F / gas mark ½.

Line two large baking trays with baking parchment, and on each draw three 10x25cm / 4x10in rectangles for a total of three rectangles. Sieve together the caster and icing sugars into a bowl. Add the egg whites to another clean dry bowl (this is essential for successful meringues) and beat with an electric mixer until foamy. With the mixer on, gradually sprinkle in all the sugar until the mixture forms stiff peaks. Use half of the meringue to evenly fill in the outlined rectangles to around 1cm / ½in thick, and reserve the other half to use for the filling. Bake in the oven for 4 hours or until dry and crisp.

To make the filling, bring a saucepan of water to a simmer and in a bowl that fits snugly on top of the saucepan (but doesn't touch the water), add the coffee, chocolate and water. Mix thoroughly over a gentle heat until melted and smooth, then set aside to cool. In another bowl, beat the butter until light and creamy, add the cooled chocolate mixture and beat well. Lastly, add the reserved meringue mixture and beat together to combine.

To make the ganache, add the cream to a medium saucepan and bring to the boil over a medium heat while stirring. Remove from the heat, add the chocolate and butter then whisk until the chocolate has melted and the ganache has thickened.

To assemble the gateau, spread an even layer of the filling onto a layer of meringue, then press another meringue on top and repeat once more to create a three-layer gateau. Cover all the sides with the ganache and set in the fridge for 1 hour. Serve at room temperature with whipped cream.

Chocolate Marquise with Crème Anglaise and Brandied Kumquats

Customers travelled to The Lime Tree especially for this dessert, which is extremely indulgent. It's a classic French chocolate dessert recipe adapted from Michel Guérard's cookbook *Cuisine Gourmande*, one of my much loved books for inspiration.

Ingredients

Serves 10-12

Marquise:

- 150g / 5¼oz dark chocolate, 70%, broken into pieces
- 7 egg yolks
- 255g / 9oz caster sugar
- 300g / 10½oz butter, softened
- 170g / 6oz dark cocoa powder
- 500ml / 18fl oz cream
- 55g / 2oz icing sugar
- 14-16 sponge finger biscuits (e.g. Boudoir or Savoiardi)
- 250ml / 9fl oz cold strong black coffee or orange flavoured syrup (p365)
- Fresh mint leaves, to decorate
- Brandied kumquats or orange segments, to serve

Brandied kumquats:

- 140g / 5oz fresh kumquats, halved and deseeded
- 150ml / 5¼fl oz cold water
- 255ml / 9fl oz sugar syrup (p365)
- 55-100ml / 2-3½fl oz brandy

Equipment:

900g / 2lb loaf tin

Serving suggestion:

If using coffee, serve with coffee bean sauce (p368); if using orange syrup, serve with orange crème anglaise (p367)

Method

Grease and line a 900g / 2lb loaf tin with clingfilm. Bring a saucepan of water to a simmer and in a bowl that fits snugly on top of the saucepan (but doesn't touch the water), add the chocolate and stir occasionally to melt, then set aside to cool. In another bowl, beat the egg yolks and caster sugar until light and fluffy. Pour the cooled chocolate into the eggs and sugar and fold to combine well. In another bowl, beat the softened butter until light and creamy, then gradually add the cocoa powder and whisk to a creamy consistency. Add the cocoa butter to the egg yolk mixture and combine the two together well.

To make Chantilly cream, pour the cream and icing sugar into a bowl, use a balloon whisk or electric hand mixer and whip the cream and sugar until slightly thick and fluffy. Combine the cream and the chocolate mixture quickly and gently fold together with a whisk. The mixture will collapse slightly, but the blending is important.

Brush the sponge fingers generously with cold coffee or the orange syrup, depending on which you have chosen.

Two options for layering:

1. Line the sponge fingers at the base. Spread over half the chocolate mixture, then line another layer of biscuits and cover with the remaining chocolate.

2. Line the sponge fingers at the base. Put in all the chocolate mix and finish with a top layer of sponge fingers.

Once layered, cover with clingfilm. Chill in the fridge for 3 hours or preferably overnight.

To serve, turn the marquise out onto a serving plate and decorate with fresh mint leaves. If using coffee, serve the marquise with coffee bean sauce (p368). Alternatively, if using orange-flavoured syrup, finish with a side of orange crème anglaise (p367). Serve with brandied kumquats (recipe below) or orange segments. Will keep for up to 1 week in the fridge.

Brandied Kumquats:

In a small saucepan, add the kumquats and water. Bring to a boil, then simmer for 10 minutes until the kumquats are soft but still hold their shape. Strain the kumquats, put them back into the pan, then add the sugar syrup to the kumquats and simmer gently for another 15 minutes. Lastly, add the brandy as desired and simmer for a further 1 minute.

Serve with the chocolate marquise. Store in a sealed jar for up to 1-2 months.

298 | Desserts & Baking

Chocolate marquise with crème anglaise and brandied kumquats (p296)

Porter Cake

This a great traditional Irish cake and it is lovely served with butter. It should be a moist cake; if it is dry then it is overbaked.

Ingredients

Serves 8-10

- 140g / 5oz sultanas
- 140g / 5oz raisins
- 90g / 3¼oz currants
- 45g / 1½oz peel
- 85g / 3oz walnuts, chopped
- ¼ tsp ground ginger
- ¼ tsp ground cinnamon
- ¼ tsp ground nutmeg
- Zest of ½ lemon
- Zest of ½ orange
- 110ml / 4fl oz Guinness
- 170g / 6oz butter
- 170g / 6oz demerara sugar
- 3 eggs, lightly beaten
- 210g / 7½oz plain white flour

Equipment:

- 900g / 2lb loaf tin

Serving suggestion:

Serve with butter

Method

Combine the sultanas, raisins, currants, peel, walnuts, ginger, cinnamon, nutmeg, lemon and orange zest and Guinness in a bowl. Cover with a damp cloth and set aside to soak for 2 days at best or overnight.

Preheat the oven to fan 140°C / 275°F / gas mark 3. Grease and line a 900g / 2lb loaf tin.

Using an electric mixer, cream together the butter and sugar until light and fluffy. Gradually beat in the eggs until well combined. Fold in the flour until combined, followed by the fruit mixture. Spread the cake batter into the prepared loaf tin. Bake in the oven for 1 hour, then turn down the temperature to fan 120°C / fan 250°F / gas mark 1 and bake for a further 30 minutes. Allow the cake to cool in the tin for 30 minutes, then turn out onto a wire rack. Store in a sealed container when the cake is completely cold. It will keep for 1 month.

Date, Orange and Sunflower Seed Loaf

This is a lovely healthy cake. Wonderful with cheese too! It is an adapted recipe from Cranks, which first opened in Soho in 1967.

Ingredients

Serves 8-10

- Butter, to grease
- 350g / 12¼oz moist dates, stoned and chopped
- 200ml / 7fl oz boiling water
- 2 tsp bicarbonate of soda
- 120g / 4¼oz butter, softened
- 55ml / 2fl oz sunflower oil
- Zest and juice of 2 oranges
- 350g / 12¼oz wholemeal flour
- ¼ tsp fine sea salt
- 85g / 3oz organic porridge oats
- 55g / 2oz sunflower seeds
- 120g / 4¼oz walnuts, finely chopped
- 160g / 5½oz golden sultanas
- 3 large eggs, lightly beaten

Equipment:

- 900g / 2lb loaf tin

Serving suggestion:

Serve with butter, local cheeses or on its own

Method

Preheat the oven to fan 140°C / fan 275°F / gas mark 3. Grease and line a 900g / 2lb loaf tin.

In a heatproof bowl add the dates, pour over the boiling water and stir in the bicarbonate of soda. Leave to soak and cool. Once cooled, add the butter and oil and mix to combine, followed by the orange juice and zest.

In a separate bowl, mix together the remaining dry ingredients. Add the dry ingredients to the date mixture and mix together by hand. Add the eggs and gently mix together until it is all well combined. Add the dough to the tin and bake in the oven for 1½ hours or until golden. Allow to cool in the tin for 5 minutes, then turn onto a wire rack to cool completely.

Serve with local cheeses, butter or simply on its own. The loaf keeps for up to 1 month in the freezer.

Desserts & Baking

Coffee & Walnut Cake

This cake is the cake for coffee lovers. It is one of the many staples on the menu at The Purple Heather. People love it, including my granddaughter.

Ingredients

Serves 8-10

Cake:

- 1½ tsp instant coffee powder
- 1½ tbsp warm milk
- 170g / 6oz butter, softened
- 170g / 6oz caster sugar
- 60g / 2¼oz walnuts, chopped
- 3 eggs, separated
- Pinch of fine sea salt
- 170g / 6oz self-raising flour

Coffee Buttercream:

- 1½ tbsp warm milk
- 2½ tsp instant coffee powder
- 170g / 6oz butter, softened
- 225g / 8oz icing sugar
- 2 tsp brandy
- Handful of walnuts, for decoration

Equipment:

- 900g / 2lb loaf tin

Serving suggestion:

Serve with whipped cream or brandy cream for an occasion

Method

Preheat the oven to fan 160°C / fan 325°F / gas mark 4. Grease and line a 900g / 2lb loaf tin.

Dissolve the coffee powder in the warm milk and set aside to cool.

Using an electric mixer, cream together the butter and sugar until light and fluffy. Add the walnuts. Sieve over the flour and salt and gradually mix into the walnut butter mixture. Add the coffee milk and egg yolks, then gently fold to combine.

In a separate bowl, whisk the egg whites to stiff peaks and fold gently into the batter. Pour the cake mix into the prepared loaf tin. Bake in the oven for 35-45 minutes or until an inserted skewer comes out clean. Allow to cool in the tin for 5 minutes, then turn out onto a wire rack to cool completely.

To make the buttercream, dissolve the coffee in the warm milk and set aside to cool. Beat the butter and icing sugar in an electric mixer until white in colour. Add the coffee milk and brandy to the creamed butter and sugar, beating well to combine. It should be light and fluffy.

To assemble the cake, use a serrated knife to split the cake horizontally so you have two layers. Fill the middle of the cake with half of the buttercream. Put the other cake layer back on top, then use the remaining buttercream to cover the rest of the cake. Decorate with the walnuts.

Desserts & Baking 303

Delicious Gateau with Coffee Bean Sauce

For the coffee and chocolate lover, this is a special rich cake fit for a celebration. It is also gluten-free.

Ingredients

Serves 8-10

Gateau:

- 7 eggs
- 255g / 9oz caster sugar
- 255g / 9oz ground walnuts, can be done in a food processor
- 25 roasted coffee beans, (or 1 heaped tsp ground coffee beans)
- ½ tsp vanilla extract

Chocolate Filling:

- 140g / 5oz butter
- 170g / 6oz dark chocolate, 70%
- 85g / 3oz caster sugar
- 3 egg yolks

Equipment:

- 20cm / 8in round cake tin

Serving suggestion:

Coffee bean sauce (p368) and whipped cream

Method

Preheat the oven to fan 160°C / fan 325°F / gas mark 4. Grease and line a 20cm / 8in round cake tin.

To make the gateau, add the eggs and sugar into a bowl and whip using an electric mixer until light and fluffy. Combine the walnuts and coffee beans (if using) and gently fold into the egg mixture with the vanilla extract using a large metal spoon. Pour the batter into the tin and bake for 40 minutes or until the cake springs back when lightly pressed. Cool in the tin for 5 minutes, then turn the cake onto a wire rack to cool completely.

To make the filling, bring a saucepan of water to a simmer and in a bowl that fits snugly on top of the saucepan (but doesn't touch the water), add the butter and chocolate and stir to melt over a medium heat. Whisk together the sugar and egg yolks, then slowly fold into the chocolate mixture, continuing for 5 minutes or until the mixture thickens. Remove the bowl from the pan and set aside to cool.

Using a serrated knife, carefully split the cake horizontally so you have two layers of cake. Spread half the chocolate filling over one layer. Place the other layer on top and spread the remaining filling to cover the rest of the cake.

Serve the gateau with the coffee bean sauce, whipped cream and a garnish of seasonal herb.

Genoise Sponge Cake with Red Berries & Grand Marnier

This is a classic light French sponge. Dusting the baking tins gives the cake a lovely crust once baked.

Ingredients

Serves 8-10

Cake:

- A little sieved flour and sieved sugar, for dusting the baking tins
- 4 eggs, at room temperature
- 125g / 4½oz caster sugar
- 55g / 2oz butter, melted and cooled
- 125g / 4½oz plain white flour, sieved with a pinch of sea salt
- 2 tbsp Cointreau or Grand Marnier

Cake Filling:

- 285ml / ½ pint cream
- 2-3 tsp caster sugar
- 250g / 9oz strawberries, hulled and sliced, or whole raspberries
- Icing sugar, for dusting
- 1 tbsp Cointreau or Grand Marnier (optional)

Equipment:

- 2 x 18-20cm / 7-8in sandwich cake tins

Serving suggestion:

Serve with extra whipped cream, if desired

Method

Preheat the oven to fan 160°C / fan 325°F / gas mark 4. To prepare the cake tins, grease both tins lightly with a little of the melted butter. Dust the sieved flour and sugar over the tins to coat, turning the tins upside down to shake off any excess.

Heat a medium saucepan of water over a medium heat, but not to boiling point – this will soon be used as a bain marie. Into a heatproof bowl that fits snugly on the saucepan, add eggs and sugar and beat immediately using an electric hand mixer. Place the bowl over the saucepan and whisk at a medium speed for 10 minutes or until the mixture holds an impression and is almost at soft peaks.

Using a hand whisk (not electric), very gently fold in the sieved flour and salt, a little at a time, into the egg mixture. Lastly, fold in the cooled melted butter using a large spoon. Pour the cake batter into the two prepared tins. Bake in the oven for 20-25 minutes or until lightly browned and the top of the cakes spring back when pressed. Leave to cool in the tin for 5-10 minutes before turning out onto a wire rack. On the cake that you will use as the base, skewer a few times and drizzle over the Cointreau or Grand Marnier. Leave the cakes to cool.

Using an electric whisk or hand whisk, whip the cream. Towards the end of the whipping add the sugar to taste. For adults, mix the berries with one of the liqueurs to enrich the cake. Fold the berries into the cream.

To assemble, spread a layer of the cream and berries on top of one of the cakes. Top with the other cake and dust with icing sugar.

Victoria Sandwich

This is a classic recipe that is widely used in Ireland. The beauty is in its simplicity and it is delicious with homemade jam and freshly whipped cream. Nearly every farmhouse in Ireland would have produced lovely homemade jams. A popular variation was an apple cake where the apples were sugared and a little cinnamon folded into the recipe. It was baked in one large tin but at the same depth as the sandwich tin. In my teashop in the early 1960s, I used this recipe for little coffee or orange layer cakes which I have given the recipe for here. For the layer cake, each sandwich was split which made a rich cake with three layers of filling and iced all over the cake as well. I used to sell them for 2s and 6d – a half crown – in the old LSD money, which has a different meaning nowadays!

Ingredients

Serves 8-10

Sponge:

- Softened butter, to grease tins
- Caster sugar and plain flour, sieved together for tin preparation
- 250g / 9oz butter, at room temperature, plus extra for greasing
- 250g / 9oz caster sugar
- 4 large eggs, at room temperature
- ½ tsp vanilla extract
- Zest of 1 lemon (if using raspberry jam) or zest of 1 orange (if using strawberry jam)
- 250g / 9oz self-raising flour with a pinch of sea salt, sieved
- 1 tbsp cold whole milk, if needed
- 6 tbsp raspberry or strawberry jam
- 300ml / 10½fl oz cream, whipped
- Icing sugar, for dusting

Equipment:

- 2 x 20cm / 8in sandwich cake tins

Coffee Cake:

- 2 tsp instant coffee, dissolved in a splash of hot water, cooled

Coffee Buttercream:

- 3 tbsp instant coffee
- 1 tbsp hot water
- 150g / 5¼oz butter, softened
- 300g / 10½oz icing sugar, sieved

Orange Cake:

- Zest of 2 oranges

Orange Buttercream:

- 150g / 5¼oz butter softened
- 300g / 10½oz icing sugar, sifted
- Finely grated zest of 2 oranges
- Juice of 1 orange
- 1 tbsp Grand Marnier (optional)

Chocolate Cake:

- 40g / 1½oz dark cocoa powder

Chocolate Fudge Icing (p288)

Chocolate Ganache (p288)

Method

Preheat the oven to fan 160°C / fan 320°F / gas mark 4.

Grease the two sandwich tins with butter, then lightly coat with the flour and sugar mixture, shaking off any excess.

Using an electric beater or a stand mixer, cream together the butter and sugar until light and fluffy. Gradually add each egg, beating well after each addition. Add the vanilla and lemon or orange zest, then gently fold in the sieved flour by hand, taking care not to overmix. The mixture should be dropping consistency; if the mixture is too stiff, fold in 1 tbsp of cold milk.

Divide the mixture evenly between the two cake tins and level the top with a spatula. Bake in the oven for 20-25 minutes or until lightly golden, slightly firm to the touch and an inserted skewer comes out clean. Leave to cool in the oven for 10 minutes then turn out onto a wire rack to cool completely.

To assemble, spread the jam on top of one of the cakes and cover with whipped cream. Top with the other cake, making a sandwich. Dust with icing sugar.

Coffee Cake:

Make the cake as instructed above, adding the cooled instant coffee when creaming the butter and sugar.

To make the buttercream, dissolve the coffee in the hot water and allow to cool. Cream together the butter and icing sugar using an electric mixer until light and fluffy. Add the dissolved coffee and beat well to combine.

Orange Cake:

Make the cake as instructed above, using the zest of 2 oranges. To make the buttercream, cream the butter and the icing sugar using an electric mixer until light and fluffy. Add the orange zest and juice and beat well to combine, adding more orange juice and Grand Marnier if you would like.

Chocolate Cake:

Make the cake as instructed above, sieving the dark cocoa powder with the self-raising flour. Make the chocolate fudge icing and chocolate ganache following the instructions on p288. Once the cake is iced, raise the cake and add a layer of ganache all over.

Tunisian Orange Cake

This is a favourite cake in my family and it was requested by my daughter and son-in-law for their wedding. I made numerous batches which were for the dessert and when I was making the main cake, my Rational oven decided to give up during the process! My good friend James Mulchrone of Jam Cafés kindly came to my rescue and produced the most exquisite large Tunisian cake. It was a work of art. This cake is worth making in double quantities just so one can be frozen for later. For a special occasion, add 2 tbsp of Grand Marnier to the syrup.

Ingredients

Serves 8-10

Cake:

- 45g / 1½oz fresh soft white breadcrumbs
- 200g / 7oz caster sugar
- 100g / 3½oz ground almonds
- 1 tsp baking powder
- Zest of 1 orange
- Zest of ½ lemon
- 200ml / 7fl oz sunflower oil
- 4 medium eggs, at room temperature

Syrup:

- Juice of 1 orange
- Juice of 1 lemon
- 70g / 2½oz sugar
- ½ cinnamon stick
- 5 star anise
- 6-7 kumquats, cut in half

Serving suggestion:

Clotted cream

Method

Line and grease a 20cm / 8in spring-form cake tin.

In a large bowl, mix together the breadcrumbs, sugar, ground almonds and baking powder, then add the orange and lemon zest. In a separate bowl, lightly whisk together the oil and eggs. Pour the egg and oil mixture into the dry ingredients and combine well. Pour the cake batter into the prepared tin and place in a cold oven. Turn the oven to fan 180°C / fan 350°F / gas mark 6 and bake for 40-45 minutes or until a skewer inserted comes out clean. Allow the cake to cool in the tin for 5 minutes, then turn out upside down onto a large plate.

To make the syrup, combine all the ingredients in a small saucepan and gently bring to the boil, stirring to dissolve the sugar. Boil for 2 minutes to a light syrupy consistency. Take out the spices and kumquats and reserve for decoration.

While the cake is still warm, use a thin steel skewer to poke holes over the cake. Slowly pour over the syrup, allowing it to be absorbed before adding more.

Decorate the cake with the reserved spices (splitting the cinnamon stick is effective), kumquats and serve with clotted cream.

Sticky Toffee Pudding

This recipe is adapted from the original Ivy's on West Street when it was owned by Chris Corbin and Jeremy King. Proven to be a true classic, A.A. Gill included this recipe n his 1997 cookbook *The Ivy*. I loved going there and it is uncanny that a local man, Arthur O' Connor from Templenoe, a parish of Kenmare, was a head door man there in its heyday welcoming both their local and celebrity customers. If making this pudding in advance, heat in the oven for a few minutes until warm, and ensure the toffee sauce is warm before pouring over the pudding.

Ingredients

Serves 10-12

Date Purée:

- 370g / 13oz dates, stoned
- 370ml / 13fl oz cold water

Toffee Sauce:

- 640ml / 22½fl oz cream
- 340g / 12oz caster sugar
- 130g / 4¾oz butter, softened

Sponge:

- 130g / 4¾oz butter
- 370g / 12oz soft dark brown sugar
- 3 eggs, at room temperature, lightly beaten
- 450g / 1lb strong plain flour
- 10g / ⅓oz baking powder
- 3g / ⅛oz bicarbonate of soda
- Pinch of sea salt

Equipment:

- Rectangle cake tin, approximately 30x24x6cm / 12x10x2½in

Method

Preheat the oven to fan 160°C / fan 325°F / gas mark 4. Line the rectangle cake tin with parchment paper.

In a small saucepan, add the dates and water and bring to a simmer over a low heat for 10-15 minutes or until soft and almost all the water is evaporated. Set aside to cool a little, then blitz using a handheld blender or food processor until smooth.

To make the toffee sauce, combine half the cream, sugar and butter in a heavy-based saucepan over a high heat and stir until the sugar has dissolved. Stop stirring, bring to the boil and continue to cook until golden brown, taking care not to burn (caramelising the toffee). Remove from the heat, allow to cool slightly, then stir in the remaining cream.

To prepare the sponge, cream together the butter and sugar in an electric mixer until light and fluffy. Gradually add the eggs, beating well after each addition, taking care as adding them too quickly could cause the mixture to split. In a separate bowl, sieve the flour, bicarbonate of soda, baking powder and salt and mix very well. Fold into the mixture gently and slowly until smooth.

Add the warm date purée and mix in well. Pour the cake batter into the prepared cake tin and smooth the top. Bake for 50-60 minutes or until the sponge is firm to the touch and an inserted skewer comes out clean. Leave the cake to cool in the tin, then transfer to a board.

Serving suggestion:

Vanilla ice-cream (p320) or crème fraîche

Turn the oven down to fan 150°C / fan 300°F/ gas mark 3. Split the cake into 3 layers, cutting horizontally, and use a thin steel skewer to pierce each layer to enable the toffee sauce to penetrate. Return the base layer of cake to the tin and cover with a layer of warm toffee sauce, then a second layer of sponge, more toffee sauce and a final layer of sponge finishing with another layer of toffee sauce. Cover the cake with foil and bake for a further 20 minutes.

For individual portions, cut a square of sticky toffee pudding on a plate (warm in the oven) and pour over a good spoon of toffee sauce and serve with vanilla ice-cream. If serving at a dinner party, serve the cake whole and pour over the warm toffee sauce.

Desserts & Baking 311

Irish Barmbrack & Butter Pudding

This is a comforting dessert perfect for winter or autumn. It is rich and custardy and ideal for a gathering. In our restaurant we were fortunate to have a wonderful family bakery in Kenmare, Moriarty's, whose speciality was their delicious rich Barmbrack that was made all year round to order. Barmbrack is a traditional yeast fruit loaf in Ireland especially associated with Halloween. Historically in Ireland it was custom at Halloween to put small objects into the cake, acting as a kind of fortune telling. It was believed that the person who got the pea wouldn't marry that year; the stick meant an unhappy marriage; cloth indicated poverty and the coin riches; while the person who found the ring would wed within the year!

Prepare the pudding the day before and bake on the day of serving. Use a rich barmbrack that is a few days old rather than a fresh brack.

Ingredients

Serves 12

- 6 large or 12-18 small slices of rich barmbrack bread, or Panettone or a rich yeasted fruit loaf as a substitute, a few days old
- 200g / 7oz butter, softened, for bread slices and greasing
- 1 whole nutmeg, for grating
- 525ml / 18½fl oz cream
- 525ml / 18½fl oz milk
- 6 eggs
- 170g / 6oz light brown sugar
- 100ml / 3½fl oz dark Jamaican rum
- Rectangular ovenproof dish, approximately 30x20cm / 12x8in

Serving suggestion:

Pouring cream

Method

Liberally spread 150g / 5¼oz of the softened butter over one side of the barmbrack slices. With the remaining butter, grease a large rectangular ovenproof dish. Using the bread slices, place one layer over the base of the dish, butter side up, followed by a grating of nutmeg. Repeat to make a total of three barmbrack layers.

In a saucepan, stir together the cream and milk, then heat to boiling point while stirring continuously. Remove from the heat. In a bowl, mix together the eggs and sugar until well combined, then gradually stir in the hot milk and cream, followed by the rum. Slowly pour the egg mixture over the prepared barmbrack to cover and soak all the bread (you may need to skewer to help with absorption). Allow to cool, cover and chill in the fridge overnight – it absorbs all the moisture and swells the dried fruit.

Preheat the oven to fan 160°C / fan 325°F / gas mark 4.

Place the pudding dish in a large deep roasting pan and pour enough water into the tray to come two-thirds of the way up the pudding dish. Bake for 45 minutes or until set. It should be golden on top. Divide into bowls and serve warm with pouring cream.

Spicy Apple & Rum Pudding

This is a lovely autumn and winter pudding. I have adapted Larry Forgione's recipe from the 1985 *Bon Appetit cookbook, New York's Master Chefs*. The rum with the apple is such a great combination and the addition of the treacle enriches the pudding.

Use a butter loaf or brioche that is a couple of days old and freshly slice it for this recipe.

Ingredients

Makes 6

- 12 slices butter loaf or brioche (about 2cm / ¾in thickness), a few days old
- 120g / 4¼oz butter, softened
- 4 tbsp light brown sugar
- 6-8 eating apples (e.g. Cox's), peeled, quartered and cut into slices (½cm / ¼in)
- 3 tbsp treacle
- 1 tsp ground cinnamon
- 4 tbsp dark Jamaican rum
- 2 tbsp fresh lemon juice
- 100g / 3½oz butter, cut into small cubes, plus extra to grease

Equipment:

- 6 ramekins

Serving suggestion:

Pouring cream or ice-cream

Method

Preheat the oven to fan 160°C / fan 325°F / gas mark 4 and grease the ramekins with butter.

Using a circle cutter, cut 12 rounds of bread to fit in the ramekins. Spread the softened butter on both sides of the bread circles and sprinkle one side of each with a little of the brown sugar. Place one bread circle, sugar side down, into the base of each ramekin.

In a stainless steel saucepan, add the apples, treacle, remaining brown sugar, cinnamon, rum, lemon juice and butter and cook over a medium heat for 4-5 minutes. Divide the mixture between the ramekins, being sure to spoon over the juices. Top each ramekin with the remaining bread circles, sugar side up.

Place the ramekins in a roasting tray and pour in enough hot water to come up 2.5cm / 1in around the ramekins. Bake in the oven for 25 minutes or until the bread is golden brown on top and the apple is cooked.

Creamy Caramelised Apple Tart

Caramelised apples, pastry and custard are a dreamy and comforting combination. This tart is best eaten on the day it is prepared. Serve with the butterscotch sauce (p316), substituting the dark rum with apple brandy or calvados. Delicious!

Ingredients

Serves 12

Pastry:

- 250g / 9oz plain white flour, sieved, plus extra
- 50g / 1¾oz icing sugar
- Pinch of sea salt
- 125g / 4½oz butter, softened
- 1 whole egg
- 2 yolks
- A little egg white, to brush the pastry

Caramel:

- 100g / 3½oz butter, melted
- 100g / 3½oz caster sugar
- 1 tsp ground cinnamon, or more to taste
- 5 large Cox's apples, peeled, cored and cut into 8 wedges

Custard:

- 250ml / 9fl oz cream
- 4 eggs yolks
- 100g / 3½oz caster sugar

Method

To make the pastry, add the flour, icing sugar, salt and butter to a food processor and pulse to a breadcrumb-like texture. Lightly beat together the egg and yolks with a fork, then add to the food processor, pulsing again until the mixture starts to form a dough, being careful not to overwork it. Wrap in clingfilm and chill for 1 hour in the fridge.

To make the caramel:

Melt the butter in a small saucepan over a medium heat. Whisk in the sugar and cinnamon until smooth, then lastly stir in the apples. Remove the apples with a slotted spoon after 5 minutes or when slightly cooked and beginning to soften. Set aside. Continue cooking the caramel to a golden brown colour, being careful not to let it burn. Remove from the heat and gently mix in the apples.

To make the custard:

In another saucepan, make the custard by bringing the cream to the boil. Meanwhile, in a separate bowl, whisk together the yolks and sugar until pale. Gradually add the cream to the egg mixture, stirring continuously. Return the mix to the saucepan and stir over a gentle heat, until the custard thickens to coat the back of a spoon.

On a lightly floured surface, roll out the pastry to 3mm / 0.1in thick and use to line a 25cm / 10in deep tart tin. Prick the base with a fork and chill in the fridge for at least 30 minutes.

Equipment:

- 25cm / 10in deep tart tin
- Baking beans or dried pulses, for blind baking

Serving suggestion:

Whipped cream and butterscotch sauce (p316, using apple brandy or calvados instead of rum), vanilla or praline ice-cream (p321)

Preheat the oven to fan 170°C / fan 340°F / gas mark 5.

Cover the pastry with baking paper, fill with ceramic baking beans or dried pulses and blind bake for 15 minutes or until sandy-like to touch. Brush a thin layer of the egg white over the base and bake again in the oven until golden to seal the pastry.

To assemble the tart, put the apple and caramel into the base and then pour over the custard. Bake in the oven for 25-35 minutes or until set and golden brown.

Desserts & Baking   315

Rum & Walnut Tart with Rum Butterscotch Sauce

This is a delicious tart for autumn and winter. The butterscotch is a very versatile sauce and is delicious with the addition of sea salt. Use calvados or brandy instead of the dark rum if serving with my creamy caramelised apple tart (p314). The recipe has been adapted from one of my favourite cookbooks, *Memories of Gascony* by Pierre Koffmann.

Ingredients

Serves 8

Pâte Sucrée:

- 125g / 4½oz plain white flour
- 55g / 2oz butter, softened
- 55g / 2oz icing sugar
- Pinch of sea salt
- 1 egg

Rum Butterscotch Sauce:

- 30g / 1oz butter
- 70g / 2½oz light brown sugar
- 70g / 2½oz golden syrup
- 90ml / 3fl oz cream
- 45ml / 1½fl oz dark Jamaican rum

Walnut Filling:

- 300g / 11oz walnuts, roughly chopped
- 150g / 5oz caster sugar
- 120g / 4½oz butter, melted
- 150g / 5¼oz honey
- 5 egg yolks
- 100ml / 3½fl oz cream
- 50ml / 2fl oz dark Jamaican rum

Equipment:

23cm / 9in flan tin

Serving suggestion:

Serve the tart with the rum butterscotch sauce and scoops of vanilla ice-cream (p320).

Method

Use a food processor to mix the flour, butter, sugar and salt to a fine crumb. Use a fork to lightly beat the egg, then add the eggs to the food processor and pulse to bring the pastry together. Wrap in clingfilm and chill for 1 hour in the fridge.

Butterscotch sauce:

Place the butter, sugar and golden syrup in a saucepan over a medium heat, stirring to dissolve the sugar. Continue to cook to a smooth and shiny syrup. Carefully add the cream (as it will splutter) and stir to combine. Bring to a gentle bubble then simmer for 3 minutes. Add the rum and remove from the heat.

Preheat the oven to fan 160°C / fan 325°F / gas mark 4. Roll out the pastry to 2-3mm / 0.1in thick and use to line a 23cm / 9in flan tin. Chill for at least 30 minutes in the fridge.

To make the walnut filling, gently mix together the walnuts, sugar, butter, honey, egg yolks, cream and rum in a large bowl. Pour the mixture into the prepared pastry and bake in oven for 50-60 minutes or until golden brown and set with a slight wobble.

Allow to set for at least 1 hour before serving.

Iced Coffee Parfait

Initially, I made coffee meringues served with whiskey cream and the dessert evolved into a parfait in the early years of Packie's. It's a lovely light dessert to follow a rich meal.

This makes a large batch in loaf tins – depending on what size tins you use. However, this is brilliant frozen and can be used instantly and sliced like an ice-cream cake. Freeze in sealed airtight containers wrapped in clingfilm. Keeps in the freezer for up to 1 month.

Ingredients

Serves 10-12

Custard:

- 425ml / 15fl oz milk
- ½ vanilla pod, split and seeds scraped
- 6 egg yolks
- 140g / 5oz caster sugar
- 425ml / 15fl oz cream
- 1½ tbsp instant coffee

Whiskey Caramel:

- 500ml / 18fl oz sugar syrup (p365)
- 2 tbsp cold water
- 4 tbsp whiskey

Whiskey Cream:

- 140ml / 5fl oz cream, for serving
- 1½ tbsp demerara sugar, or more to taste
- 55ml / 2fl oz whiskey

Equipment:

- 2 small loaf tins or 1 large loaf tin

Desserts & Baking

Method

Line 2 small loaf tins or 1 large loaf tin with clingfilm, leaving sufficient overhang to later cover the parfait.

In a small saucepan, add the milk, vanilla seeds and pod, bring to the boil then reduce the heat to a simmer for 2 minutes, stirring with a whisk. Remove from the heat and set aside to infuse with the lid on.

Use an electric mixer to beat the egg yolks and sugar together until light and creamy and the consistency of whipped cream. It should leave a little trail when lifted out.

Remove the vanilla pod from the milk. Gradually pour the milk into the eggs while whisking. Return the custard to a clean saucepan and stir over a very low heat until the custard thickens. It should coat the back of a wooden spoon. Stir in the coffee until it dissolves. Cool the custard quickly over a bowl of ice, stirring constantly. Whip the cream to soft peaks, then fold the custard into the cream.

Pour the parfait mix into the prepared tin and seal well with clingfilm. Enclose in a sealed airtight container and set it in the freezer overnight, where it will keep for up to 1 month.

To make the caramel:

Prepare a shallow basin of iced water sufficient for the base of the saucepan to rest inside. Simmer the sugar syrup over a low heat in a saucepan, not stirring. When the syrup starts to turn golden at the edges, swirl the saucepan occasionally until it goes a deep golden colour, then place the saucepan immediately into the shallow iced water to stop the cooking process for a few minutes. Return the saucepan to a very low heat and add the cold water to loosen the caramel, swirling the saucepan gently, being careful that it doesn't splutter. The caramel should now be loose or liquefied; only then add the whiskey and swirl around gently over the low heat. Cool before serving with the parfait. The caramel can be stored in a sealed jar for up to 1 month.

To make the whiskey cream:

Whip the cream and sugar together to soft peak stage, then fold in the whiskey.

Turn out the parfait. Cut two slices measuring 1.5cm / ½in in width, then place one at an angle over the other and serve with a good dollop of whiskey cream and a drizzle of whiskey caramel around it.

Homemade Vanilla Ice-Cream

My maternal grandmother was known in Kenmare as Nonie Crowley Hanley. She came from Drombouhilly in Tuosist, a parish outside Kenmare on the Beara Peninsula. She crossed the Atlantic twice as a very young girl and travelled to Boston working with a family in their home and eventually as their cook. When she returned to Kenmare for the second time, she built No. 35 Henry Street and opened a shop in 1926. This is where Packie's is today. She was famous for her hare soup and stew and most importantly delighted Kenmare people with hand churned ice-cream from 1929. Kenmare had a railway line at that time and she had blocks of ice sent to her from the train weekly. She made her own custard with milk and cream over the stove.

The ice-cream was hand churned. A metal container inside in a bigger cylinder was used. The crushed ice went on the outside and in the centre, with the blade the custard was poured in and they used the handle which came up out of centre twisting it and that churned it. They used blocks of ice to keep it cool. We still have her old shop ice-cream sign from the 1930s.

Ingredients

- 8 egg yolks
- 225g / 8oz caster sugar
- 570ml / 1 pint milk
- 1 large vanilla pod, split and seeds scraped
- 570ml / 1 pint cream

Equipment:

- ice-cream machine

Serving suggestions:

Praline ice-cream is lovely on its own with butterscotch sauce (p317) or with spicy apple rum pudding (p313) or sticky toffee pudding (p310)

Nonie's original 1930's ice-cream sign

Method

In a large heavy saucepan, warm the milk with the split vanilla pod and vanilla seeds scraped into the saucepan over a low heat, stirring continuously. Remove from the heat just before it boils. Set aside to infuse with the lid on for 10 minutes.

Using an electric mixer, beat together the eggs yolks and sugar until light and fluffy. Add the warm milk gradually, stirring continously with a whisk. Return the mixture to the saucepan and stir over a low heat until the custard coats the back of a wooden spoon, it must not boil, then remove from the heat. Transfer to a cold bowl or saucepan and continue to stir for 2 minutes. Immediately cover the custard with clingfilm over the surface to prevent a skin forming and set aside to cool completely. This can also be done over an ice-bath or in a sink of cold water to speed up the process.

Combine the custard with the cream using a whisk. Transfer to an ice-cream machine and follow the instructions for churning times. Transfer the ice-cream to an airtight container and keep in the freezer for up to 1 month.

Praline Ice-Cream:

For praline ice-cream you prepare the exact same as for the Vanilla ice-cream above, adding 85g / 3oz praline coarsely crushed or bashed praline (see bitter chocolate praline tart, p290) once it begins to freeze and thicken in the ice-cream machine.

Prepare custard as with the vanilla ice-cream method.

Combine the custard with the cream using a whisk. Transfer to an ice-cream machine and follow the machine's instructions for churning times. As the ice-cream starts to thicken, gradually add praline so it is well dispersed throughout the ice-cream. Transfer the ice-cream to an airtight container and keep in the freezer for up to 1 month.

Zabaglione Ice-cream with a Rum Caramel Syrup

I attended a course at Ballymaloe by Ruth Rogers and Rosie Gray of the River Café in London in the 1980s; this is one of their signature ice-creams. It is a deliciously rich ice-cream and could be served on Christmas Day as an alternative to Christmas pudding.

Ingredients

Ice-cream:

- 10 egg yolks
- 225g / 8oz caster sugar
- 470ml / 16½fl oz cream
- 100ml / 3½oz dark Jamaican rum
- 100ml / 3½oz Bristol Cream Sherry

Rum Caramel:

- 500ml / 18fl oz sugar syrup (p365)
- 4 tbsp cold water
- 6 tbsp dark Jamaican rum

Method

Using an electric mixer, beat together the yolks and sugar until light and fluffy. Warm the cream in a medium saucepan over a low heat, stirring continuously and removing from the heat just before it boils. Add cream to the sugar and egg mixture to combine, stirring continuously with a whisk. Stir in half the rum and sherry, then return the mixture to the saucepan and stir constantly over a low heat until the custard coats the back of a wooden spoon (it must not boil), then remove from the heat. Transfer to a cold bowl or saucepan and continue to stir for 2 minutes. Immediately cover the custard with clingfilm over the surface to prevent a skin forming and set aside to cool completely. This can also be done over an ice bath or in a sink of cold water to speed up the process. Once cool, stir in the remaining alcohol. Churn in an ice-cream maker and freeze in a sealed container.

To make the caramel:

Prepare a shallow basin of iced water sufficient for the base of the saucepan to rest inside. Simmer the sugar syrup over a low heat in a saucepan, not stirring. When the syrup starts to turn golden at the edges, swirl the saucepan occasionally until it goes a deep golden colour for a few minutes, then place the saucepan immediately into the shallow iced water to stop the cooking process. Return the saucepan to a very low heat and add the cold water to loosen the caramel, swirling the saucepan gently, being careful that it doesn't splutter. Add the rum and swirl around gently. Cool before serving with the ice-cream. The caramel can be stored in a sealed jar for up to 1 month.

Tuilles

These are a French classic and Paul Bocuse, the famous French chef, did a wonderful almond version rolling them around a rolling pin. Because of my excessive use of butter, I often justify it with Paul's famous quote: "du beurre, encore du beurre, toujours du beurre!" He was such an amazing man.

One of my daughter's favourites, I served these tuilles in abundance in The Lime Tree and people were upset if I didn't have them. The recipe below is a particularly delicious version; the orange zest gives them a lift and balances the sweetness. These are fantastic to hold a dessert, such as a mousse, parfait or ice-cream, providing a pleasing contrasting texture. The tuilles will need to be made in small batches as it is a very hands-on method.

Ingredients

- 125g / 4½oz butter, room temperature
- 225g / 8oz caster sugar
- 225g / 8oz egg whites
- 225g / 8oz plain white flour, sieved
- 1 tsp natural vanilla extract
- Zest of 1 orange, finely grated

Method

Preheat the oven to fan 190°C / fan 375°F / gas mark 6½. Line a baking tray with parchment. Use a pencil to draw two or three 12.5cm / 5in circles. Be sure to leave sufficient space, around 7½cm / 3in, between the circles as the batter will spread. Have 8-10 small, deep round bowls placed upside down ready, such as a ramekin or small soup bowl; these will be moulds for the tuilles.

Beat the butter in an electric mixer until pale in colour. Add the sugar, beating until light and fluffy. Add the egg whites and beat to combine. On a low speed or by hand, gently mix in the flour, vanilla and orange zest.

With a dessert spoon, drop the batter into the centre of the prepared circles and spread a little with the back of the spoon. Bake in the oven for 4-5 minutes or until the edges are brown. Take them out immediately and with a thin fish slice or small palette knife lift the biscuits off the tray and gently place over the moulds, using your hand to press them down. This must be done immediately while they are warm. If they do harden, return to the oven for a few seconds to soften and try again.

Leave the tuilles on the moulds until completely cold. Be sure to handle with care as they are fragile. Repeat the process with the remaining batter. Stored in an airtight container they will keep for 2-5 days.

Thos' Lemon Posset with Shortbread

I got this recipe originally from one of two dear friends who retired to our area and who had the most wonderful dinner parties. She kindly gave me this simple but delicious recipe back in the late 1970s. My son Thos has perfected it for his café Pyro on Henry Court, refining my friend's recipe and adding vanilla pods. His is a technical recipe designed for a professional kitchen and has the perfect balance in flavours. The recipe here is a simplified version and is bursting with flavour.

When Thos was a young boy he used to sell homemade biscuits around the town, particularly at Henry Court. All the locals would buy from him. He had ginger, shortbread, chocolate chip and hazelnut biscuits. Now he serves delicious pizzas with local ingredients and divine pots of pleasure for dessert on the same lane!

This recipe is quick and easy but bursting with zing, ideal for dinner parties in the summer months – a total cinch! It can be made the night before and chilled in the fridge; take it out just before serving. Thos' biscuits can also be made in advance and put into the posset just before serving.

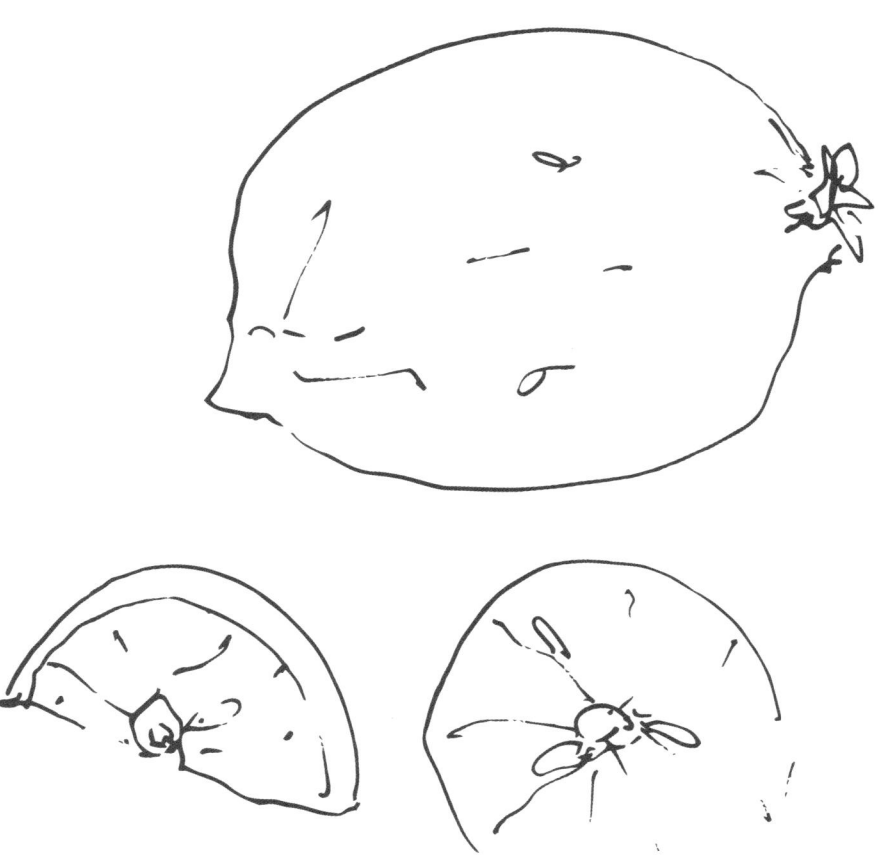

Ingredients

Makes 4

Posset:

- 600ml / 20fl oz good quality whipping cream with a high fat content (minimum 35% fat)
- ¼ vanilla pod, scraped
- 155g / 5½oz caster sugar
- Zest and juice of 3 unwaxed lemons

Shortbread:

- Sunflower oil, to grease
- 225g / 8oz unsalted butter, room temperature
- 140g / 5oz caster sugar
- Zest of ½ lemon
- 325g / 11½oz plain white flour
- Pinch of sea salt

Serving suggestion:

Sprig of mint, to garnish

Method

To make the posset:

Place the cream, vanilla and sugar into a small saucepan. Bring to the boil over a medium heat, stirring continuously. Stir in the lemon zest and juice. Bring it back to the boil and continue on a rolling boil for around 30-40 seconds, stirring continuously with a small sauce whisk, ensuring it does not burn. Set aside and allow to cool for 30 minutes, stirring occasionally. Pour the posset mix into ramekins. Allow to cool a little, then chill in the fridge overnight.

To make the shortbread:

Preheat the oven to fan 160°C / fan 325°F / gas mark 4. Lightly grease an oven tray with a little butter and press down a layer of parchment paper on top to line. Use an electric mixer to cream together the butter, sugar and lemon zest. Add the flour and mix thoroughly. Roll the mix into a sausage shape, wrap in clingfilm and chill for 30 minutes in the fridge. They can also be frozen for up to 1 month. Using a thin sharp knife, slice the rolled dough into biscuits, around 4-5mm / 0.2 inches thick. Place on the lined baking tray and bake in the oven for 10-15 minutes or until lightly golden.

Serve the posset with a shortbread biscuit each. Garnish with a sprig of mint.

Thos working in his kitchen at Pyro

Desserts & Baking 327

John Desmond's Island Cottage White Chocolate Mousse

Heir Island is one of my favourite havens in this world. The island itself is beautiful, tucked off the coast of west Cork near Cunnamore Pier. To me, it is most special because of John and Ellmary of Island Cottage. Their restaurant is in a charming cottage and it is such a unique experience. Since John and Ellmary's opening my family and I go there annually in September. Each year we look forward to the day out; our stops along the way include Levis and Rosie's in Ballydehob, Minihanes bar closer to the pier, our journey on the ferry with John Moore and our walk along the country road to the restaurant (or on occasion packing into island vehicles because of pouring rain!). The food is exquisite and the whole evening is magical. We love visiting John's gallery before our meal and I always come away from the island refreshed and energised. Pure perfection!

This white chocolate mousse is divine. John gave me the recipe when I attended one of his courses at Ballymaloe in the 1980s. It was so popular that I couldn't take it off the menu at The Lime Tree. I served it in a slice and I gave my customers the option of the chocolate sauce or a strawberry & Grand Marnier sauce. My youngest daughter used to drink glasses of puréed strawberry without the Grand Marnier – smoothie of the 1980s! Here is John's White Chocolate Mousse with his Chocolate Sauce.

Desserts & Baking

Ingredients

Serves 12

Mousse:

- 250g / 9oz white chocolate (e.g. Lidl white chocolate)
- 50g / 2oz cream
- 3.5g / 0.1oz gelatine powder
- 3 egg yolks
- 500ml / 18fl oz cream
- 50g / 2oz sliced almonds, toasted, to serve

Chocolate Sauce:

- 62.5g / 2¼oz Green & Black's cocoa
- 62.5g / 2¼oz sugar
- 30g / 1oz unsalted butter
- 125ml / 4¾fl oz hot water

Strawberry Sauce:

- 125g / 4½oz Irish strawberries
- 1 tbsp sugar syrup (p365)
- 1 tbsp Grand Marnier

Method

To make the mousse:

Melt the white chocolate over a hot water bath until totally melted. Do not overheat.

In a separate saucepan, add the cream, bring to the boil and take off the heat. Add the gelatine powder, whisk until all the gelatine is dissolved, then add to the melted white chocolate and whisk. Add the egg yolks, whisk and let cool.

Whisk the cream until you get soft peaks, then fold into the white chocolate mixture.

Put into a container 4cm / 1.5in high and leave in the fridge until firm (at least 6 hours). Put away the remainder in an airtight container and keep in the freezer for up to 1 month. When needed for a special dinner, take out the day before and keep in the fridge. Make your sauce fresh.

To make the chocolate sauce:

Put all the above ingredients in a saucepan, put over a medium heat and whisk until coating consistency.

To make the strawberry sauce:

Add all the ingredients to a blender and blitz.

To serve, thickly slice the mousse to around 2.5cm / 1in and lay on a plate. Spoon a little chocolate or strawberry sauce around the mousse, sprinkle over the almonds and garnish with mint leaves.

Grainne's Christmas Pudding with Brandy Butter

Grainne has been making this wonderful pudding for years. It is a very old recipe and it is without doubt my favourite part of the Christmas meal. Make 4-5 weeks in advance to the allow the flavours to intensify.

Ingredients

Makes 4 puddings

Puddings:

- 225g / 8oz muscatel grape raisins
- 340g / 12oz seedless raisins
- 340g / 12oz sultanas
- 225g / 8oz candied mixed fruit peel, finely chopped
- 170g / 6oz blanched almonds slivers
- 1 Bramley cooking apple, peeled, cored and roughly chopped
- 1 small carrot, peeled and roughly chopped
- Zest of 2 oranges
- Zest of 1 lemon
- 225g / 8oz butter, melted
- 225g / 8oz plain white flour
- 110g / 4oz soft fresh white breadcrumbs
- 225g / 8oz light brown muscovado sugar
- ½ tsp ground ginger
- ½ tsp cinnamon
- 1 tsp freshly grated nutmeg
- 1 tsp sea salt
- 6 eggs
- 140ml / ¼ pint Guinness
- 4 tbsp brandy
- 4 tbsp fresh orange juice
- 3 tbsp fresh lemon juice
- 1 tbsp brandy, for flaming each pudding

Brandy Butter:

- 55g / 2oz butter, softened
- 100g / 3½oz caster sugar
- 2½ tbsp brandy
- ½ tsp grated orange zest

Equipment:

- 4 x 850ml / 1½ pint plastic pudding basins with lids

Method

Into a large deep bowl, add the raisins, sultanas, candied fruit peel, almonds, apple, carrot, orange and lemon zest and mix thoroughly. Stir in the flour, breadcrumbs, sugar, ginger, cinnamon, nutmeg and salt thoroughly and then stir into the fruit mix. Finally, add the melted butter and mix.

In a separate bowl, beat the eggs lightly and mix in the Guinness, brandy, orange and lemon juice. Pour the egg and Guinness mixture over the fruit mixture and mix thoroughly with a wooden spoon until all the ingredients are well combined. Cover the bowl with a damp tea towel and allow to macerate at room temperature overnight or for up to 24 hours.

Divide the mixture between the four pudding basins, filling them to within 5cm / 2in from the top, pressing the mixture down with the back of a spoon. Grease 1.3cm / ½in strip of foil with butter and wrap around the edge of the pudding bowl. Cover the bowl with a double layer of parchment paper and seal with a long piece of kitchen string around the edge of the bowl and seal with the lid.

Place each pudding basin in 4 separate saucepans and pour in enough boiling water to come three-quarters of the way up the sides. Bring the water to the boil over a high heat, cover the pan tightly, then reduce the heat to the lowest point and steam the puddings for 8 hours. Check occasionally and top up the saucepans with additional boiling water from the kettle to ensure there is sufficient water to steam the puddings.

When the puddings are done, remove them from the water and allow to cool to room temperature. Store the puddings in a cool, well aired larder or pantry for at least 3 weeks before serving.

To serve a pudding on Christmas Day, bring a medium saucepan of water to the boil then add the pudding basin to the saucepan, topping up with additional boiling water from the kettle so the water comes three-quarters of the way up the sides of the basins. Bring to the boil over a high heat, cover the pan and reduce to a very low heat to gently simmer for 2 hours. Check occasionally and top up with boiling water from the kettle if required.

Remove the basin from the water and the lid. Run a knife along the inside edges of the basin and, grasping the top of the basin and a plate firmly together, invert the pudding onto a serving plate. The pudding should slide out easily.

If you would like to serve the pudding alight, pour the brandy over the pudding and light.

Serve with a spoon of brandy butter.

To make the brandy butter:

Use an electric beater to cream together the butter and sugar until light and fluffy. Add the brandy and orange zest and further mix until smooth. Store in the fridge for up to 2 weeks. Remove from the fridge prior to serving, soften and bring to room temperature.

Grainne's Wholemeal Shortbread Biscuits

The wholemeal flour gives these biscuits a nutty texture. An alternative to this very simple and easy recipe is to add toasted hazelnuts for a crunchy variation.

The biscuits will keep for up to 1 week in an airtight container.

Ingredients

- 100g / 3½oz caster sugar
- 100g / 3½oz light muscovado sugar
- 450g / 1lb butter
- 285g / 10oz plain white flour
- 285g / 10oz stoneground wholemeal flour

Hazelnut Variation:

- 55g / 2oz hazelnuts, toasted and roughly chopped

Method

Preheat the oven to fan 160°C / fan 325°F / gas mark 4.

Line a large baking tray with baking paper.

Using an electric mixer, cream together the butter and sugar until light and fluffy. Reduce the mixer to a medium speed and gradually add in the flour, mixing until smooth. If making the hazelnut biscuits, fold in the hazelnuts.

Lightly flour the work surface to roll out the dough. For rectangle or triangle shaped biscuits, roll out the dough into a rectangle shape (around 25x20cm / 10x8in) to a thickness of 1cm / ½in. Chill in the fridge for 30 minutes or 10 minutes in the freezer; this will help with cutting the biscuits. Cut the rectangle into smaller rectangles or triangles. Alternatively, for round biscuits, roll the dough into a large sausage shape, chill, then cut round biscuits off the log, around 1cm / ½in thick.

Place the shaped dough on the baking tray and prick once or twice with a fork. Bake in the oven for 10-12 minutes or until lightly golden in colour. Store in an airtight container for up to 1 week.

Grainne's Oatmeal Biscuits

These are traditional Irish biscuits, dating back centuries. They go very well with cheese and are served in The Purple Heather with the Irish Farmhouse Cheese Plate (p71).

The biscuits will keep for up to 1 week in an airtight container.

Ingredients

- 100g / 3 ½oz plain white flour
- 1 tsp baking powder
- 225g / 8oz medium oatmeal
- 1 tsp sea salt
- 65ml / 2¼fl oz water
- 45g / 1½oz butter
- 2 tbsp pinhead oatmeal

Method

Preheat oven to fan 160°C / fan 325°F / gas mark 4.

Lightly grease a baking tray with butter and line with parchment paper.

Sieve the flour and baking powder into a large bowl. Add the oatmeal and salt. Mix thoroughly and make a well in the centre. In a saucepan, heat the water over a medium heat, add the butter, bring to the boil and then immediately pour into the centre of the dry ingredient mixture. Mix and bring together to form a stiff dough. Add a little more water if needed.

Sprinkle a work surface with the pinhead oatmeal and roll out the dough to a thickness of 0.5cm / ¼in. Cut the dough into wide rectangles (4x7x0.5cm / 1½x2¾x¼in), place on the tray and bake for about 35-40 minutes or until a pale golden colour. Gently transfer to a wire rack to allow to cool.

Sauces, Stocks & Staples

Sauces, Stocks & Staples

Sauces, Stocks & Staples

Savoury Sauces

Hollandaise Sauce	342
Paloise Sauce	343
Béarnaise Sauce	344
Sauce Choron	344
White Sauce	345
Mornay or Cheese Sauce	345
Beurre Blanc	346
Cream Reduction Sauce	347
Garlic Cream Sauce	347
Tarragon Cream Sauce	348
Wholegrain Mustard Cream Sauce	348
Simple Wholegrain Mustard Cream Sauce	349
Fennel Cream Sauce	349
Seafood Sauce	352
Rouille with Garlic Croûtons	353
Tartare Sauce	354
Chermoula	355
Pesto	356
Tomato & Caper Salsa	356
Salsa Verde	357
Thai Dipping Sauce	358
Cumberland Sauce	358
Basic Brown Sauce	359
Red Wine Jus	360
Fast Red Wine Jus	360
Red Wine, Rosemary & Garlic Sauce	360
Dijonnaise Sauce	361
Green Peppercorn Sauce	361
Port & Cashel Blue Cheese Sauce	362
Fruity Curry Sauce	363

Sweet Sauces

Apple Sauce	364
Apple Syrup	364
Sugar Syrup	365
Crème Anglaise	366
Orange Crème Anglaise	367
Coffee Bean Sauce	368

Stocks

Chicken	370
Fish	371
Beef	372
Shellfish	373
Vegetable	374

Staples

Clarified Butter	376
Garlic Butter	376
Thyme Butter	377
Citrus Butter	377

Sauces, Stocks & Staples

Chutneys & Pastes

Apple Chutney	378
Garlic Confit Paste	379

See also
Red Pepper Relish (p164)
Sweet & Sour Aubergine Relish (p164)

Salad Dressings

Apple & Walnut Oil Dressing	380
Citrus Herb Vinaigrette	381
Hazelnut Vinaigrette	381
Shallot Vinaigrette	382
Simple Balsamic Dressing	382
Simple Citrus Dressing	383
Purple Heather Balsamic Dressing	383
Purple Heather Vinaigrette	384

Hollandaise Sauce

My first encounter with hollandaise was in a Swiss restaurant, Maison Suisse, owned by two sisters in London in the 1950s. My aunt brought me there as a teenager on special occasions. I remember vividly the chicken dish with a white wine cream sauce, the one both my aunt and I especially went for. They also served globe artichokes with hollandaise, and, being my first taste of the sauce, I was in awe. To this day it is still one of my favourite sauces.

This is a basic swift hollandaise which I learned from Sonia Stevenson in the early 1980s. For the 20 years before this time, my method of making hollandaise involved continuously whisking the eggs and water in a bowl over a saucepan of hot water to make a light foamy mixture. I would then slowly add the cold butter, cube by cube, making sure it had emulsified before adding the next cube. I then flavoured the sauce with either lemon juice or the traditional reduction. This swift method is thanks to Sonia and to a food processor. The butter must be hot and foaming and initially added slowly to the processor.

Ingredients

Egg Base:

Makes 200–250ml / 7–9fl oz

- 2 egg yolks
- 2 tbsp cold water
- 225g / 8oz butter

Swift Method:

- 1 tbsp fresh lemon juice, more to taste if needed

Method

Swift Method

In a small saucepan, melt the butter until it starts to boil then remove from the heat. Meanwhile, place the water and yolks in a food processor and blend until pale and fluffy. Very gradually start to pour the hot foaming butter via the funnel into the processor, keeping the motor running, until it starts to emulsify. You can then add the remaining butter more swiftly while still hot. If using lemon juice, add via the funnel and blend. Add more to taste if needed. Transfer the hollandaise into the saucepan used to melt the butter and cover with a lid. If not serving immediately, place the saucepan over another saucepan of hot water to keep warm until serving.

Traditional Reduction:

- 30g / 1oz butter

- 3 black peppercorns, lightly crushed in a pestle and mortar

- 50g / 1¾oz finely diced shallots (around 2 shallots, but will depend on size)

- 150ml / 5¼fl oz white wine vinegar

- 75ml / 2½fl oz white wine

- 75ml / 2½fl oz water

Paloise:

- Egg base (opposite)

- Traditional Reduction

- 2 tbsp of chopped mint leaves

Traditional Reduction

Melt the butter in a small saucepan over a low heat. Add the shallots and pepper. Cover and sweat for 10 minutes or until the shallots are soft but not coloured, stirring occasionally. Add the vinegar and wine and reduce for 5-8 minutes or until it reaches a syrupy consistency. Add the water and boil to reduce by two thirds. Strain the reduction through a sieve, pressing gently to obtain as much liquid as possible and discard the shallots and peppercorns. If necessary, further reduce the liquid to about 1 tbsp by returning the liquid to the pan.

Add the reduction into the egg base (no lemon juice) in the food processor via the funnel (as above).

Paloise Sauce

The paloise sauce is magical with roast lamb, like a classic béarnaise with fillet steak. To make the paloise, make the egg base with the traditional reduction, then remove from the food processor and stir in 2 tbsp of chopped mint leaves.

Sauces, Stocks & Staples

Béarnaise Sauce

Béarnaise is one of the great egg sauces, wonderful with fillet steak. While the steak is resting, a little juice from the fillet can be added to the sauce. It also goes very well with prawns or crab. The sauce includes the egg base from the hollandaise with a tarragon reduction.

Ingredients

Makes 400ml / 14fl oz

Tarragon reduction:

- 30g / 1oz butter
- 75g / 2½oz finely diced shallots (around 3 shallots, but will depend on size)
- 2 whole peppercorns, crushed in a pestle and mortar
- 150ml / 5¼fl oz tarragon vinegar (p34)
- 75ml / 2½fl oz water
- Egg base (p342)
- 1 tbsp chopped fresh tarragon

Sauce Choron:

- 1 tsp butter or olive oil
- 4 medium tomatoes (best quality firm but ripe), skinned, deseeded and finely diced
- 1 garlic clove, peeled
- 1 sprig of thyme
- 1 tsp good quality tomato purée
- Béarnaise (above)

Tarragon reduction:

Melt the butter in a small saucepan over a low heat. Add the shallots and pepper. Cover and sweat for 10 minutes or until soft but not coloured, stirring occasionally. Add the tarragon vinegar and reduce for 5-8 minutes or until it reaches a syrupy consistency. Add the water and boil to reduce by two thirds. I prefer not to strain the sauce, but I do remove any large chunky peppercorn pieces.

Stir the reduction into the egg base and stir in the chopped fresh tarragon. Cover with a lid. If not serving immediately, place the saucepan over another saucepan of hot water to keep warm until serving.

Sauce Choron:

This is a very tasty sauce, beautiful with fish or shellfish. I serve this sauce with the Brochettes de Fruits de Mer (p190). The sauce consists of a tomato base added to the béarnaise.

In a small stainless steel saucepan, heat the olive oil or butter. Add the tomatoes, garlic and thyme and cook over a medium-high heat, stirring regularly, until all the liquid has evaporated and the tomatoes are smooth and thick. Mix in the tomato purée, then remove the thyme and garlic. Add the tomato mixture to the warmed béarnaise sauce. Cover with a lid. If not serving immediately, place the saucepan over another saucepan of hot water to keep warm until serving.

White Sauce

This is a simple white sauce, without the infusion of the onion, peppercorns and bay leaf used in a classic béchamel sauce. There is generally no cream in a white sauce, however for my recipe I prefer to use cream to enrich the sauce. The white sauce can be used as a base for a cheesy Mornay sauce, as below.

Ingredients

Makes 250ml / 9fl oz

- 30g / 1oz butter
- 30g / 1oz plain white flour
- 420ml / ¾ pint whole milk
- 140ml / ¼ pint cream
- Sea salt and cracked black pepper

Mornay or Cheese Sauce:

- White Sauce (above)
- 55g / 2oz grated Coolea Matured (or a mature cheddar would also work)
- 30g / 1oz Parmigiano Reggiano, freshly grated
- Sea salt and cracked black pepper

Method

To make the sauce, melt the butter in a saucepan over a low heat. Add the flour and stir for 2-3 minutes. Gradually pour in the milk, continuing to stir until you have a smooth consistency. Continue to cook gently for 15 minutes, stirring continuously, until the sauce has thickened. Add the cream and stir until the sauce has a thick coating consistency. Season to taste. If a thinner coating sauce is desired, add a little more milk.

Mornay or Cheese Sauce:

Make the white sauce as above. Remove from the heat and stir in the cheese until blended. Season to taste.

Beurre Blanc

This is a classic French sauce that is well flavoured, buttery and wonderful with fish. This is my variation as cream is not in a true beurre blanc, but it is a brilliant help for emulsifying.

Ingredients

Makes 500ml /17.5fl oz

- 100g / 3½oz finely diced shallots (around 4-5 shallots, but will depend on size)
- 20g / ¾oz butter
- 100ml / 3½fl oz white wine vinegar
- 100ml / 3½fl oz dry white wine
- 50ml / 1¾fl oz cream
- 400g / 14oz cold butter, cut into small pieces
- Sea salt and cracked black pepper

Method

In a small saucepan over a low heat, add the shallots with butter, cover and sweat for 10 minutes or until soft but not coloured, stirring occasionally. Add the vinegar and white wine, then reduce the liquid over a high heat until barely any remains.

Add the cream, bring to the boil then reduce to a very low heat. Gradually whisk in the butter to make a smooth and creamy sauce – you may need to occasionally remove the pan from the heat to prevent the mixture from overheating and splitting. Season to taste.

If not serving immediately, cover and keep warm over a pot of hot water and stir before serving.

Cream Reduction Sauce

This sauce should taste good enough to use by itself – for example, when cooking chicken you can deglaze the pan with this sauce and serve with the chicken. It can be used as a base for many sauces, featuring garlic, tarragon, fennel or mustard, as detailed below and overleaf.

Ingredients

Makes 600-650ml / 21-23fl oz

- 200g / 7oz finely diced shallots (around 8-10 shallots, but will depend on size)
- 30g / 1oz butter
- 75ml / 2½fl oz good quality dry white wine
- 250ml / 8¾fl oz Noilly Prat
- 500ml / 17½fl oz stock, chicken (p370), vegetable (p374) or fish (p371), depending on your accompanying dish
- 400ml / 14fl oz cream
- Sea salt and cracked black pepper

Garlic Cream Sauce:

Makes 200ml / 7fl oz

- 1 tbsp garlic confit paste (p379)
- 200ml / 7fl oz cream reduction sauce (p347)
- Sea salt and cracked black pepper

Method

In a saucepan over a low heat, add the shallots with butter, cover and sweat for 10-15 mins or until soft but not coloured, stirring occasionally. Add the wine, Noilly Prat and stock, then bring to the boil and reduce over a high heat until it has reduced by two thirds. Add the cream and reduce to a coating consistency over a low heat. Blitz using a hand blender, or in a food processor. If using a food processor, return to the saucepan to heat through.

Season to taste.

Garlic Cream Sauce:

This sauce is wonderful with lamb. In the springtime, wild garlic grows in abundance. If you have access to wild garlic, chop around 4 tbsp of the tender leaves and add to the sauce instead of the garlic confit.

In a saucepan, bring the cream reduction sauce to the boil, then reduce to a low heat. Add 1 tbsp of the garlic confit paste to the heated cream reduction sauce. Season to taste, adding more garlic if desired.

Sauces, Stocks & Staples

Tarragon Cream Sauce:

Makes 180ml / 6¼fl oz

- 1 tbsp butter
- 75g / 2½oz finely diced shallots (around 3 shallots, but will depend on size)
- 1 tbsp tarragon vinegar (p34)
- 200ml / 7fl oz cream reduction sauce (p347)
- 60g / 2oz fresh tarragon leaves
- Sea salt and cracked black pepper

Tarragon Cream Sauce:

Tarragon is in season in summer in Ireland. Depending on what stock is used, this sauce can accompany pasta, fish or chicken with rice (p213).

In a small saucepan, melt the butter over a low heat then add the shallots, cover and sweat for 10 minutes or until soft but not coloured, stirring occasionally. Add the vinegar and reduce for 5 minutes over a medium-high heat until the liquid has evaporated. Add the cream reduction sauce, bring to the boil, then turn down the heat and simmer for a few minutes. Blitz using a hand blender, or in a food processor. If using a food processor, return to the saucepan to heat through. Season to taste. Add the tarragon leaves to a sieve and plunge into a saucepan of boiling water for 1 minute. Remove the sieve with the leaves and refresh under cold running water.
Pat the leaves dry with kitchen paper. Snip the leaves into the sauce and stir.

Wholegrain Mustard Cream Sauce:

Makes 200ml / 7fl oz

- 2 tbsp wholegrain mustard
- 200ml / 7fl oz cream reduction sauce (p347)
- 1 tsp honey
- Lemon juice, to taste
- Sea salt and cracked black pepper

Wholegrain Mustard Cream Sauce:

This sauce works very well with ham or also with sea bass. This version has more depth than the simple wholegrain mustard sauce.

In a saucepan, bring the cream reduction sauce to the boil, then reduce to a low heat. Stir the wholegrain mustard into the heated cream reduction sauce. Add the honey and lemon juice to taste. Season to taste.

Simple Wholegrain Mustard Cream Sauce:

Makes 150ml / 5¼fl oz

- **150ml / 5¼fl oz cream**
- **2 tbsp wholegrain mustard**
- **1 tsp honey**
- **1 tbsp lemon juice, or more to taste**
- **Sea salt and cracked black pepper**

Simple Wholegrain Mustard Cream Sauce:

Heat the cream in a saucepan over a low heat. Stir in the mustard and honey. Add the lemon juice to taste and season to taste. Use immediately (as cream has not been boiled).

Fennel Cream Sauce:

Makes 200ml / 7fl oz

- **1 tbsp fresh snipped fennel leaves**
- **1 tbsp Pernod**
- **200ml / 7fl oz cream reduction sauce (p347), made using fish stock**
- **Salt and black cracked pepper**

Fennel Cream Sauce:

This sauce is for any fish of your choice. Use fish stock in the cream reduction sauce. Alternatively, the sauce goes well with pasta when using a vegetarian stock.

In a saucepan, bring the cream reduction sauce to the boil, then reduce to a low heat. Stir in the fennel and Pernod. Season to taste.

The Purple M

Appetizers
- Soup of the Day — 1-6
- Melon with Maraschino — 2-0
- Fruit Juice — 1-3
- Fresh Prawn Cocktail — 6-
- Smoked Kerry Salmon — 6
- Homemade Paté & Cumberland Sauce — 4-

Seafoods
- Fresh Dover Sole on the Bone — 13
- Grilled or Poached Fresh Roughty River Salmon with Hollandaise Sauce — 1:
- Fresh fillets of Plaice with Tartare Sauce

Grills
- Mixed Grill
- Half Chicken & Bacon
- Half Chicken in Wine Sauce
- Steak Sirloin
- Sausage & Bacon

Egg Dishes — *Cooked in Butter*
- Plain Omelette
- Ham, Cheese, Tomato, Mushroom Omelette
- Purple Heather Omelette

Heather.

Old Purple Heather menu from the early 1970s which includes hollandaise, Cumberland sauce, tartare sauce and red wine sauce

Telephone KENMARE 71

Salads
Fresh Salmon Mayonnaise	13-6
Cheese Salad	7-6
Ham Salad	9-6
Chicken & Ham	11-6

Vegetables *tossed in Butter*
Broccoli	2-6
French Beans	1-6
Mushrooms	1-6
Peas	1-6
Tossed Salad	1-6
Potatoes Creamed or Chipped	1-6

Sweets *Fresh cream served with all sweets.*
Icecream and Chocolate Sauce	1-6
Apple Tart	1-9
Gateau	2-0
Fresh Fruit Salad with Kirsch	2-6
Asst. Cheeses	2-0

Tea or Coffee inclusive.

Irish Coffee 4-6

Fully Licenced.   Wine List.

Seafood Sauce

This is a rich, creamy sauce and is wonderful with any white fish, in particular turbot, brill, John Dory and Dover sole. This sauce could be served with the seafood sausage or mousse (p122) instead of the beurre blanc.

Ingredients

Makes 300ml / 10½fl oz

- 570ml / 1 pint shellfish stock (p373)
- 285ml / ½ pint cream
- 50ml / 1¾fl oz brandy
- 1 tbsp chopped fresh tarragon leaves

Method

In a medium saucepan, reduce the stock to half over a high heat. Pour in the cream and brandy and bring to the boil. Reduce the heat to medium and simmer for 10 minutes or until it reaches a coating consistency. Add the tarragon and stir to combine.

Rouille with Garlic Croûtons

Rouille is French for 'rust', and in this case it is a hot garlic mayonnaise with a rust-like colour. I serve it with the Wild Atlantic Seafood Soup (p80) on the side with garlic croutons to dip into the rouille. The rouille also works well as a dip for crudités.

Ingredients

Serves 6–8

Rouille:

- A few pinches of saffron threads or ¼ tsp saffron powder
- 2 egg yolks
- 4 garlic cloves, peeled and crushed
- ½ tsp cayenne pepper
- ¼ tsp dried chilli flakes
- 250ml / 8¾fl oz olive oil

Garlic Croûtons:

- 4 tbsp olive oil
- 1 stale French stick or narrow baguette, cut into thin slices
- 2 garlic cloves

Method

Preheat the oven to fan 150°C / fan 300°F / gas mark 3.

Soak the saffron threads or powder in 1 tbsp warm water and add to a food processor, along with the egg yolks. Blend until light and fluffy. Add the garlic, cayenne pepper and chilli flakes and blend again. With the machine still running, very slowly trickle in the oil through the funnel, being careful to avoid splitting. Once the mixture starts to emulsify and thicken, the oil can be added more confidently and quickly.

To make the garlic croûtons, pour the oil onto a lipped baking tray and spread to cover. Spread the sliced baguette onto the baking tray, dipping the bread in the oil to coat both sides. Bake in the oven for 15-20 minutes or until golden and crisp. Remove from the oven and allow to cool. Rub the garlic along both sides of the croûtons; the hard bread abrades like sandpaper, so only rub a little as it absorbs easily.

Serve the rouille with the croûtons and a generous bowl of hot Atlantic seafood soup (p80).

Tartare Sauce

Tartare sauce is a classic sauce for deep fried fish or any fried fish in general. The key to this sauce is its piquancy. I serve it with crab cakes (p116) and smoked cod cakes (p126). Capers grow wild in a bush in the Mediterranean and should be much more expensive given that they must be handpicked, only when ripe and at a specific time of day. They are also cultivated, but even then they cannot be picked by machine.

If using salted capers, ensure you rinse off the salt. Large capers can be chopped; if using small capers, do not chop.

Ingredients

Makes 250ml / 9fl oz

- 2 egg yolks, room temperature
- 15g / ½oz English mustard
- 215ml / 7½fl oz sunflower oil
- 1½ tbsp white wine vinegar
- 2 tbsp chopped chives
- 2 tbsp chopped parsley leaves, flat leaf or curly
- 3 tbsp capers, rinsed and chopped if large or whole if small
- Sea salt and cracked black pepper

Method

Beginning with the base of a mayonnaise, place the egg yolks and mustard in a food processor and start the machine running. Very slowly, trickle in the oil through the funnel, being careful to avoid splitting the mayonnaise. Once the mixture starts to thicken, the oil can be added more confidently and quickly. Add the vinegar, adding more mustard if desired.

Tip into a bowl and finish by mixing through the chives, parsley and capers. Season to taste.

Chermoula

Chermoula depends very much on personal taste and preference, so you can vary the amount of herbs, citrus and spice. Denis Cotter has a delicious recipe, and this is an adaptation of his. Denis is a superb vegetarian chef and his food is astounding. I have two vegetarians in my family and Denis's cooking has offered great inspiration for me over the years.

This is very useful for people who love grains and it is a vegan recipe. Chermoula delivers fast flavour, great to have in a jar ready to serve.

Ingredients

Makes 450ml / 16fl oz

- 1 tsp coriander seeds
- 1 tsp cumin seeds
- 85g / 3oz coriander, stems and leaves
- 60g / 2oz flat leaf parsley, leaves and fine stems
- 50g / 1¾oz mint leaves
- 4 garlic cloves, peeled
- 3 tsp smoked paprika
- Pinch of cayenne
- Zest of 1 orange and 1 tbsp of juice
- Zest of 1 lemon and 1 tbsp of juice
- Zest of 1 lime
- 300ml / 10½fl oz olive oil
- Sea salt

Method

In a dry frying pan, toast the coriander and cumin seeds over a low heat for a few minutes or until fragrant and turning lightly golden. Crush in a pestle and mortar to a fine powder.

Place the herbs and garlic in a food processor and blitz to roughly chop. Add the remaining ingredients with crushed spices and blitz again to the texture of pesto or a salsa verde.

Pesto

At first, customers at The Lime Tree in the mid 1980s weren't familiar with pesto. I had a regular customer who always asked for "more of the green stuff". Now into the mainstream, I continue to serve pesto with fish, pasta or just simply with bread. A critical point when making pesto is not to use pre-grated cheese; use freshly grated Parmigiano Reggiano or Pecorino and a good extra virgin olive oil.

Ingredients

Makes around 1 jar

- 255ml / 9fl oz good quality extra virgin olive oil
- 55g / 2oz pine nuts, lightly toasted
- 3 garlic cloves, peeled
- 85g / 3oz Parmigiano Reggiano or Pecorino freshly grated
- 55g / 2oz basil leaves, washed and stems removed
- Sea salt and cracked black pepper

Method

Add all the ingredients into a food processor and blitz to chop and combine well.

Season to taste.

Tomato & Caper Salsa

Ingredients

- 30g / 1oz butter
- 4 tomatoes, seeds removed, diced very finely
- 1 tbsp small 'nonparielle' capers (leave whole)
- 1 tsp lime juice
- ½ tbsp chopped flat leaf parsley
- Lime wedges, to serve

This salsa is lovely with fillets of fish such as lemon sole and is particularly good with plaice

Method

Melt the butter in a small saucepan, add the tomatoes, capers and lime, and warm through for about 1 minute. Sprinkle with chopped parsley and serve with lime wedges.

Salsa Verde

A piquant herby green sauce of pesto-like consistency. It almost works with everything and is excellent with fish. There are many variations and it can be tweaked to your liking. Some include chopped anchovies; here is my version.

For a vegan version, omit the mustard and add an extra tablespoon of olive oil.

Ingredients

Makes around 1 jar

- 2 tbsp finely chopped flat leaf parsley
- 2 tbsp finely chopped mint leaves
- 2 tbsp finely sliced basil leaves
- 2 garlic cloves, finely chopped
- 2 tbsp small capers, strained, leave whole
- 8 gherkins, finely chopped
- 1 tbsp Dijon mustard
- 1 tbsp red wine vinegar
- Zest of 2 limes and 2 tbsp lime juice
- 4 tbsp good quality extra virgin olive oil
- A pinch of sugar or honey, optional

Method

In a bowl, mix together the herbs with the garlic, capers and gherkins. In a small bowl, combine the mustard with red wine vinegar, lime juice and zest and then stir into the herb mixture. Mix in the olive oil and taste. If too bitter, stir in a pinch of sugar or some honey.

Thai Dipping Sauce

This is a very useful sauce to have to hand to enhance many sauces, soups and even dressings for grain-based salads. It can also be used as a dipping sauce (p162) for battered fish, and I use it in my red pepper relish (p164) to add spiciness and piquancy. A larger quantity can be made and kept in the fridge for 1 month.

Ingredients

Makes 150ml / 5¼fl oz

- 300ml / 10½fl oz red wine vinegar
- 2 tbsp caster sugar
- 2 garlic cloves, peeled and finely chopped
- 3 medium red chillies, deseeded and finely chopped

Method

In a small saucepan, add the vinegar and sugar. Bring to the boil then simmer until the vinegar has reduced by half. Remove from the heat and then add the garlic and chilli. Set aside to cool. Store in a sterilized glass jar and seal. Serve cold.

Cumberland Sauce

This is served with the chicken liver pâté in The Purple Heather. It's a very simple sauce, delicious with chicken or ham and is super easy to make.

Ingredients

Makes around 1 jar

- 370g / 13oz redcurrant jelly
- Juice and zest of 1 orange
- Juice and zest of ½ lemon
- ¾ tsp English mustard
- 100ml / 3½fl oz port
- Sea salt and cracked black pepper

Method

Place all the ingredients in a medium saucepan over a medium-high heat, stirring gently and bring to boil. Then turn down the heat and stir occasionally until smooth. The sauce has a fairly thin consistency. Allow to cool, pour into a sterilised glass jar and seal. The sauce will keep for up to two weeks in the fridge.

Serve cold with meats.

Basic Brown Sauce

This sauce is similar to a demi-glace and is ready to use as it is. It is an excellent base for other sauces such as the steak sauces: Dijonnaise, port & Cashel Blue and green peppercorn sauce as well as red wine jus and red wine rosemary and garlic sauce. I recommend making the sauce in a large quantity as it is very versatile and can be frozen in batches keeping for up to 3 months. Take it out when required to make a rich sauce full of depth and flavour.

Ingredients

- 1x 400g / 14oz tin good quality tomatoes
- 4 tbsp clarified butter (p376)
- 2 tbsp plain white flour
- 450g / 1lb onions, peeled and finely chopped
- 450g / 1lb carrots, peeled and finely chopped
- 2 celery sticks, washed and finely chopped
- 2 leeks, washed and finely chopped
- 140g / 5oz mushrooms, finely chopped
- 2.5 litres / 4½ pints beef stock (p372) or a good quality bought stock
- 300ml / 10½fl oz red wine
- 300ml / 10½fl oz port
- 150ml / 5¼fl oz Madeira
- 1 tbsp cornflour mixed with 1 cup cold water

Method

Strain the tomatoes from the tin and discard the liquid. Finely chop the tomatoes removing as many of the seeds as possible.

To make the brown roux, heat 2 tbsp of the clarified butter in a medium saucepan and add the flour. Cook over a medium heat, stirring continuously until golden brown.

In a separate large saucepan, heat the remaining 2 tbsp clarified butter, then add all the vegetables except the tomatoes and sauté until brown. Stir frequently and be careful not to burn (if it does it is not usable). Add the finely chopped tomatoes to the vegetables and cook until the liquid evaporates and it starts to brown and caramelise. Add the brown roux to the vegetables. Stir well. Add the beef stock and bring to the boil. Reduce to a low heat, then simmer uncovered for 2 hours.

Strain the sauce through a sieve – do not press, instead allow it to drip out. Return the strained liquid to a saucepan and add the cornflour mix over a high heat. Stir continuously. Add the wine, port and Madeira to the pot and simmer over a gentle heat for 30 minutes.

Allow to cool, then store in the fridge for 2-3 days or freeze in batches for up to 3 months.

Serves 3–4

- 150ml / 5¼fl oz basic brown sauce (p359)
- 50ml / 1¾fl oz port
- 50ml / 1¾fl oz red wine
- Sea salt and cracked black pepper

Red Wine Jus:

This is suitable with lamb during spring and summer or chicken at any time of the year.

In a saucepan, add the basic brown sauce, port and wine and bring to the boil. Turn down the heat to low and simmer for 15 minutes to cook out the red wine. Season to taste.

Serves 6

- Residue, juices and remaining 1 tsp of fat in meat roasting pan
- 1 tsp plain white flour
- 240ml / 8½fl oz red wine
- 240ml / 8½fl oz water
- 1 tbsp redcurrant jelly
- Sea salt and cracked black pepper

Fast Red Wine Jus:

This is delicious with roast lamb or chicken. If serving the jus with roast beef, substitute the jelly for 2 tbsp port. This sauce is made in the roasting pan using the residue and flavour from the roasted meat.

Strain off the excess fat from the pan in which the meat was roasted, leaving the residue and juices and at least 1 tsp of fat in the roasting pan. Over a low heat on the stove, sprinkle the flour into the roasting pan and mix well, being sure to scrape the bottom the pan to keep the precious sediment. Increase the heat to medium and add the wine and water, then simmer for 10 minutes to cook off the alcohol. Transfer to a medium saucepan and reduce the liquid over a high heat to around 250ml / 8¾fl oz. Stir in the redcurrant jelly and season to taste.

Serves 3–4

- 150ml / 5¼fl oz basic brown sauce (p359)
- 50ml / 1¾fl oz red wine
- 50ml / 1¾fl oz port
- 2 sprigs of fresh rosemary
- 1 tbsp garlic confit (p379)
- 1 tbsp redcurrant jelly
- Sea salt and cracked black pepper

Red Wine, Rosemary & Garlic Sauce:

This is delicious with lamb, especially in the autumn.

In a small saucepan, heat the basic brown sauce, red wine, port and rosemary over a medium heat for 15 minutes. Add the redcurrant jelly and garlic confit and bring to the boil, stirring continuously until the jelly is dissolved. Remove the rosemary sprigs, shaking off any sauce. Season to taste.

Dijonnaise Sauce:

Serves 3–4

- 75ml / 2½fl oz basic brown sauce (p359)
- 100ml / 3½fl oz cream
- 1 tbsp brandy
- 2 tbsp good quality Dijon mustard

The combination of flavours in this sauce is wonderful with steak.

In a small saucepan, combine the basic brown sauce, cream and brandy and bring to the boil over a medium-high heat, then reduce to a medium heat and simmer for 5 minutes. Add the mustard and mix well. The consistency should be slightly thicker than coating consistency. Season to taste.

Green Peppercorn Sauce:

Serves 4

- 150ml / 5¼fl oz basic brown sauce (p259)
- 55ml / 2fl oz port
- 2 tbsp brandy
- 55ml / 2fl oz cream
- 1 tbsp green peppercorns, add more if you'd like (well rinsed if in brine)
- Sea salt

Black, green and white pepper all come from the same plant, the piper nigrum plant which originated in India. The green peppercorns are the really unripe berries. They now usually come in a jar with brine. This sauce is wonderful with both steak and chicken; we served it at The Lime Tree with fillet steak, one of the most popular dishes there. Serve only a few tbsp per person.

In a small saucepan, combine the basic brown sauce, port and brandy and bring to the boil over a medium-high heat, then reduce to a medium heat and simmer for 5 minutes. Add cream and bring back to the boil, then turn the heat down and simmer for 5 minutes or until it reaches coating consistency. Add the peppercorns just before serving. Season to taste with sea salt.

Port & Cashel Blue Cheese Sauce

Divine with sirloin steak (p232), and what could also be a luxurious sauce inside beef burgers, the intensity of this sauce stands up well to the flavour of the beef. Cashel Blue cheese is a very intense salty blue cheese from the Grubb family in Tipperary. In 1984, when I was restoring The Lime Tree, which was originally a derelict school, Jane and Louis were creating Cashel Blue cheese on their farm. The same family produce Crozier Blue, which is a sheep's blue cheese and one of my daughter's favourites – it is similar to Roquefort, which is a ewe's milk cheese. The Cashel Blue works very well in this sauce. I started using the cheese at The Lime Tree when I opened in 1985, and I still serve it on my cheese board at Shelburne Lodge today.

Ingredients

Serves 3–4

- 150ml / 5¼fl oz basic brown sauce (p359)
- 55ml / 2fl oz port
- 1 tbsp brandy
- 75ml / 2½fl oz cream
- 30g-55g / 1-2oz Cashel Blue cheese, amount depends on personal taste
- Cracked black pepper

Method

In a small saucepan, combine the basic brown sauce, port and brandy and bring to the boil over a medium-high heat, then reduce to a medium heat and simmer for 5 minutes. Add cream and bring back to the boil, then turn the heat down and simmer for 5 minutes or until it reaches coating consistency. Crumble the blue cheese into the sauce, remove from the heat and stir to melt the cheese. Season to taste with cracked black pepper.

Fruity Curry Sauce

This curry sauce can be made in advance and stored in the fridge for a few days or frozen for up to 3 months in batches.

Ingredients

Makes 700ml / 1¼ pints

- 55g / 2oz butter

- 200g / 7oz finely diced shallots (around 8-10 shallots, but will depend on size)

- 4 garlic cloves, finely chopped

- 2 tbsp plain white flour

- 5 tbsp curry powder

- 3 tsp coriander seeds, toasted and crushed in a pestle and mortar

- 3 tsp cumin seeds, toasted and crushed in a pestle and mortar

- 1 tbsp freshly grated ginger

- 3 Cox's apples, peeled, cored and chopped

- ½ ripe pineapple, finely chopped

- 250ml / 8¾fl oz coconut milk

- 1 tbsp apple chutney (p378)

- 2 tsp tomato purée

- Juice and zest of 2 limes

- 700ml / 1¼ pint vegetable (p371) or chicken stock (p370)

- Sea salt and cracked black pepper

Method

In a large saucepan, melt the butter over a low heat. Add the shallots and garlic. Cover and sweat for 10-15 minutes or until softened but not coloured, stirring occasionally. Add the flour, curry powder, crushed toasted coriander and cumin seeds and stir over a gentle heat for 2-3 minutes to cook out the flour. Turn up to a medium heat and add all the remaining ingredients, stirring well. Bring the sauce to a boil then turn down to a very low heat. Cover and simmer for 1½ hours, stirring occasionally. I prefer a chunky sauce. If desired, purée the sauce using a hand blender or food processor.

Season to taste.

Apple Sauce

Ingredients

Makes 500ml / 17.5fl oz

- 4-6 medium cooking apples (such as Bramley), peeled, cored and sliced
- 15g / ½oz butter
- 55ml / 2fl oz cold water
- 1-2 tbsp demerara sugar
- Zest of 1 lemon
- Zest of 1 orange, if serving with duck or goose

Method

In a saucepan add the apples, butter, water, sugar and zest and bring to the boil over a medium heat, stirring frequently. Reduce to a low heat to cook the apples until soft, stirring occasionally. Taste and add more sugar if required. Serve hot or allow to cool and store in the fridge for up to 3 days and serve cold.

Apple Syrup

This apple syrup can be served with Drop Scone Pancakes (p58) or porridge. It also works very well with yoghurt or vanilla ice-cream. To further enrich the sauce, 2 tbsp of Longueville Irish Apple Brandy can be added at the end. Use farm pressed apple juice for this recipe.

Ingredients

- 350ml / 12¼fl oz Irish Farm Pressed Apple Juice (e.g. Attyflin Estate or Ballyhoura Apple Farm)
- 200g / 7oz caster sugar
- 2 tbsp water

Method

In a heavy-based stainless steel saucepan, pour in sugar and water and stir over a medium heat to dissolve the sugar. Turn up the heat and do not stir again, allowing the sugar to caramelise by swilling the pan over the heat. The edges will colour first – when a lovely golden colour all over, remove from the heat. Gradually pour in the apple juice, being very careful as it will splutter and splash. Place the pan back over a high heat and swill to combine the juice with the caramel which will be partly solidified. Watch it carefully until all is combined and continue to boil for 3 minutes until a syrupy consistency. Remove from the heat. Cool and store in sterilised bottles for up to 2 weeks in the fridge.

Sugar Syrup

Sugar syrup is very useful for imparting further flavour, texture and natural sweetness. This syrup is in several of the fruit compotes in the breakfast section. I have provided a recipe here for a large quantity and it can be adapted to how much you need. It keeps for up to one month in the fridge.

This simple sugar syrup can be used as a base for different flavoured syrups using 300ml / 10fl oz of warmed syrup and allowing the flavours to infuse for up to 30 minutes before serving. For an orange syrup, add the zest and juice of 1 orange. For a lime syrup, add the zest and juice of 1 lime. For a passion fruit syrup, split a passion fruit across the middle (not from top to tail), scoop out the seeds and add to the syrup just before you take it off the heat. For an elderflower syrup, add two flower heads and strain by firmly pressing through a sieve to obtain maximum flavour. Cover all these once off the heat.

Ingredients

Makes around 1 litre / 35fl oz

- 570ml / 1 pint cold water
- 800g / 1lb 12oz caster sugar

Method

In a small saucepan, add the sugar and water. Stir over a medium heat until the sugar dissolves then stop stirring, turn up the heat and bring to the boil. Continue to boil for 2-3 minutes or until the sugar syrup is clear. Allow to cool completely.

The sugar syrup can be stored in the fridge for up to 1 month.

Crème Anglaise

This can be made a few hours in advance and should be used on the same day as serving. If you wish to serve the custard warm, it must be kept warm over hot water. Cold custard is delicious and traditional. It is very much a personal choice!

Ingredients

Makes 280ml / 10fl oz

- 285ml / ½ pint whole milk
- 1 vanilla pod, moist and split with seeds scraped (see p35 for further description)
- 75g/ 2½oz caster sugar
- 3 egg yolks

Method

In a small heavy-based saucepan, add the milk and split vanilla pod with scraped seeds. Turn the heat up to high and bring to the boil, stirring continuously to prevent any sticking. Take the pan off the heat, cover and allow to infuse for 10 minutes.

In a bowl, whisk the egg yolks and sugar for a few minutes until pale and creamy.

Remove the split vanilla pod from the saucepan. Squeeze the pod from top to bottom, adding any remaining seeds into the milk. Set aside and keep for vanilla sugar (p35).

Pour the infused milk into the egg and sugar mixture, stirring continuously. Pour the mixture back into a clean saucepan and stir constantly over a low heat to thicken. Be careful not to boil, as this will give you scrambled eggs with sugar! The finished custard should coat the back of a spoon. When it has thickened to this point, remove from the heat and transfer to a clean bowl and continue to stir in the bowl for another minute. Cover immediately with clingfilm to prevent a skin from forming.

If serving warm and not serving immediately, keep warm over a bowl or saucepan of hot water.

Orange Crème Anglaise:

- **285ml / ½ pint cream**
- **125ml / 4½fl oz whole milk**
- **Zest of 2 large oranges**
- **3 egg yolks**
- **50g / 1¾oz caster sugar**

Orange Crème Anglaise:

This crème anglaise is best served cold.

In a saucepan, bring the cream, milk and orange zest to the boil. Beat the egg yolks and sugar together until pale, then pour in the hot milk, stirring continuously. Pour back into a clean saucepan and return to a low heat, stirring continuously until the custard starts to thicken and coats the back of a spoon. When it has thickened to this point, remove from the heat, transfer to a clean bowl and continue to stir in the bowl for another minute. If not serving immediately, cover with clingfilm to prevent a skin from forming and allow to cool. Store in the fridge for up to 1 day.

Coffee Bean Sauce

This sauce is best served cold.

Ingredients

Makes 280ml / 10fl oz

- **285ml / ½ pint whole milk**
- **75g / 2½oz caster sugar**
- **1 tsp fine freshly ground coffee**
- **3 egg yolks**

Method

In a small saucepan, bring the milk and 35g / 1¼oz of the sugar to the boil, stirring to prevent any sticking. When the milk comes to the boil, turn off the heat and stir in the coffee. Cover the saucepan with a lid and leave to infuse for 15 minutes. Return the pan to a medium heat and bring to the boil.

In a bowl, whisk the egg yolks with the remaining sugar for a few minutes until pale and creamy. Pour the coffee-infused milk into the egg and sugar mixture, stirring continuously. Pour the mixture back into a clean saucepan and stir constantly over a low heat to thicken, being careful not to boil as this would give you coffee flavoured scrambled eggs! The finished custard should coat the back of a spoon. When it has thickened to this point, remove from the heat and transfer to a clean bowl, not straining out the coffee grains as they help to give the sauce texture. Continue to stir for another minute in the bowl.

Cover immediately with clingfilm to prevent a skin from forming and allow to cool completely. Store in the fridge for up to 1 day.

Stocks

Using a homemade stock where possible intensifies the flavours of soups and sauces. If you are making a stock, it is worth making it in large quantities as it is a slow process and the stocks can be frozen in batches for up to 3 months (fish or shellfish stock for up to 1 month). If using a readymade stock, ensure it is of the best quality with natural ingredients. Stocks are always cooked uncovered at the simmering stage as it allows you to spoon off the scum easily.

Chicken Stock

Ingredients

Makes around 2-2 ½ litres / 3 ½ - 4 ½ pints

- 1.5kg / 3lb 5oz chicken carcasses (fat removed) roughly chopped or wings
- 4 shallots, roughly chopped
- 2 onions, roughly chopped
- 2 garlic cloves, peeled and roughly chopped
- 4 sticks of celery, roughly chopped
- 2 leeks, cleaned using white parts only and roughly chopped
- 285ml / ½ pint dry white wine
- 3 sprigs of fresh thyme
- 4 litres / 7 pints cold water

Method

In a large tall stock pot, add the chicken bones and cover with the cold water. Over a high heat, bring to the boil. then reduce to a low heat and add the vegetables, wine and thyme and barely simmer uncovered for 3 hours, skimming off any scrum periodically.

Strain the stock through a fine mesh sieve then through a colander with a double layer of muslin or a J-cloth to remove any extra impurities.

Keep in the fridge for up to a week or freeze in batches for up to 3 months.

Fish Stock

Ingredients

Makes 2 litres / 3½ pints

- 3 tbsp clarified butter
- 6 shallots, finely chopped
- 2 garlic cloves, crushed and then skins removed
- 3 carrots, finely chopped
- 6 sticks of celery, finely chopped
- 3 leeks, cleaned and finely chopped
- 2 fennel bulbs, thinly sliced
- Zest of 1 lemon
- 1 star anise
- 200ml / 7fl oz dry white wine
- 200ml / 7fl oz Noilly Prat
- 2kg / 4lb 6½oz fish bones – preferably sole bones, alternatives are turbot, brill or cod heads (no oily fish), well washed and no blood
- 2 litres / 3½ pints cold water (ensure there is enough to cover the ingredients well)

Method

In a large tall stock pot, heat the butter over a low heat then add the shallots and garlic, cover and sweat until soft but not coloured, stirring occasionally. Remove the lid, add the vegetables, lemon zest and star anise and cook until soft, stirring regularly to stop any caramelisation. Add the wine and Noilly Prat, turn up to a high heat and bring to the boil then reduce by half, stirring occasionally. Add the fish bones and cover with the cold water. Bring to the boil over a high heat, then reduce to a medium heat and simmer for 30 minutes, skimming off the scum periodically. Strain the stock through a sieve into a deep container and stand in a sink of cold water to allow to cool quickly.

Store in the fridge for up to 2 days or freeze in batches for up to 1 month.

Beef Stock

Ingredients

Makes 2 ½ litres / 4½ pints

- 2kg / 4lb 6½oz beef bones and trimmings, chopped into small pieces (your butcher can do this)
- 55g / 2oz clarified butter (p376), melted (for the bones)
- 45g / 1½oz clarified butter (p376)
- 1 x 400g / 14oz tin good quality whole tomatoes
- 1kg / 2lb 3oz onions, peeled and finely chopped
- 400g / 14oz carrots, peeled and finely chopped
- 2 celery stalks, roughly chopped
- 3 garlic cloves, crushed
- 1 Granny Smith apple, peeled, cored and roughly chopped
- 2 sprigs of fresh thyme
- 1 bay leaf
- 4 black whole peppercorns
- 300ml / 10½fl oz dry white wine
- 240ml / 8fl oz cold water, plus enough to cover the bones well

Method

Preheat the oven to fan 190°C / fan 375°F / gas mark 6½.

On a roasting tray, lay out the bones and trimmings and brush with the clarified butter. Roast in the oven, turning occasionally, for 45 minutes or until golden brown and well caramelised. Pour off the excess fat.

Strain the tomatoes from the tin and discard the liquid. Chop the tomatoes and remove as many of the seeds as possible.

While the bones are roasting, in a large stock pot heat the remaining clarified butter and sauté the vegetables, apple, herbs and black pepper over a medium heat, stirring regularly, until all are golden brown. Be careful not to burn, as this will result in a bitter stock. Reduce to a low heat, add the chopped tomatoes and sauté carefully until the liquid evaporates and the tomatoes start to brown and caramelise. Pour in the wine and continue to cook for a few more minutes.

Transfer the roasted bones and trimmings into the stock pot, then deglaze the roasting tin with the cold water to release all the caramelised flavour on the base of the pan. Add this liquid to the stock pot, followed by enough cold water to completely immerse the bones. Bring to the boil over a high heat, then reduce to a low heat and simmer gently for 4 hours, uncovered, skimming off any scum periodically. Strain the stock and discard the solids. Allow the stock to cool to room temperature and chill overnight in the fridge. Remove from the fridge and remove the solidified fat from the top of the stock.

Keep in the fridge for up to 3 days or freeze in batches for up to 3 months.

Shellfish Stock

Roasting the shells intensifies the flavour. This is required for the Wild Atlantic seafood soup (p80) and the seafood sauce (p352)

Ingredients

Makes around 1 ½ litres / 2 pints

- 2.7kg / 6lb prawns or lobster shells, crushed
- 5 tbsp butter
- 5 tbsp olive oil
- 2 carrots, peeled and roughly chopped
- 1 leek, washed and finely chopped
- 1 fennel, washed and finely chopped
- 1 celery stick, finely chopped
- 2 onions, roughly chopped
- 2 banana shallots, roughly chopped
- 2 garlic cloves, unpeeled and crushed
- 1 small bouquet garni (p394)
- 3 tbsp Armagnac or brandy
- 3 tbsp port
- 285ml / ½ pint dry white wine
- 3 tomatoes, peeled, diced and seeds removed
- 1 tbsp tomato purée
- Cold water to cover all the ingredients well
- Sea salt and cracked black pepper

Method

Preheat the oven to fan 180°C / fan 350°F /gas mark 6.

Roast the shells with 1 tbsp butter and 1 tbsp oil in the oven for 30 minutes.

Heat the remaining oil and butter in a large saucepan over a medium heat. Add the vegetables, onions, shallots, garlic and bouquet garni, cover with a lid and sweat over a medium heat for 10-15 minutes or until soft, stirring occasionally.

Remove the lid and add the roasted shells. Deglaze the roasting pan with Armagnac or brandy and port on the stove over a medium heat and scrape to keep all the goodness. Using a spatula, add all the glaze into the saucepan, then add the white wine, tomatoes, tomato purée and enough cold water to cover the contents of the saucepan well. Over a high heat, bring to the boil then reduce to a medium heat and simmer gently for 1 hour, uncovered, skimming off any scum periodically. Strain through a sieve, pressing down the shellfish and vegetables with a ladle to extract all the juice and flavour. Allow to cool. Store in the fridge for up to 2 days or in the freezer for up to 1 month.

Vegetable Stock

Ingredients

Makes 2 litres / 3½ pints

- 1½ tbsp clarified butter
- 400g / 14oz onions, peeled and roughly chopped (keep the skins)
- 3 shallots, roughly chopped (keep the skins)
- 1 garlic clove, crushed
- 3 carrots, roughly chopped
- 3 sticks of celery, roughly chopped
- 2 leeks, cleaned and roughly chopped
- 1 fennel bulb, thinly sliced
- Zest of ½ lemon
- 100ml / 3½fl oz dry white wine
- 100ml / 3½fl oz Noilly Prat
- 3 sprigs of fresh thyme
- 3 sprigs of parsley
- 3 litres / 5¼ pints cold water

Method

Preheat the oven to fan 190°C / fan 375°F / gas mark 6½.

In a large tall stock pot, heat the butter over a low heat then add the onions, shallots and garlic, cover and sweat until soft but not coloured, stirring occasionally. Remove the lid, add the vegetables and lemon zest and cook until soft, stirring regularly to stop any caramelisation. Add the wine and Noilly Prat, turn up to a high heat and bring to the boil, then reduce by half, stirring occasionally. Mix in the onion and shallot skins and the herbs.

Cover the vegetables well with the cold water. Bring to the boil over a high heat then reduce to a low heat and simmer gently for 2 hours, uncovered, skimming off any scum periodically.

Strain the stock through a sieve into a deep container and stand in a sink of cold water to allow it to cool quickly.

Store in the fridge for up to 2 days or in batches in the freezer for up to 3 months.

Sauces, Stocks & Staples 375

Clarified Butter

Clarified butter is great to use for pan-frying food. By clarifying butter, you reduce the sediments and it can be cooked at a high temperature without burning, since clarification removes impurities. It keeps well and can be stored in the fridge for 3 weeks.

Ingredients

- 225g / ½lb salted butter

Method

Heat the butter in a saucepan over a low heat until it melts. When it has finished foaming, take it off the heat and let it stand for 30 minutes. The salt and milky residue settles at the base and you will have a liquid like oil with a froth on top. Skim off the froth. Gently pour off the liquid (clarified butter), leaving the milky residue in the base. Allow to cool, then store the clarified butter in an airtight container in the fridge.

Garlic Butter

Ingredients

- 225g / ½lb good quality salted butter, at room temperature, chopped into cubes
- 3 garlic cloves, peeled and roughly chopped
- 2 tbsp chopped flat leaf parsley

Method

Add the butter, garlic and parsley to a food processor and blend until combined. Store in an airtight container and keep for up to 1 week in the fridge. When using, allow the butter to come to room temperature.

Thyme Butter

Ingredients

- 225g / ½lb good quality salted butter, at room temperature, chopped into cubes
- 2 tbsp thyme leaves (no stalks)

Method

Add the butter and thyme to a food processor and blend. Store in an airtight container and keep for up to 1 week in the fridge. When using, allow the butter to come to room temperature.

Citrus Butter

This is best made fresh as it does not lend itself well for storing. It is delightful and simple to make. Use any one of the citrus fruits – lemon, orange or lime.

Ingredients

- 55g / 2oz salted butter
- 2 tbsp freshly squeezed citrus juice

Method

Melt the butter in a small saucepan over a medium heat, then add the juice and stir continuously to combine. It will form a slight emulsion.

Apple Chutney

Ingredients

Makes 4-6 jars

- **1kg / 2lb 3oz cooking apples, peeled and coarsely chopped**
- **340g / 12oz onions, peeled and finely chopped**
- **200g / 7oz sultanas**
- **310g / 11 oz brown sugar**
- **350ml / 12½fl oz malt vinegar**
- **2 tsp yellow mustard seeds**
- **1 heaped tsp mixed pickling spice**
- **½ tsp ground ginger**
- **½ tsp cayenne pepper**

Method

In a large saucepan or pot, stir together all the ingredients. Bring to the boil over a medium heat, stirring occasionally. Reduce to a low heat and simmer the chutney for 2 hours or until the liquid has reduced and is thick and pulpy – a chutney consistency. Remove the pot from the heat and allow to cool. Spoon the chutney into clean, dry and sterile jars and seal. Store in a cool dark place sealed for up to 4-6 months.

Once opened, store in the fridge for up to 1 month.

Garlic Confit Paste

This is very handy if you want to add extra flavour. It is great with sauces, tomatoes, pasta, salad dressings, stir fries or even crostini. It is very simple to make and can be stored in the fridge where it will keep for up to 1 week.

Ingredients

- 2 garlic bulbs
- 1 tbsp olive oil
- Extra virgin olive oil, to store

Method

Preheat the oven to fan 120°C / fan 250°F /gas mark 1.

Place both the garlic bulbs on a sheet of foil and drizzle over the oil. Wrap the garlic in the foil, place on a baking tray and slowly roast in the oven for 1-1½ hours or until soft. Allow to cool, then squeeze the garlic cloves into a bowl and mix to form a paste.

Transfer to a sterilised jar and pour a small layer of extra virgin olive oil on top to help preserve the confit.

Store in the fridge for up to 1 week.

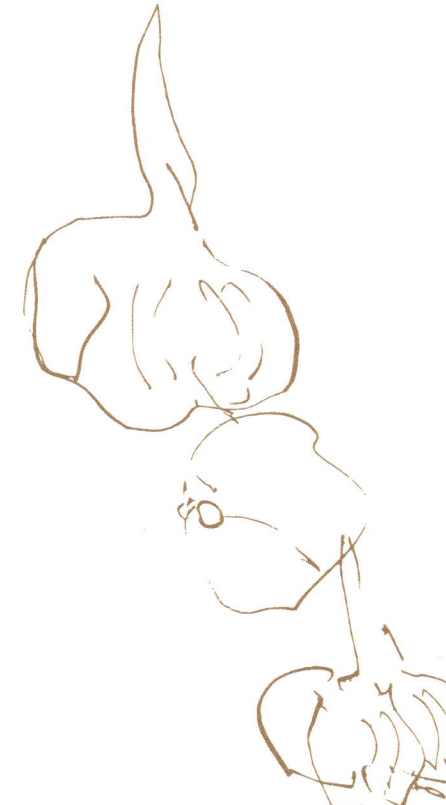

Apple & Walnut Oil Dressing

This is a delicious combination with the acidity of the apples, the nut oil and the sweetness of the honey. We first used this in The Lime Tree when nut oils were very fashionable, and we did a lot of experimenting. They are wonderful with cheese and fruit combinations.

We serve a fantastic farm pressed apple juice from Limerick in Shelburne Lodge. The Attyflin Estate is based near Adare in Co. Limerick, my beloved Tom's county! Many years ago, there was a wonderful restaurant run by the young Glancy's and it was on the very same estate. Brian and Bridget O'Connell and their family produce delicious apples. They now have a great Attyflin apple cider vinegar, too.

Ingredients

- 1 tbsp Attyflin apple cider vinegar
- 2 tsp local honey (warmed to help it combine)
- 3-4 tbsp lemon juice
- 3 tbsp walnut oil
- 3 tbsp olive oil or mild oil of your choice
- Sea salt and cracked black pepper

Method

Put the vinegar, honey and juice into a jar, tightly seal and shake vigorously. Add the oil and seasoning and shake again.

Taste and adjust to your liking.

Citrus Herb Vinaigrette

Ingredients

- 2 tbsp orange or lemon juice
- 2 tsp local honey (warmed to help it combine)
- 1 tsp Dijon mustard
- 4 tbsp extra virgin olive oil
- 1 tbsp chopped herbs of choice: tarragon, chives, coriander, oregano or basil (depending on salad ingredients)
- Sea salt and cracked black pepper

Method

Put the juice, honey and mustard into a jar, tightly seal and shake vigorously. Add the oil, herbs and seasoning and shake again.

Taste and adjust to your liking.

Hazelnut Vinaigrette

Ingredients

- 1½ tbsp apple cider vinegar
- 3 tbsp olive oil
- 1 tbsp hazelnut oil
- 1 tsp local honey (warmed to help it combine), plus extra to taste
- Sea salt and cracked black pepper

Method

Put all the ingredients into a jar, tightly seal and shake vigorously. Add local honey and seasoning to taste, then shake again.

Taste and adjust to your liking.

Shallot Vinaigrette

This is delicious with smoked salmon, trout or mackerel, also great served with cheeses.

Ingredients

- 1 tbsp balsamic vinegar
- 1 tbsp lemon juice
- 1 tsp Dijon mustard
- 3 small shallots, finely chopped
- 6 tbsp extra virgin olive oil
- Sea salt and cracked black pepper

Method

Put the vinegar, juice and mustard into a jar, tightly seal and shake vigorously. Add the oil, shallots and seasoning and shake again.

Taste and adjust to your liking.

Simple Balsamic Dressing

Ingredients

- 2 tbsp balsamic
- 2 tsp local honey (warmed to help it combine)
- 1 tsp Dijon mustard
- 6 tbsp extra virgin olive oil
- Sea salt and cracked black pepper

Method

Put the vinegar, honey and mustard into a jar, tightly seal and shake vigorously. Add the oil and seasoning and shake again.

Taste and adjust to your liking.

Simple Citrus Dressing

Ingredients

- 3 tbsp fresh orange juice
- 1 tbsp lemon juice
- 1 tbsp local honey (warmed to help it combine)
- 6 tbsp extra virgin olive oil
- Sea salt and cracked black pepper

Method

Put the juice and honey into a jar, tightly seal and shake vigorously. Add the oil, season and shake again.

Taste and adjust to your liking.

Purple Heather Balsamic Dressing

Ingredients

- 2 tbsp balsamic vinegar
- 1 tsp wholegrain mustard
- 1 tsp dark muscovado sugar
- 1 garlic clove, kept whole
- 4 tbsp olive oil
- Sea salt and cracked black pepper

Method

Put all the ingredients into a jar, tightly seal and shake vigorously. Store in the jar with the garlic clove inside.

Taste and adjust to your liking.

Purple Heather Vinaigrette

Omit the mustard to make the dressing gluten-free.

Ingredients

- 1½ tsp English mustard
- 1½ tsp sugar or local honey (warmed to help it combine)
- 150ml / 5¼fl oz sunflower oil
- 55ml / 2fl oz white wine vinegar
- Sea salt and cracked black pepper

Method

Put all the ingredients into a jar, tightly seal and shake vigorously.

Taste, season and adjust to your liking.

Dinner Parties

You don't have to cook fancy or complicated masterpieces — just good food from fresh ingredients.
— Julia Child

Dinner Parties

Planning your menu is important, and will help you to enjoy the evening as much as your guests.

- It is a good idea when you invite your guests to enquire about any dietary requirements which will help you plan your menu.
- Aim to keep food seasonal and simple and think about the balance of courses and how they complement each other; for example if you have a heavy and rich main course, choose something light as a starter.
- Dishes that can be partially or fully prepared in advance will cause less stress and therefore create a relaxed atmosphere. Soft lighting is also conducive in creating a relaxed environment, especially during evening or night-time.
- If you are having wine, make sure you have a good supply of whatever wines you have chosen to serve for your guests.

What follows is a sample of seasonal and themed menus which can act as a guide to your planning, accompanied by exquisite paintings by my friend Pauline Bewick. Enjoy!

Pauline Bewick

Pauline lived in Kenmare as a young girl and hoped to return to Kenmare in later years but founded her home by the splendid Caragh Lake where she still resides. I love all her art and followed many of her exhibitions, most recently in the City Hall in London last year. Over the years we developed a friendship; Pauline also loved The Lime Tree and was a customer when we owned it. I love the colours, subjects and sensual nature of her paintings which are so beautiful. Pauline has kindly sourced these works from her private collectors.

'Eating Passion Fruit in Bed', Pauline Bewick

Spring / Summer Menu

Starters

Chicken Liver Pâté with Cumberland Sauce
Smoked Cod Mousse
Roast Red Pepper & Tomato Soup or Asparagus Soup
Salad of Summer Fruits with St Tola Divine Irish Goat's Cheese
Crab & Coriander Bundles
Soused Mackerel

Mains

Chicken with Lime & Lemongrass
Baked Fillet of Wild Salmon with Gooseberry, Elderflower & Lime Sauce
or Wild Sorrel Hollandaise
Baked Fillet of Turbot en Papillote with Noilly Prat and Basil Orange Sauce
Rack of Lamb with Puy Lentils and a Red Wine Sauce
Seared Scallops with Curried Vermicelli
Cyril's Atlantic Prawns Roasted with Garlic Butter or Béarnaise Sauce

Desserts

Thos' Lemon Posset with Shortbread
John Desmond's Island Cottage White Chocolate Mousse
with Chocolate or Strawberry Sauce
Iced Coffee Parfait served with Whiskey Caramel and Whiskey Cream
Bitter Chocolate Praline Tart
Tuilles served with choice of Ice-Cream & Summer Berry Compote
Génoise Sponge with Red Berries & Grand Marnier

'Mouton Rothschild', Pauline Bewick

Winter / Autumn Menu

Starters

Leek & Potato Soup
Confit of Duck Leg with Pear & Ginger Salad
Prawn & Spinach Pastries
Twice Baked Hazelnut Cheese Soufflé
Crab Cakes with Tartare Sauce
Rocket, Pear & Irish Blue Cheese Salad (or cheese of choice)
with Apple & Walnut Oil Dressing

Mains

Duck Casserole with Red Wine & Prunes
Chicken Vallée d'Auge with Caramelised Apples
Beef & Guinness Casserole
Roast Beef with Yorkshire Pudding,
Roast Potatoes and Turnip Purée
Roast Monkfish with Red Pepper Relish or Beurre Blanc
Roast Cod Mornay with Coolea Matured Cheese
Crumbed Scallops with Herb or Garlic Butter

Desserts

Chocolate Pots
Sticky Toffee Pudding
Irish Barmbrack & Butter Pudding
Creamy Caramelised Apple Tart
Spicy Apple & Rum Pudding

'Holly's Cooking Dinner', Pauline Bewick

Vegetarian Menu

Starters

Wild Chanterelle Mushrooms with Bruschetta or Tagliatelle
Celeriac & Apple Soup
St Tola Goat's Cheese Salad with Warm Red Pepper Salad

Mains

Goat's Cheese Parcels with Toasted Hazelnuts and Apple
Vegetarian Java
Red Onion Tart with Kerry Blue Cheese

Desserts

Delicious Gateau with Coffee Bean Sauce
Chocolate Marquise with Crème Anglaise and Brandied Kumquats
Zabaglione Ice-Cream with Rum Syrup served with Tuilles

Glossary

A few cookery terms and explanations, especially those referred to frequently throughout the book.

Bain marie
A warm water bath that cooks food gently with hot water either in a bowl over a pot of hot water or in a deep roasting tray filled with water.

Beurre manié
Directly translated from French as 'kneaded butter', this is equal quantities of softened butter (not melted) and plain white flour used to thicken sauces. It is uncooked, not like roux. Use one tablespoon of flour to one tablespoon of butter, and add a little to a simmering sauce to thicken, adding more if needed to reach your desired consistency.

Blanch and refresh
Plunging vegetables into boiling water with a pinch of salt for a few minutes and then straining and refreshing in cold or iced water.

Blind bake
Baking pastry prior to adding the filling. This helps to ensure the pastry is fully baked when the tart is complete and prevents it from becoming soggy.

Bouquet garni
A bundle of herbs tied together with string to infuse soups, sauces, stocks, casseroles and stews. Usually consisting of half a celery stick, 2 thyme sprigs, 1 parsley sprig and a bay leaf. Other herbs can be added, such as sage, rosemary or dill, to suit what you're cooking.

Butterflied
Deboned, split and opened out.

Cartouche
A circle of greaseproof paper used to cover ingredients while cooking. Prevents burning or keeps food submerged in a liquid.

Chiffonade
A slicing technique used for leafy green vegetables or herbs. The leaves are stacked, rolled and then finely sliced.

Coating consistency
A consistency of sauce that coats the back of a wooden spoon. When a finger is drawn through the sauce, it keeps the path.

Concasse
Peeled, deseeded and chopped tomatoes. To do so, bring a small pot of water to the boil. Remove the stems and score a cross on the bases. Plunge the tomatoes into the water for 30 seconds, then immediately remove and refresh in ice-cold water. The skins of the tomatoes should now be easy to peel off. Roughly chop and use as per recipe.

Confit
Directly translated from French as 'to preserve', this refers to the method of preservation of salting and then cooking meat or vegetables at a very low heat submerged in fat. Stored in the fridge, the food can then be finished in a hot pan to caramelise and add extra flavour.

Deglaze
Adding liquid to the residue of a pan or roasting tray, scraping well to remove the precious sediment which has maximum flavour for sauces.

Demi-Glace
Made from a combination of a classic brown sauce and brown stock reduced to make a rich brown sauce. Used to enhance other sauces and add a further depth of flavour.

Draw
Removing the insides of a bird.

Julienne
A cutting technique used for vegetables, to slice them into thin strips resembling matchsticks.

Medallion
Meat or fish cut into rounds the size and shape of a medallion.

Nappé
The motion of coating food with a sauce or glaze.

En papillote
Cooking (typically baking) in a sealed package which keeps in the juices.

Reduce
Cooking over a high heat rapidly to reduce the liquid content and intensify the flavour or to reduce a sauce to reach a desired consistency.

Sear
Cooking briefly, generally in a hot pan with a smear of oil or butter.

Skim
Removing from cooking juices any fat or scum that rises to the surface. Skimming is especially vital to prevent stocks becoming cloudy due to the scum or fat cooking back into the liquid.

Sweat
Softening vegetables in butter over a low to medium heat and sealed with a tight-fitting lid on.

Index

A
apricot
  dried prune & apricot fruit compote 50
apples
  apple chutney 378
  apple sauce 364
  apple syrup 364
  apple & walnut dressing 380
  blackberry or blackcurrant & apple compote 53
  celeriac & apple soup 92
  chicken vallée with caramelised apples 207
  creamy caramelised apple tart 314
  drop scone pancakes with dry cured bacon and apple syrup 58
  spiced apple & cinnamon compote 48
  spicy apple & rum pudding 313
artichokes
  globe artichokes 102
asparagus
  asparagus soup 88
aubergines
  sweet & sour aubergine relish 164

B
bacon
  drop scone pancakes with dry cured bacon and apple syrup 58
  roast confit of duck breast with bacon 225
  smoked bacon and bread stuffing rolls 129
balsamic vinegar
  Purple Heather balsamic dressing 383
  simple balsamic dressing 382
basic brown sauce 359
béarnaise sauce 344
beef
  beef & Guinness casserole 235
  beef stock 372
  roast beef with Yorkshire pudding 236
beetroot
  roast beetroot & orange 277
biscuits
  Grainne's oatmeal biscuits 333
  Grainne's wholemeal shortbread biscuits 332
  shortbread 324
  tuilles 323
blackberries, blackcurrants
  blackberry or blackcurrant & apple compote 53
black pudding 44
  Irish black pudding, caramelised apple & citrus vinaigrette salad 134
brandy
  brandy butter 330
  brandy cream sauce 156
bread
  bread sauce 226
  fresh thyme bread stuffing 243
  Irish brown soda bread 46
breakfast 41
broccoli
  purple sprouting broccoli 272
butter 33
  béarnaise sauce 344
  beurre blanc 346
  beurre manié 394
  buttered cabbage with ginger 278
  citrus butter 377
  clarified butter 376
  garlic butter 376
  garlic buttered rainbow chard or kale 271
  lemon butter 160
  lime & coriander butter 177
  thyme butter 377

C

cakes *see also* desserts & baking 283-333
  chocolate cake   288
  chocolate marquise   296
  coffee & walnut cake   302
  date, orange & sunflower seed loaf   301
  Génoise sponge cake   305
  porter cake   300
  Tunisian orange cake   308
  Victoria sandwich   306

carrots
  carrot & coriander soup   89
  new baby carrots with coriander   257
  carrot purée   258

Cashel Blue cheese
  Irish farmhouse cheese selection   71
  port & Cashel Blue cheese sauce   362

cauliflower
  cauliflower soup   83

celeriac
  celeriac & apple soup   92
  celeriac purée   259

cheese
  blue cheese
    port & Cashel Blue cheese sauce   362
    red onion tart with Kerry Blue cheese   96
    rocket, pear, Irish blue cheese salad   114
  Coolea Matured cheese
    roast cod mornay with Coolea Matured cheese   168
  goat's cheese
    goat's cheese parcels   108
    St Tola Irish goat's cheese & warm red pepper salad   111
    salad of summer fruits with St Tola Irish goat's cheese   112
  Irish farmhouse cheese selection   71
  mornay or cheese sauce   345
  twice baked hazelnut cheese soufflé   106

chermoula   355

chicken   207-218
  chicken coconut with pineapple or mango salsa   215
  chicken with coriander & lime butter   212
  chicken Java   210
  chicken with lime & lemongrass   217
  chicken liver pâté   133
  chicken mousseline   132
  chicken stock   370
  chicken with tarragon cream sauce   213
  chicken in a thyme & mustard crumb   209
  chicken vallée d'Auge   207
  roast chicken with thyme & honey jus   218

chocolate
  bitter chocolate praline tart   290
  chocolate cake   288
  chocolate marquise   296
  chocolate coffee meringue   294
  chocolate pots   289
  coffee chocolate meringue gateau with chocolate ganache   288, 294
  delicious gateau   304
  John Desmond's Island Cottage white chocolate mousse   328

choron sauce   344

Christmas   241-247
  Christmas ham with a honey & mustard glaze   241
  Grainne's Christmas pudding with brandy butter   330
  Maura's Christmas turkey with all the trimmings   242

cinnamon
  spiced apple & cinnamon compote   48

clarified butter   376

citrus butter   377

citrus herb vinaigrette   381

coffee
  chocolate coffee meringue   294
  coffee bean sauce   368
  coffee & walnut cake   302
  delicious gateau & coffee bean sauce   304
  iced coffee parfait   318

compote
  spiced apple & cinnamon compote   48
  gooseberry & elderflower compote   49

dried prune & apricot fruit compote   50
summer berry compote   51
blackberry or blackcurrant & apple compote   53
rhubarb & orange compote   54
spicy plum compote with star anise   55
colcannon   262
courgettes
  pan-fried courgettes   272
  tempura courgettes   275
crab
  crab cakes with tartare sauce   116
  crab & coriander bundles   117
cream
  brandy cream sauce   156
  cream reduction sauce   347
  fennel cream sauce   349
  garlic cream sauce   347
  tarragon cream sauce   348
  wholegrain mustard cream sauce   348
  whiskey cream   60, 318
creamed leeks   268
creamed potatoes   264
crème anglaise   366
  orange crème anglaise   367
Cumberland sauce   358

D
desserts *see* desserts & baking   283-333
Dijonnaise sauce   361
Dover sole
  Dover sole meunière   154
  Dover sole stuffed with Atlantic prawns & brandy cream sauce or garlic butter   156
  Dover sole stuffed with spinach, mushrooms & Noilly Prat sauce   156
duck
  confit of duck   222
  confit duck leg with pear & ginger   131
  duck casserole with red wine & prunes   220
  roast confit of duck breast with bacon, thyme bread stuffing, spicy plum sauce   225
  roast confit of duck breast with thyme bread stuffing, apple sauce and a red wine jus   224

E
eggs
  béarnaise sauce   344
  hollandaise sauce   342
  meringues   294
  see omelettes
  scrambled eggs with smoked salmon   68
  Shelburne Lodge eggs Benedict, Florentine and Royale   66
elderflower
  baked fillet of wild salmon with gooseberry, elderflower & lime sauce   178
  gooseberry & elderflower compote   49

F
fennel
  fennel cream sauce   349
  roast fennel   270
fish   139-197
  cod
    cod provençale   170
    roast cod with herb crust   167
    roast cod mornay with Coolea cheese   168
    roast cod with chilli, garlic & rosemary oil   169
    smoked cod cakes   126
    smoked cod mousse   128
  crab
    crab cakes with tartare sauce   116
    crab & coriander bundles   117
  Dover sole *see* Dover sole
  John Dory
    Fillet of John Dory or brill with pears, leeks and Noilly Prat sauce   176
  lemon sole
    Lemon sole with tomato & caper salsa or toasted almonds   160
  lobster
    baked stuffed lobster   193
    lobster Thermidor   191
  mackerel

pan-fried mackerel in an oatmeal crust
    with salsa verde or caper salsa   174
  soused mackerel   124
monkfish
  monkfish in a ginger & garlic crust with
    Thai dipping sauce   162
  roast monkfish with red pepper relish or
    sweet & sour aubergine relish   164
mussels
  baked stuffed garlic mussels   197
  moules marinière   194
prawns
  Cyril's Atlantic prawns roasted with garlic
    butter or béarnaise sauce   187
  Dover sole with Atlantic prawns   156
  prawn & spinach pastry with
    mousseline sauce   119
salmon
  baked fillet of wild salmon with
    gooseberry, elderflower & lime sauce
    or wild sorrel hollandaise   178
  baked fillet of wild salmon with lime
    & coriander butter   177
  scrambled eggs with smoked salmon
    and a chive crème fraîche   68
sea bass
  roast sea bass with wholegrain mustard
    sauce   166
scallops
  crumbed scallops with garlic butter   186
  seared scallops with curried vermicelli   183
  scallops with Noilly Prat & mushroom
    sauce   185
turbot
  baked fillet of turbot en papillote with
    Noilly Prat and basil orange sauce   181
  fillet of turbot en papillote with salsify
    and red wine sauce   182
Wild Atlantic seafood soup   80
fruity curry sauce   363

G
game chips   265
garlic
  baked stuffed garlic mussels   197
  crumbed scallops with garlic butter   186
  garlic butter   376
  garlic buttered rainbow chard or kale   271
  garlic confit paste   379
  garlic cream sauce   247
  garlic croûtons   353
  garlic & rosemary roast potatoes   266
  Cyril's Atlantic prawns roasted with garlic
    butter   187
  monkfish in a ginger & garlic crust with
    Thai dipping sauce   162
  red wine, rosemary & garlic sauce   360
  roast cod with chilli, garlic & rosemary
    oil   169
gateaux
  chocolate coffee meringue gateau with
    chocolate ganache   294
  delicious gateau with coffee
    bean sauce   304
ginger
  buttered cabbage with ginger   278
  confit duck leg with pear
    & ginger salad   131
  monkfish in a ginger & garlic crust   162
  poached pear in ginger   57
gooseberries
  gooseberry & elderflower compote   49
  baked fillet of wild salmon with gooseberry,
    elderflower & lime sauce   178
green peppercorn sauce   361

H
ham
  Christmas ham with a honey
    & mustard glaze   241
hazelnuts
  bitter chocolate praline tart   290
  goat's cheese parcels with toasted hazelnuts
    and apple   108

hazelnut vinaigrette   381
twice baked hazelnut cheese soufflé   106
herbs   34
hollandaise   342
  wild sorrel hollandaise   178

I
ice-cream
  homemade vanilla ice-cream   320
  iced coffee parfait   318
  vanilla & praline ice-cream   321
  zabaglione ice-cream with a rum caramel syrup   322

J
John Dory
  fillet of John Dory with pears, leeks and Noilly Prat sauce   176

L
lamb
  rack of lamb with puy lentils   229
leeks
  gratin of leeks or creamed leeks   268
  leek & potato soup   93
  fillet of John Dory or brill with pears, leeks and Noilly Prat sauce   176
lemon
  Thos' lemon posset with shortbread   324
lemongrass
  chicken with lime and lemongrass   217
lemon sole
  Lemon sole with tomato & caper salsa or toasted almonds   160
lobster
  baked stuffed lobster   193
  lobster Thermidor   191

M
mackerel
  pan-fried mackerel in an oatmeal crust with salsa verde or caper salsa   174
  soused mackerel   124

meat   201-243
  beef *see* beef
  chicken *see* chicken
  duck *see* duck
  ham
    Christmas ham with a honey & mustard glaze   241
  lamb   *see* lamb
  pheasant   *see* pheasant
  steak
    Maura's steak   232
  turkey
    Maura's Christmas turkey   242
meringue
  chocolate coffee meringue gateau   294
monkfish
  monkfish in a ginger & garlic crust with Thai dipping sauce   162
  roast monkfish with red pepper relish or sweet & sour aubergine relish   164
mornay sauce   345
mousse
  chicken mousseline   132
  John Desmond's Island Cottage white chocolate mousse   328
  prawn & spinach pastry with mousseline sauce   119
  seafood mousse   122
  smoked cod mousse   128
mushrooms
  mushroom soup   87
  wild chanterelle mushrooms with bruschetta or tagliatelle   99
  Dover sole stuffed with spinach, mushrooms & Noilly Prat sauce   156
  scallops with Noilly Prat & mushroom sauce   185
mussels
  baked stuffed garlic mussels   197
  moules marinière   194
mustard
  chicken in a thyme & mustard crumb   209
  Christmas ham with a honey & mustard

glaze   241
roast sea bass with wholegrain mustard sauce   166
simple wholegrain mustard cream sauce   349
wholegrain mustard cream sauce   348

N
nettle
  nettle & spinach soup   84
Noilly Prat   35
  Baked fillet of turbot en papillote with Noilly Prat and basil orange sauce   181
  Dover sole stuffed with spinach, mushrooms & Noilly Prat sauce   156
  Fillet of John Dory or brill with pears, leeks and Noilly Prat sauce   176
  Scallops with Noilly Prat & mushroom sauce   185

O
omelettes
  Shelburne Lodge omelette with gubbeen chorizo   62
  Purple Heather omelette   64
  Smoked salmon omelette   65
orange
  rhubarb & orange compote   54
  basil orange sauce   181
  braised chicory in orange   271
  roast beetroot & orange   277
  date, orange & sunflower seed loaf   301
  Tunisian orange cake   308
  orange crème anglaise   367

P
paloise   343
pancakes
  drop scone pancakes   58
  potato pancakes   94
parsnip
  curried parsnip soup   82
pastry
  bitter chocolate praline tart   290

creamy caramelised apple tart   314
goat's cheese parcels with toasted hazelnuts and apple   108
Moroccan vegetable parcels   104
red onion tart with Kerry Blue cheese   96
rum & walnut tart   316
pears
  poached pears in ginger   57
  rocket, pear & Irish blue cheese salad with apple & walnut oil   114
  confit of duck leg with pear & ginger salad   131
  fillet of John Dory or brill with pears, leeks and Noilly Prat sauce   176
pesto   356
pheasant
  roast pheasant with bread sauce   226
porridge
  organic porridge with whiskey cream   60
port & Cashel Blue cheese sauce   362
potatoes
  colcannon   262
  creamed potatoes   264
  game chips   265
  leek & potato soup   93
  potato pancakes   94
  potato stuffing   265
  garlic & rosemary roast potatoes   266
plum
  spicy plum compote with star anise   55
  roast confit of duck breast with a spicy plum sauce   225
prawns
  Cyril's Atlantic prawns roasted with garlic butter or béarnaise sauce   187
  Dover sole with Atlantic prawns   156
  prawn & spinach pastry with mousseline sauce   119
prune
  dried prune & apricot fruit compote   50
  duck casserole with red wine & prunes   220
puddings
  sticky toffee pudding   310

Irish barmbrack & butter pudding   312
spicy apple & rum pudding   313
Grainne's Christmas pudding with brandy butter   330
Purple Heather balsamic dressing   383
Purple Heather omelette   64
Purple Heather vinaigrette   384

R
raspberries
  salad of summer fruits with St Tola Irish goat's cheese   112

red onions
  red onion tart with Kerry Blue cheese   96
red peppers
  roast red pepper & tomato soup   86
  St Tola Irish goat's cheese & warm red pepper salad   111
  red pepper relish   164
red wine
  duck casserole with red wine & prunes   220
  fillet of turbot en papillote with salsify and red wine sauce   182
  red wine fish sauce 182
  red wine jus   360
  red wine, rosemary & garlic sauce   360
  rack of lamb with puy lentils and a red wine sauce   229
  roast confit of duck breast with thyme bread stuffing, apple sauce and a red wine jus   224
rhubarb
  rhubarb & orange compote   54
roast beef with Yorkshire pudding   236
roast chicken   218
roast confit of duck breast   224-225
roast pheasant with bread sauce   226
roast potatoes   266
roast vegetables   261
rouille with garlic croûtons   353
rum
  rum & walnut tart with rum butterscotch sauce   316
  spicy apple & rum pudding   313
  zabaglione ice-cream with a rum caramel syrup   322

S
salads
  St Tola Irish goat's cheese & warm red pepper salad   111
  salad of summer fruits with St Tola Irish goat's cheese   112
  rocket, pear & Irish blue cheese salad   114
  salad suggestions   115
  pear & ginger salad   131
  Irish black pudding, caramelised apple & citrus vinaigrette salad   134
  salad dressings   380-384
salmon
  baked fillet of wild salmon with gooseberry, elderflower & lime sauce or wild sorrel hollandaise   178
  baked fillet of wild salmon with lime & coriander butter   177
  scrambled eggs with smoked salmon and a chive crème fraîche   68
salsas
  caper salsa   174
  pineapple or mango salsa   215
  tomato & caper salsa   356
  salsa verde   357
sauces   342-368
  savoury sauces   342-363
  sweet sauces   364-368
scallops
  crumbed scallops with garlic butter   186
  seared scallops with curried vermicelli   183
  scallops with Noilly Prat & mushroom sauce   185
sea bass
  roast sea bass with wholegrain mustard sauce   166
seafood *see* fish   139-197
  seafood sauce   352
shallot vinaigrette   382

Index   403

shellfish   183-197
  shellfish stock   373
spinach
  nettle & spinach soup   84
  prawn & spinach pastry   119
  Dover sole stuffed with spinach, mushrooms & Noilly Prat sauce   156
  wilted fresh spinach 278
soda bread   46
soufflé   106
soups   80-93
  asparagus soup   88
  carrot & coriander soup   89
  cauliflower soup   83
  celeriac & apple soup   92
  curried parsnip soup   82
  leek & potato soup   93
  mushroom soup   87
  nettle & spinach soup   84
  roast red pepper & tomato soup   86
  Wild Atlantic seafood soup   80
starters   75-134
steak
  Maura's steak   232
strawberries
  salad of summer fruits with St Tola Irish goat's cheese   112
stuffing
  fresh thyme bread stuffing   243
  potato stuffing   265
  smoked bacon and bread stuffing rolls   129
stocks   370-374
  beef stock   372
  chicken stock   370
  fish stock   371
  shellfish stock   373
  vegetable stock   374
sugar snaps with fresh mint   274
sugar syrup   365

T
tarragon
  tarragon cream sauce   348
  tarragon vinegar   34
tartare sauce   354
  crab cakes with tartare sauce   116
tarts
  bitter chocolate praline tart   290
  creamy caramelised apple tart   314
  red onion tart with Kerry Blue   96
  rum & walnut tart with rum butterscotch sauce   316
Thai dipping sauce   358
Thos' lemon posset with shortbread   324
thyme butter   377
tomatoes
  roast red pepper & tomato soup   86
  tomato & caper salsa   356
turbot
  baked fillet of turbot en papillote with Noilly Prat and basil orange sauce   181
  fillet of turbot en papillote with salsify and red wine sauce   182
turkey
  Maura's Christmas turkey   242

V
vegetables   251-278
  roast vegetables 261
vegetable stock   374
vegetarian Java   210
vinaigrettes *see also* salad dressings   380-384
  citrus herb vinaigrette   381
  hazelnut vinaigrette   381
  Purple Heather vinaigrette   384
  shallot vinaigrette   382

W

walnuts
  apple & walnut dressing   380
  coffee & walnut cake   302
  rum & walnut tart   316
wholegrain mustard *see* mustard
wine *see* red wine
whiskey
  whiskey cream   60, 318
white sauce   345

Y

yoghurt
  organic whole natural yoghurt with honey, nuts & seeds   61
Yorkshire puddings   236

Z

zabaglione ice-cream with a rum caramel syrup   322

Acknowledgements

Thanks to my dear family for their love and support. I have had many wonderful years cooking and continue to enrich my life with my number one passion. Thanks to all the great food people who inspired me and kept the spark going, I am hugely grateful. A special thanks to all my loyal customers, friends, suppliers and fantastic team of staff who have been with me over the years.

Maura

> "If you're afraid of butter, use cream."
>
> Julia Child

For my husband; Tom, our five children, Senga, Jane, Thos, Grace and Christina; and our grandchildren, Liam, Louis, Julia, Diarmuid and Ben. And for Grainne, my sister, and our parents, John and Agnes.